Slaves, Peasants, and Rebels

Blacks in the New World

Edited by
August Meier and John H. Bracey

A list of books in the series
appears at the end of this book.

Slaves, Peasants, and Rebels

Reconsidering Brazilian Slavery

Stuart B. Schwartz

6

University of Illinois Press
Urbana and Chicago

Library of Congress Cataloging-in-Publication Data

Schwartz, Stuart B.
    Slaves, peasants, and rebels : reconsidering Brazilian
slavery /
    Stuart B. Schwartz.
    p. cm. — (Blacks in the New World)
    Includes bibliographical references and index.
    ISBN 0-252-01874-5
    1. Slavery—Brazil. I. Title. II. Series.
HT1126.S39 1992
306.3′62′0981—dc20   91-21938
                                                          CIP

To the memories of

Peter Eisenberg, historian of Brazil
Andrés "Tony" Ramos Mattei, historian of Puerto Rico
Susan Schneider, historian of Portugal

friends and colleagues whose spirits live on in the histories
they wrote.

CONTENTS

Preface   ix

List of Abbreviations   xiii

1. Recent Trends in the Study of Brazilian Slavery   1

2. Sugar Plantation Labor and Slave Life   39

3. Peasants and Slavery: Feeding Brazil in the Late Colonial Period   65

4. Rethinking Palmares: Slave Resistance in Colonial Brazil   103

5. Opening the Family Circle: Godparentage in Brazilian Slavery   137

6. Reconsiderations   161

Index   165

PREFACE

Allow me to be perfectly clear at the outset. This is a volume of essays conceived and written at various times over the last two decades, during which much of my scholarly life was dedicated to the study of slavery in Brazil. Scholars often prefer to republish old essays as they were originally written because they represent a particular moment in the state of a field and in the author's thinking. Also, it is often easier to leave well enough alone; however, I have not chosen that path. Instead, I have sought to reconsider a number of themes that have become central to the study of Brazilian slavery by either recasting or enlarging earlier articles or even by writing new essays on subjects I have considered in the past. While the essays deal with disparate topics, all emphasize the role of slaves in the shaping of their own lives and in the construction and operation of the Brazilian slave system. Slaves were not independent historical actors able to mold their own destiny at their will, but masters too were limited, sometimes by the actions and attitudes of slaves. The equation of power and opportunity was, of course, unequal, but both masters and slaves constantly tried to redefine that formula. The constraints and opportunities that limited both have preoccupied my research. And the complex and dynamic relationship of slaves, masters, and other groups in slave society provide a central and unifying theme to these essays.

My interest in Brazilian slavery was of course tied to my own experience. The struggle for civil rights and the concern with race relations in the United States moved many men and women in my academic generation to turn toward the history of slavery and of Afro-American peoples as a way to understand and explain the present. In the United States, Brazil, Spanish America, the Caribbean, and Europe the 1960s marked a period of renewed interest in slavery and race relations. For North American specialists in Brazilian history like me, the study of slavery offered a double attraction. The Afro-American experience was obviously crucial for an understanding of Brazilian history, and, in addition, the contrasts and parallels between slavery and race relations in Brazil and the United States seemed to offer fruitful comparisons that might illumine and explain the course of contemporary events in both countries.

The study of slavery provoked many controversies—political, theoretical, and historiographical. My own research and writing were usually done with attention to these debates about the nature of slave-based economies, the role of patriarchalism in slave regimes, the autonomy of slaves, the meaning and nature of slave resistance, the structure of the slave population, and many other questions. My writing profited from the criticism and comments of those who agreed or disagreed with my interpretations or use of data. My work both influenced and was influenced by others in the normal give and take of scholarly debate; so over time I have been forced to continually reassess my earlier findings and interpretations. I have used this volume to reconsider some of my earlier work, to restate or to alter some earlier interpretations in the light of criticism, and to focus attention on a few themes that have preoccupied students of Brazilian slavery in recent years.

The book begins with a historiographical review and discussion of the predominant trends in the study of Brazilian slavery in the last few decades. While in no way complete, it identifies the major scholars and their most important works and seeks to place them in the context of developments in slavery studies beyond Brazil. An earlier version of this essay was published in the *Luso-Brazilian Review* (25:1 [Summer, 1988], 1–27), but it included only works by Brazilian scholars. The present chapter has been changed and expanded to include the work of non-Brazilians as well.

The remainder of the chapters in this volume, then, take up a number of those themes noted in the historiographical review: work, slavery and the economy, resistance, and the family. In some ways these essays are either debates with or comments on the field; some are the reexamination of problems that have preoccupied me in the past. Chapter 2, "Sugar Plantation Labor and Slave Life," was originally prepared for a conference titled "Slave Life and Culture" at the University of Maryland in 1989. Published here for the first time, it retraces some of the steps I took in an earlier monograph on the economy and society of the sugar plantation region of Bahia in order to place work at the core of historical analysis of slavery. Work requirements set the stage upon which masters and slaves engaged in a series of negotiations that opened some "social space" to the slaves. To ignore the centrality of labor is to miss the point of what slavery was all about. To study slave culture, slave life, or even resistance without reference to—and a clear understanding of—the labor required of slaves and the way it determined their existence is misleading. In this essay, I do not deal with all the myriad types of labor required of Brazilian slaves, but I seek to delineate the relationship between slave work and slave life in a particular context. Slaves clearly formed communities and social structures not always controlled by their masters, but these were peculiar communities in which decisions and forms were constrained in a variety of ways by the servile status of their members. This chapter, then, begins at the heart of slavery. Appended to chapter 2 are two documents that are discussed in the text and that have themselves been the focus of considerable debate. Although I originally published these in the *Hispanic American Historical Review* (57:1 [1977], 69–81) and they have subsequently been republished by others, they are included here for the convenience of the reader.

In chapter 3, "Peasants and Slaves," I move outward to the slave system as it operated in Brazil. Here, I address a question of the larger relationship between slavery and the Brazilian economy during the transition at the end of the eighteenth century. In this essay, which I originally prepared for a Conference on Colonial Brazil at the University of Toronto in 1987 but never published, I seek to underline both the pervasiveness of slavery in Brazil and its remarkable adaptability to new economic conditions and opportunities. I argue that the expansion of Brazil's slave-based export economy was accompanied by a parallel expansion of internal markets for foodstuffs supplied by large and small producers, many of whom could be called peasants, and that these turned increasingly to slavery for their labor needs. In this essay, I also seek to close the ideological and historiographical gap between slaves and peasants by demonstrating that the two forms of agriculture intersected in unexpected ways.

In the following essay, "Slave Resistance in Colonial Brazil," I step outside or beyond the slave regime to examine the nature of some forms of slave resistance, specifically the runaway communities that became a continual feature of slavery in Brazil. Here, I have combined earlier published research on Bahia with comparative materials from the Brazilian mining zones to establish parallels in the nature of fugitive communities and to better understand how they functioned. The development of African history has opened new possibilities and lines of research for the study of Afro-American life. Using the example of the great fugitive community of Palmares, I suggest that these fugitive communities may have had an internal organization and a cultural content that has escaped observers and that they must be approached with an understanding of the African cultural heritage that Brazilian slaves possessed. A version of this chapter appeared in Portuguese ("Mocambos, Quilombos e Palmares: resistencia escrava do Brasil colonial," *Estudos Econômicos,* 17 [1987], 61–88). It appears in English here for the first time.

In recent years, the study of the slave family in Brazil has finally begun to receive the attention it deserves, but studies of the slave family in Brazil must keep in mind the peculiar features and structures of the Brazilian family. In chapter 5, "Opening the Family Circle," I examine a social and spiritual dimension of the slave family by analyzing the choice of godparents by or for slaves in Paraná and Bahia—two very different and widely separated regions of Brazil. Here, I not only demonstrate some clear patterns in godparent selection, indicating ties and preferences within the slave community, but I also raise questions about the much-touted paternalism of Brazilian slave owners, who are noticeably absent as godparents for their slaves. This chapter follows an earlier collaborative examination of the problem done in conjunction with my colleague, anthropologist Stephen Gudeman; and here, I test those earlier findings with new data and expand the geographical and chronological limits of that earlier study. Chapter 5, then, is an essay in which I reconsider, expand upon, and reconfirm earlier findings.

These essays are the fruit of over twenty-five years of teaching and researching the history of Brazil. The number of debts to students, colleagues, archivists, librarians, research assistants, and to those who Lewis Hanke once called "frank and fearless friends" is impossible to calculate. I hope that they will not mind this collective statement of thanks. Those chapters presented as conference papers have benefited from the comments of critics and discussants such as Linda Lewin. I do owe a special debt of thanks to Dauril Alden, Katia Mattoso, Herbert Klein, Russell Menard, Richard Graham, and Stanley Engerman, all of whom have provided help and guidance over the years.

ABBREVIATIONS

Archives

ACS	Arquivo da Câmara Municipal do Salvador
ACMP	Arquivo da Cúria Metropolitana de Paraná (Curitiba)
ACMB	Arquivo da Cúria Metropolitana da Bahia (Salvador)
AGS	Archivo General de Simancas
AHU	Arquivo Histórico Ultramarino (Lisbon)
ANRJ	Arquivo Nacional de Rio de Janeiro
ANTT	Arquivo Nacional da Torre do Tombo (Lisbon)
APB	Arquivo Público (do Estado) da Bahia (Salvador)
ARSI	Archivum Romanum Societatis Iesu (Rome)
BA	Biblioteca da Ajuda (Lisbon)
BGUC	Biblioteca Geral da Universidade de Coimbra
BI	Biblioteca do Itamaraty (Rio de Janeiro)
BNL	Biblioteca Nacional de Lisboa
BNRJ	Biblioteca Nacional de Rio de Janeiro
IHGAP	Instituto Histórico, Geográfico, e Arquelógico Pernambucano (Recife)
Stl/VFL	Saint Louis University/Vatican Film Library

Collections

Con. ultra.	Conselho ultramarino
Corp. cron.	Corpo cronológico
CSJ	Cartório dos Jesuitas
Ord. reg.	Ordens régias
pap. avul.	papéis avulsos
Pres. da Prov.	Presidência da Provincia
sec. prov.	Secretarias provinciales

Printed Sources

ABNRJ	*Anais da Biblioteca Nacional de Rio de Janeiro*

ACB	*Atas da Câmara. Documentos históricos do Arquivo Municipal*, 6 vols. (Salvador, 1944–65?)
CHLA	*Cambridge History of Latin America*, Leslie Bethell, ed., 5 vols. to date (Cambridge, 1984–)
CPSNWS	*Comparative Perspectives on Slavery in New World Plantation Societies*, Vera Rubin and Arthur Tuden, eds. (New York, 1977)
HAHR	*Hispanic American Historical Review*
HISLA	*Revista Latinoamericana de Historia Economica y Social* (Lima)
M.A.N.	*Mensário do Arquivo Nacional* (Rio de Janeiro)

1 Recent Trends in the Study of Brazilian Slavery

In 1988 Brazilians commemorated the centenary of abolition, an important event not only in the history of Brazil but in the Americas as a whole. A century before, Brazil, the last nation of the Western hemisphere to abolish slavery, had ended its over three centuries of experience with that institution. Although slavery was a moribund institution in Brazil by May 13, 1888, the date of the "Golden Law," the final act of abolition officially marked the end of slavery in the Americas. What came after was not always better for the former slaves and their descendants, but it was certainly different.

In recognition of the centenary, Brazilians of all colors took stock of the nation's past and the role of people of Afro-American extraction within it. Coverage in the popular media was extensive. Political movements sought to mobilize black awareness, and some black leaders spoke out against any celebration of what, from their perspective, seemed to be a hollow event, given the disadvantages under which persons of color still live in Brazil. Nevertheless, a number of national commissions were established to plan a variety of public and academic events. Over one hundred books—some classics and others new—were published with the support of the CNPq (The National Council of Scientific and Technological Development), and other volumes appeared without that support. Large academic congresses and symposia were held across Brazil, and many scholarly journals dedicated entire issues to the question of slavery in Brazilian life.[1] For at least a year slavery and race caught the attention of Brazilians and students of Brazil in an unprecedented

manner. Since 1988 that interest has abated. Other events such as
the centenary of the establishment of the Republic in 1989, which
coincided with the return to electoral democracy in Brazil, have captured popular and academic attention. Research and publication on
slavery continues, but the crest of the wave has passed for the moment. The centenary of 1988 thus presents a good vantage point
from which to review the preceding three decades of scholarship,
during which considerable advances had been made in understanding how slavery operated in Brazil and what it has meant to that
nation and its people.[2] This review does include some publications
subsequent to 1988, but their small numbers indicate the pattern of
publication and a shift of interest to other themes.

Slavery molded the contours of Brazilian life in innumerable
ways, and ever since the publication of Gilberto Freyre's classic,
Casa grande e senzala (1933), Brazilians and students of Brazil have
devoted considerable attention to the nature of Brazilian slavery and
its impact on the society, economy, and culture of Brazil. Freyre
himself represented a long tradition of fascination with, and sometimes rejection of, Brazil's African past, but it was really after
Freyre's book that slavery and the African were given a central place
in the historical formation of Brazil. In that sense, his book marked
a watershed in the interpretation of Brazilian history. While subsequent generations of Brazilian and Brazilianist scholars have departed from Freyre's interpretations of the nature of slavery, the
patriarchal relationship of master to slave, and the system of postemancipation race relations, the centrality of slavery to the Brazilian experience remains a leitmotiv of modern Brazilian historiography and a continuing legacy of Freyre's insight.[3]

The study of slavery, however, encompassed a variety of
themes and approaches. Freyre's principal concern had been the
impact of slaves and their culture on the formation of the Brazilian
family, and, through it, on Brazilian society as a whole. While his
work drew on the studies and sometimes followed the interpretative
lines of earlier students of Afro-Brazilian life, it was the impact of
Indians—both as slaves and as servants—and especially of African
slaves on the general society that preoccupied his work. The phenomena of miscegenation, cultural adaptation, and what he perceived to be "milder" race relations served as central themes that
oriented his studies; and he argued in *Casa grande e senzala* (translated into English in 1946 as *The Masters and the Slaves*) and in
books like *O mundo que o português criou* (1940) that the Portuguese colonists had been particularly suited to the cultural fusion

that took place in Brazil. Freyre's wide-ranging scholarship and acute sensitivity to the unwritten codes and nuances of Brazilian life dominated popular and academic thinking in Brazil about these issues. This situation was certainly aided by the political usefulness of his interpretation in its exaltation of Brazilian culture and in the implication that the existing social structures might be modified by gradual change.

However, Brazilians were not the only ones concerned with the history of slavery and race relations in their nation. Frank Tannenbaum's *Slave and Citizen* (1947) used Freyre and other Latin American scholars to pose a sharp contrast between the slave systems of Protestant North America and Catholic Latin America, seeing in the legal codes, traditions, and state intervention of the latter a series of factors that mitigated the rigors of slavery and inserted themselves between the economic relationship of master and slave. Tannenbaum assumed that the differences in contemporary race relations flowed directly from the contrast in the historical systems of slavery.[4] Subsequent scholarship in the United States divided between those like Stanley Elkins (1959) and the early Herbert Klein (1967), who followed Tannenbaum's lead, and those like Marvin Harris (1964) and David B. Davis (1966, 1984), who criticized his assumptions and sources and found instead a disheartening similarity in the American slave systems.

The debate continued, as Carl Degler's (1971) comparison of slavery and race relations in the United States and Brazil demonstrated. In many ways Tannenbaum's critics gained the upper hand, but there remained an unanswered question: the apparent differences in race relations between Latin America and North America. The very question that fascinated Freyre and Tannenbaum. Recent scholarship has often rejected Tannenbaum's cultural explanations in favor of demographic and economic ones, although elements of Tannenbaum's approach have infused the comparative work of Eugene Genovese (usually noted as a Marxist but also a former student of Tannenbaum). Genovese (1971, 1979), more than any other North American historian, has used a comparative perspective to inform and illumine his analysis of slavery in the United States. Other scholars have simply rejected the idea that the major differences lie in slavery per se; they seek the roots instead in postemancipation history. Scholars like Toplin (1972) have taken the comparative approach from slavery to postemancipation societies. In any case, the lasting contribution of Tannenbaum was to assure that a comparative perspective, if at times only implicit, was essential for an

understanding of slavery and race relations in the Americas, although, in truth, students of Latin America have been more inclined
to that perspective than have those concerned with North America.

If indeed some anglophone scholars like C. R. Boxer (1963),
David B. Davis, and Marvin Harris were dissatisfied with
Tannenbaum's formulation of the comparison and criticism of the
sources on which it was based, by the 1950s Brazilian scholars were
responding to the intellectual and sociopolitical dynamics of their
own reality and were also launched on a revisionist course. Much of
the criticism leveled at Freyre, and which mounted in Brazil in the
decades of the 1950s and 1960s, came from young social scientists
from São Paulo who were strongly influenced by Marxian approaches and a materialist vision of society. Less concerned with cultural
phenomena per se, they sought ultimately to understand the impact
of the slave system—or what in Portuguese is called *escravismo*—
on the general development of the Brazilian economy and, in some
cases, on the subsequent system of race relations. The detailed regional studies of Emilia Viotti da Costa (1966) on São Paulo,
Fernando Henrique Cardoso (1962) on Rio Grande do Sul, and Octávio Ianni (1962) on Paraná, and the more general theoretical works
of Paula Beiguelman (1967, 1968) on the slave system and Florestan
Fernandes (1969, 1972) on race relations all addressed in different
ways the central question of the slave system's effects on economy,
polity, and society. With considerable differences among them, their
collective vision of slavery's impact and of master-slave relations
was far more negative than Freyre's assessment had been. The sociologists and historians of the "São Paulo School" concentrated primarily on the nineteenth century and on southern Brazil; and their
work was to that extent limited, but their theoretically informed
and well-documented monographs provided a new standard of analysis that made the economic and social effects of slavery the central
issue of study.[5]

The work of these scholars in the 1960s contributed to the continuing development of comparative studies of slavery and served as
an impetus for an intensification of concern with slavery in Brazil.
In the past two decades the historiography of slavery in Brazil has
undergone significant changes in orientation, method, and interpretation. Much of the development has been strongly regional, presented as detailed monographs on some aspect of slavery within a
regional context. At the same time, the new Brazilian historiography
of slavery is in a way a national historiography. There are a number
of ongoing debates in Brazil that are particularly Brazilian and that

the regional monographs often address, although sometimes only implicitly. Was the slave plantation and, by extension, Brazilian slavery, feudal or capitalist? What were the dimensions of patriarchalism? Could slaves be peasants? What was the relationship between resistance and oppression? Such are the questions that infuse many of the monographic studies. In addition, this historiography also reflects the broad international trends and tendencies of slave studies as well as the general trends within the discipline of history. For example, quantitative methods were increasingly used in Brazilian studies of slavery during the 1970s and early 1980s and remain an important element in the historiography of slavery, although interest in aspects of intellectual and cultural history have gained a new popularity in the field. The creation of graduate programs in a number of Brazilian universities and the professionalization of history has resulted in modern studies that speak to issues and concerns of scholars who study the phenomena of slavery and race elsewhere.

In my bibliographic review, I concentrate on the work of Brazilian and foreign scholars in the last three decades in order to discuss some important tendencies in studies on Brazilian slavery and to identify the major authors, works, and debates in one of the most continually active areas of Brazilian historiography.[6] Since slavery so permeated Brazilian life until at least 1870, almost every book on its history touches on slavery or its effects to some extent, although a recent book by Moura (1990) argues that many of the classic histories of Brazil ignored or marginalized blacks. Nevertheless, to include them all would go far beyond the scope of this essay.

The authors and themes noted here are intended to represent major bodies of work, and the review is necessarily highly selective. While it concentrates on Brazilian scholarship, it also includes work produced by foreigners. In the 1960s a considerable division arose between Brazilian scholarship and that produced by "Brazilianists," foreigners—especially North Americans—who wrote on Brazil. During the dark days of military repression, resentment of the financial advantages enjoyed by Brazilianists combined with critiques of Yankee empiricism and sometimes suspicions of ulterior motives to create a certain tension between Brazilian and foreign scholars. That tension also had its roots in scholarly differences in emphasis, methodology, and theoretical approach. This gap has now closed considerably. Many Brazilian scholars have been trained abroad and a number of foreign-born scholars who have long resided in Brazil have influenced a generation of students there, while being influenced by Brazilian scholarship themselves. Many Brazilian historians have taught in the United States and Europe with similar effects, becoming what Fernando Novais has called "Brazilian Brazilianists." Presently the continual intellectual exchange among historians of slavery properly ignores national boundaries and national origins. It is now difficult to tell the Brazilians from the Brazilianists or the Brazilian Brazilianists. This intellectual cross-fertilization is also reflected in the growing awareness of the trends in the historiography of U.S. slavery and to a lesser extent Caribbean slavery studies among students of Brazilian slavery. In that sense, the modern scholars of Brazilian slavery are all, like it or not, the godchildren of Freyre and Tannenbaum.

Reflecting not only the international trends but also the dynamics of Brazilian reality, one of the most noticeable developments in this field has been the study of what might be called the internal nature of slavery (*escravidão*), rather than a primary concern with the effects of slavery as a system (*escravismo*) on the economy and society as a whole, which tended to be the orientation of the studies of the 1950s and 1960s.[7] Of course, in the best studies these two approaches are integrated, but there has been a considerable growth of studies of slave life and culture using modern techniques and going far beyond the older traditional approach of folkloric studies and the description of "African traditions," which previously had characterized the study of slave life, and which had been too far removed from the central concerns of many historians and social scientists. The new historiography of Brazilian slavery makes clear the importance of understanding how slavery was organized and how it worked both as a labor form and as a social and cultural system in order to understand its broader theoretical and systemic implications for an understanding of Brazil's national history and its place within the development of the world economy. This trend, unwelcome to some, parallels similar developments in the United States and the Caribbean. Jacob Gorender (1990) sees in this attention to slave life and culture an attempt to "rehabilitate" Freyre's patriarchal model of slavery and to detract from an understanding of slavery's power as a coercive system.

Tannenbaum and his followers had stressed the importance of civil and religious constraints on slavery in the Iberian tradition by arguing that Roman law and church doctrine provided a set of principles in which the slave was viewed as a person and as a member of society, albeit a disadvantaged one. A more critical investigation of legislation and religious doctrine is now under way by some scholars (Carneiro da Cunha 1983; Freitas Brandão 1973; Titton 1973). They have shown that the law provided little protection to the slave. A. J. R. Russell-Wood (1978) has studied Portuguese attitudes toward slavery, while Ronaldo Vainfas (1986) has examined the classic texts on colonial slavery for their ideological and religious bases. Changes in the eighteenth century and discrepancies between thought and action have merited attention. Falcon and Novais (1973) have studied the economic forces that underlay the Pombaline abolition of slavery in Portugal, emphasizing its mercantilist goals, while MacLachlan (1979) has argued for the impact of the Enlightenment on judicial decisions involving slaves. In any case, laws regarding slavery and their enactment are being subject to close scrutiny, and efforts to examine the dynamic relationship between law and practice has become a major area of interest in the study of slavery.

The operation of the slave system and its implications for economic development has long been a matter of primary concern, as the syntheses of Caio Prado, Jr. (1942), Frédéric Mauro (1983), and Jurgen Hell (1986) demonstrate. The subject still preoccupies many Brazilian scholars. Much of the present debate has been framed within the categories of Marxian analysis and dependency theory, although Wallerstein's union of dependency theory and Braudelian categories is also attractive in Brazil, where French historical currents have long had great impact (Wallerstein 1974-80). Fernando Novais's (1972, 1979) provocative study of the crisis of the ancien régime in eighteenth-century Brazil concentrates on the Portuguese and indeed Atlantic economic system, emphasizing the mercantilist nature of the colonial regime and the role of slavery and the slave trade in the "primitive accumulation of capital" necessary in the Marxian framework for the beginnings of capitalist development. His interpretation, which places emphasis on the mercantile capitalist nature of slavery in Brazil, has been hotly debated with major attacks coming from Barros de Castro (1977, 1980) and Ciro Cardoso (1979, 1982), both of whom, in different ways, emphasize distinct productive relations rather than commerce as the key to understanding slavery as a system. These debates have been presented and ably summarized in two works by José Roberto do Amaral Lapa (1980, 1982). Perhaps the most ambitious attempt to create a theory of slavery in Brazil is Jacob Gorender's *O escravismo colonial* (1985), which from a Marxist viewpoint seeks to establish a series of laws of colonial slavery. The ideological commitment of this work sometimes overshadows its considerable erudition and insight, but it

clearly establishes the existence or not of a "colonial slave mode
of production," as a topic of central concern among Brazilian scholars of slavery.

One of the theoretical debates is represented by the work of
Ciro Cardoso and others on the "peasant breach," the desire and
ability of slaves to grow and market their own food. Gorender (1983)
and others have viewed the slave system as one of unmitigated
exploitation with little room for maneuver or negotiation by slaves.
Ciro Cardoso (1979, 1983, 1984, 1987), Barros de Castro (1977, 1980),
Reis (1983), and Reis and Silva (1988) have found empirical evidence
of slaves operating as peasants by growing and even marketing their
own food, a fact that raises questions about the definitions of
"modes of production" and economic roles. How common slave
personal production was and how it was incorporated into the overall network of economic and social relations (Maeyama 1981) is a
matter of great dispute because, to some extent, the answer rests
on a vision of the nature of slavery itself. It is a good example of
the important implications of theoretical issues on Brazilian historical scholarship and should serve as an antidote to the sometimes
rudderless empiricism of North American historians. Here, I do not
wish to imply that a clear theoretical agenda necessarily produces
better historical scholarship, but simply that studies often appearing
to be purely empirical and devoid of any particular ideological or
theoretical orientation are never free of such biases. Whatever their
intellectual and theoretical preferences, Brazilian scholars are rarely
naive about their ability to write "value free" history.

The application of techniques of historical demography to
questions of Brazilian slavery has been one of the most notable advances in the study of slavery. Historical demography itself is a relatively new development in Brazil. A major turning point in this
field occurred in 1968 with the publication of Maria Luiza Marcílio's
La ville de São Paulo (1968). The first application of the modern
techniques of historical demography to the Brazilian population,
this study has served as a model and as a starting point for a whole
generation of students; and the Centro de Estudos de Demografia
Histórica da América Latina at the University of São Paulo under
her direction continues to publish (Pinto Venâncio, 1986). Parallel
to Marcilio's work was the development in Curitiba of a graduate
program at the Universidade Federal do Paraná under Altiva Pilatti
Balhana. This program began to produce graduate theses of high
quality and technical skill, many of which included analyses of the
enslaved elements in the population. However, in truth, the first

modern demographic studies could give little attention to the slave population because of the lack of adequate sources and the problems of linking records when so few slaves had family names that permitted them to be traced over time or from one source to another. To overcome these difficulties historians have become increasingly inventive, or, like Robert Slenes and Pedro Carvalho de Mello, have concentrated their demographic studies on the period between 1872, the date of Brazil's first national census and the end of slavery.[8] Their sophisticated methods have produced solid analyses of fecundity, life expectancy, and age distribution, as well as of the economic profitability in the final years of slavery. Scholars are now trying to link the recent demographic findings to other aspects of slave historiography (Cardoso 1983). Notable in this regard is Kuznesof's (1986) study of São Paulo's urbanizing economy and its changing population structure.

Concern with demographic issues now characterizes many books on Brazilian slavery. Alden's (1963) early article based on colonial regional censuses set the context for more specific studies based on local data. Schwartz (1985) has examined the unhealthy demographic regime on Bahian sugar plantations and Karasch (1987) has included a chapter on slave demography in Rio de Janeiro. Kiple's (1989) article on nutrition and mortality is an important new departure linking medical and social history.

In recent years, the greatest advances in the study of slave demography has been concentrated regionally on Minas Gerais.[9] There, the continual government desire to control and profit from the output of gold by registering and taxing the slave population produced a documentation that, along with traditional parish and census materials, provides a rich documentary basis for modern demographic analysis. The center of these studies has been the Instituto de Pesquisas Economicas of the University of São Paulo, where two scholars, Iraci del Nero da Costa and Francisco Vidal Luna, have produced individually and in collaboration a number of important studies of the demography and ownership structure of the slave population of Minas Gerais in the colonial period (Nero da Costa 1978, 1983; Vidal Luna 1981, 1986; Vidal Luna and Nero da Costa 1979, 1981, 1982, 1982a). These two scholars are now applying their methods to similar data from São Paulo and Paraná and they have been joined more recently by Horácio Gutiérrez, who is also connected with the same institution (Vidal Luna and Nero da Costa 1983; Gutiérrez 1985, 1986). Their detailed studies have demonstrated the predominance of small-scale slaveholding, the economic diversity of slave occupations, and the presence of persistent family structures among slaves. These studies also suggest that the negative demographic characteristics found in the plantation sectors did not invariably characterize other areas of Brazilian slaveholding. Independently, the American scholar Donald Ramos (1975, 1975a, 1979) has produced a series of demographic and social studies of Minas Gerais, which parallel the work done in Brazil and add considerably to our knowledge of the population of the mining zones.

Of a more controversial nature has been the work of two Mineiro scholars trained in the United States, Amilcar Martins Filho and Roberto Borges Martins (Borges Martins 1980, 1983; Martins Filho and Borges Martins 1983). They have emphasized the expanding economy of Minas in the nineteenth century and its orientation toward internal markets, and they have examined the demography of the slave population to measure that growth. They argue that Minas presents a seeming anomaly of an expanding slave-based economy with only secondary links to the export sector. Other scholars like Slenes (1985) and Cano and Vidal Luna (1985) are less convinced of the autarkic nature of the Mineiro economy and the extent to which the size of the slave force resulted from natural growth; but the debate on slavery in Minas demonstrates the manner in which demographic analyses of the slave population can provoke an examination of some of the most hallowed and repeated beliefs about slavery in Brazil.

One extension of the interest in slave demography has been a rebirth of concern with the slave family, once dismissed as virtually nonexistent (Fernandes 1969). Whereas Freyre had sought to examine the impact of the slave on the Brazilian, i.e., planter family, the recent studies are concerned with the slave household and family. Here the influence of North American historiography, especially Herbert Gutman's *The Black Family in Slavery and Freedom* (1977) is reflected in many recent studies of the slave family in Brazil. An important early article on an atypically large plantation by Graham (1976) was an important turning point. Mesquita Samara (1981, 1981a) and Marcílio (1972) have analyzed household structure and the role of slaves within it. Nizza da Silva (1980, 1983, 1984) has examined marriage in general and slave marriages in particular from a juridical viewpoint. Using census data Nero da Costa, Gutiérrez, and Slenes have suggested that the traditional image of fractured, single-parent families usually associated with slaves must be changed in some places where mixed economies and a low level of importation characterized the structure of slavery, and that variables such as size of the slaveholding and the type of economic activity must be considered. São Paulo seems to have had higher rates of slave marriage than other areas of Brazil, but the reasons for this are still unclear. The work of these scholars, along with that of Metcalf (1987) and Fragoso and Florentino (1987) in a special issue of *Estudos Econômicos* (17:2 [1987]), indicates the complexity of the issue of the slave family. That complexity and the need to go beyond models developed from European studies of the family is made clear in works like that of Gudeman and Schwartz (1984) on godparentage and of Goldschmidt (1987) on mixed slave/nonslave marriages.

The new more nuanced view of the Brazilian slave family can be reconciled with the overall negative demographic conditions of Brazilian slavery because of regional and temporal variations. In certain areas and under certain conditions more stable family structures and healthier demographic regimes prevailed among Brazilian slaves. Recent studies are seeking to establish where, when, and why such conditions prevailed. Despite their differences, almost all of these studies make clear that the traditional vision of the slave family in terms of a social pathology is in need of serious revision, and that the absence of formal church-sanctioned unions and thus a high rate of illegitimacy among slaves does not by itself prove the absence of family life. Once freed of the former preconceptions, fresh approaches are possible. Mattoso's work (1988) on nineteenth-century Bahian families gives considerable attention to families of former slaves and their descendants. Her work, like that of many other Brazilians and Brazilianists working on the slave family, demonstrates a familiarity with parallel studies done in the United States; but it seeks to avoid a simple transposition of questions and results from the North American context. To understand the form, function, and meaning of the slave family, the Brazilian family and its place in society must be understood. However, historians are only just beginning to address this task. Students of the slave family in Brazil have not yet established the extent to which the norms of slave family life reflected an autonomous development or were encouraged and molded by the masters who imposed their own paternalistic sense of morality.

The negative demographic regime that usually characterized Brazilian slavery made constant resupply from Africa an essential feature of the institution, but the slave trade is a topic that in Brazil has received less concern in recent years than many others. The question of volume was most carefully addressed in Mauricio Goulart's (1949) study (which was republished in 1975). Goulart suggests low figures and total numbers of between 2.5 and 3 million slaves introduced by the Atlantic trade to Brazil. These figures were closely followed by Philip Curtin (1969) in his classic census of the Atlantic slave trade. However, these estimates have been questioned more recently by Robert Conrad (1986), who places the number at close to 5 million, and a number of other Brazilian authors are also not convinced by the Goulart figures (Alencastro 1979). Perhaps, it will only be through careful regional and local studies of the slave trade that the gross figures will be adjusted. The work of Westphalen (1972) on Paranaguá, Ribeiro Júnior (1973) on Pernambuco, Antônio Carreira (1979, 1983) on Pará and Maranhão, Postma (1990) on Dutch Brazil, and Medeiros dos Santos (1978, 1980) and Wehling (1973) on Rio de Janeiro are steps in that direction, although in their studies slaves are simply one aspect of the commerce that interests them. More studies are needed in Brazil on the structure and volume of the trade like Herbert Klein's *Middle Passage* (1978), which has been recently translated into Portuguese. His chapters on the slave trade to Brazil may provoke further inquiry in this area. Klein has also contributed an excellent review essay on the demography of the trade (1987).

A few Brazilian authors are presently concerned with other aspects of the slave trade. Portuguese and Brazilian connections to the market for slaves in Spanish America in the seventeenth century remains a topic of interest (Gonçalves Salvador 1981). Luiz-Felipe de Alencastro (1979, 1984) has written on quantitative and nonquantitative aspects of the slave trade. He has examined the structure of the Angola-Brazil slave trade and he has argued that the common interest in the slave trade during the nineteenth century contributed to the creation of a national unity. A major study from an African perspective is Miller's 1988 study of the Angolan slave trade and its connections to Brazil. Miller's complex book essentially documents the old seventeenth-century saying that "without sugar, no Brazil, without slaves, no sugar, without Angola, no slaves." He discusses also the attempts by Brazilian merchants to shift the center of the slaving business from Lisbon to Rio de Janeiro.

The movement to abolish the slave trade, coupled with the relationship between British pressure and Brazilian concerns, has also been the focus of the recent studies by the Bahian historian Luís Henrique Dias Tavares (1967, 1988), who, building on the previous work of Alan Manchester and Leslie Bethell (1970), concentrates on Brazilian motives and aims in the movement for abolition of the trade. David Eltis (1987) has included Brazil in his complex discussion of the suppression of the Atlantic slave trade. Finally, those interested in the slave trade from a Portuguese perspective should begin with the articles of Carreira (1979) and Latour da Veiga Pinto (1979), who both outline major historiographical trends and seek to summarize findings, but who do not deal in depth with the complex social and political forces that influenced changing Portuguese policy.

The early origins of the slave trade and its subsequent rhythms are related to the question of alternate labor sources. Indians as well as Africans were enslaved in Brazil or coerced to work under a variety of labor arrangements. Novais (1972) has suggested the European mercantilist origins of Atlantic slave trade and the reasons for moving from Indian to African workers. Schwartz (1978) demonstrated the transition on northeastern sugar plantations and argued that the causes were to be found in Brazil and were essentially a combination of Indian demographic decline, shifting levels of supply and price for the two kinds of laborers, the productivity and skills of Africans, and the increasing efficiency of the slave trade. Menard and Schwartz (1990) have examined these conditions in a comparative perspective using case studies of Mexico, South Carolina, and Barbados as well as Brazil. Monteiro (1988, 1988a) has studied the workings of Indian slavery in São Paulo, and Alden (1983) and MacLachlan (1973) have examined the process in the Amazon region.

A new economic history of slavery characterized by modern quantitative approaches has begun to flourish in Brazil, influenced to some extent by the cliometric histories of North Americans. The questions of prices (Marcílio 1978), markets (Slenes 1986), and especially the profitability of slavery (Carvalho de Mello 1978; Oliveira Portocarrero de Castro 1973) have all received some attention, although many Brazilian scholars have remained skeptical of the implicit neoclassical economics that serve as the basis for such studies. However, economists and historians have generated important statistical series in these studies. Good case studies of specific sectors of the economy are beginning to appear (Libby 1984, 1988). Graham (1981) has shown how the general impact of slavery on economic development (the other central concern of the cliometric historians of the United States) can be addressed in a comparative perspective.

Quantitative and nonquantitative techniques have been used in a number of new monographic studies examining the structure and history of slavery from a regional perspective or within a particular economic setting. Stanley Stein's *Vassouras* (1957), a study of the Paraíba river valley, set a standard for this approach. Reis de Queiroz (1977) and Dean (1976) on São Paulo, Queirós Mattoso (1974, 1976) and Schwartz (1985) on Bahia, Eisenberg (1974) and Barros dos Santos (1985) on Pernambuco, Mott (1974, 1976) on Piauí, Vasconcelos Ferreira (1973, 1984) on Goiás, and Oscar (1985) on the Province of Rio de Janeiro are examples of a growing body of slave studies that have carefully analyzed the institution from a limited geographical perspective and have attempted to demonstrate the specificity of the institution in particular settings. Studies of activities such as whaling (Ellis 1973), ranching (Mott 1986), mining (Palacin 1973), and salt meat packing (Maestri Filho 1984a) represent an important tendency of work specific studies while Karasch (1987), Sousa Andrade (1988), and Silva (1988) have examined slaves and freed people in the urban labor force.

Concern with slave resistance has increased greatly in the last two decades. This is due in part to an increasing awareness of racial inequality in Brazil, a self-conscious search for historical example and tradition by revisionist and Afro-Brazilian intellectuals, and to a general historical climate in which the actions of slaves are given increasing attention (Chiavento 1980; Moura 1983). A number of general studies, like José Alípio Goulart's *Da fuga ao suicídio* (1972), report many incidents and types of resistance and reprint selected documents (Goulart 1971; Freitas 1976). More interpretative are the works of Clóvis Moura, who concentrates on fugitive slave communities (*quilombos*) and on rebellions (Moura 1981, 1987). Palmares, the great *quilombo* of the seventeenth century, continues to draw interest in works such as Décio Freitas's (1982) often reprinted interpretation, but little new evidence on Palmares has come to light since the classic books of Edison Carneiro (3d ed., 1966) and Ernesto Ennes (1938) of over forty years ago. The recent volume by Alves Filho (1988) incorporates primary sources from Portuguese archives, but does not alter the main outlines of the story.

The growth of a regional historiography of slave resistance has been an important development. Local studies such as Mário José Maestri Filho (1979, 1984) on Rio Grande do Sul, Vicente Salles (1971) on Pará , Waldemar de Almeida Barbosa (1972) on Minas Gerais, Pedro Tomás Pedreira (1973) on Bahia, Luiz Mott (1976a, 1980, 1986b) and Ariosvaldo Figueiredo (1977) on nineteenth-century Sergipe have considerably enriched the knowledge of slave resistance.

The best of these studies attempt to link the form and frequency of slave actions to broader social and economic conditions (Gama Lima 1981). In general, these studies either emphasize long-term conditions specific to the slave population, such as African ethnicities or local work regimes, or they portray a slave population sometimes aware of broad political and social trends and ready to seize the moment as they did in the years just preceding abolition.

Slave actions were often a matter of police concern and a number of scholars are now exploiting previously unused police records to analyze master-slave relations and slave crimes. Aufderheide's (1976) still-unpublished thesis has influenced a number of these studies. Among the notable examinations of slave crime are Machado (1987), Mezan Algranti (1988), and the recent book by Hunold Lara (1988) on master-slave relations in the area of Campos, Rio de Janeiro, in the late eighteenth century, which makes extensive use of police and court records. Police and judicial records of slave resistance are also being published. The official inquest into the 1838 revolt of Manuel Congo in Rio de Janeiro province indicates the kind of documentation that is available (Pinaud et al., 1987). The recent book and article by Mezan Algranti (1988, 1988a) on slave crime in the city of Rio de Janeiro and Pereira Toledo Machado's book (1987) on rural São Paulo represent this trend and demonstrate the usefulness of these materials. Work by Reis (1988) and Holloway (1989) are good examples of how police records of repression of black cultural manifestations like *capoeira* (African martial arts clubs) and African religious practices can be used to penetrate the inner life of slaves.

Finally, important new scholarship on the major slave rebellions of the early nineteenth century has emphasized the role of slave culture in understanding these movements. While a number of the general works on slave resistance have analyzed slave rebellions, the work of João José Reis (1986) on the Malê rebellion of 1835 and the government's repression of it (1985) has been a breakthrough demonstrating once again the utility of police and judicial records that, in this case, demonstrate the existence of a vibrant slave culture and community often suspected but rarely perceived by contemporaries or by later historians. Reis's analysis of the Malê movement emphasized the deeply African nature of Bahian slave culture and its influence on resistance. That position stands in stark contrast to Genovese's (1979) attempt to link slave rebellions of the late eighteenth and nineteenth centuries to the wider political movements of the "Atlantic Revolution." Clearly both historians of Brazilian and North American slavery have turned toward cultural explanations of slave motives and actions, but their interpretations may vary greatly not only because of their own intellectual differences but because of the very different historical contexts of Brazilian and U.S. slavery. Reis's work is a good example of the union of broad theoretical concerns with a detailed and informed analysis of slave life and culture, not because it is "exotic" but because an understanding of its dynamics illumines and helps to explain the historical process. This topic promises to demand continuing attention. In 1988, as part of the centenary commemoration, *Estudos Econômicos* dedicated two issues to the theme of "Slave Protest."

Curiously, while studies of slave protest have flourished in the last two decades and have turned increasingly toward cultural interpretations, studies of slave culture and by extension African cultures in Brazil have not received similar attention. The obvious strength of Afro-Brazilian culture in slavery times and the broad diffusion of African elements in Brazilian culture as a whole have led to a somewhat tacit acceptance of slave culture as a given. The idea of cultural survival as a kind of resistance that has gained some popularity in the United States has not informed recent Brazilian historiography, where the focus has been on the way in which slave culture molded or stimulated resistance.

The study of slave culture in Brazil grew from an earlier ethnographic tradition. The works of Nina Rodrigues (1974), Manuel Querino (1938), and Artur Ramos (1951, 1979), which Freyre continued, were often folkloric in nature and did not generate great interest in the years after 1950, at least among historians who turned increasingly toward economic approaches to slavery. Some of these earlier classics were republished but had little impact on historical research. Conversely, important work on slave culture was and still is often done by anthropologists, some of them non-Brazilians. Here we must mention Pierre Verger's (1966, 1968, 1975, 1981, 1985) historical, anthropological, and photographic works, which collectively bring the historical past and present together on the theme of African cultural diffusion. Roger Bastide's *African Religions in Brazil* (1960, 1973) provides a general and still provocative overview, and detailed monographs like Elbein dos Santos (1984) on the Yoruba cult of death in Bahia demonstrate the complexity of the topic. The work of D. M. Dos Santos, Edison Carneiro, and others continued to investigate African culture but often outside a historical framework. Some attempts to link the two approaches can be seen in the linguistic studies of Yeda Pessoa de Castro (1980), who is associated with the Institute of African Studies of the University of

Bahia, which irregularly publishes the journal *Afro-Ásia*. Much remains to be done by historians, but the situation is changing. Reis, it should be noted, is presently writing a history of *candomblé* (Yoruba religion) in Bahia based on police records. The wealth of these sources is revealed in his 1988 discussion of an African cult raided in Cachoeira in 1785. Luiz Mott (1986a) has used Inquisition records in Portugal to demonstrate the existence of *acontundá*, or syncretic religious forms, among slaves in eighteenth-century Minas Gerais, and he is completing a biography of a remarkable African woman who went from slave prostitute to widely acclaimed and revered holy woman in late colonial Rio de Janeiro (Mott 1987). Finally, the Africanist John Thornton (1988), in his examination of African contacts with Christian conversion in both Africa and the Americas and his emphasis on a dynamic process of religious syncreticism, offers a new line of research with interesting prospects.

This new trend in the historiography of Brazilian slavery reflects the growing interest in popular culture and *mentalites*, which has captured the attention of historians in Europe and the United States. In a country so profoundly affected by slavery, the impact of slaves, slavery, and racial attitudes on varieties of popular culture is easily understood. Laura de Mello e Souza (1986) demonstrated how African beliefs and practices were confused with European concepts of witchcraft by the Portuguese Inquisition. Sexuality, morality, and popular religion have been the focus of a number of these studies, like those of Vainfas (1988) and Mott (1988).

Historians have been active in examining the participation of slaves and freed persons in the institutions of Brazilian life. Excellent studies of religious brotherhoods (*irmandades*), like that of Caio César Boschi (1986) on Minas Gerais and Julita Scarano (1976) on black brotherhoods in particular, have demonstrated the way in which the records of certain types of institutions can be particularly revealing of slave life and culture when used creatively. Here, the work of Russell-Wood (1968, 1971, 1974) has been a useful model and example. Other institutions await investigation, as Berrance de Castro (1969) has shown with the National Guard.

Studies of the process of manumission and of the former slaves and their descendants have been a major achievement of Brazilian scholarship. Katia de Queirós Mattoso and her students in Bahia have led the way. Her general study of Brazilian slavery (1986) contains much material on the freed population based on her own monographic studies (1972, 1976, 1979) and also incorporating work done under her direction, like that of Côrtes de Oliveira (1979).

Mattoso has also recently completed an exhaustive study of the free people of color of Salvador. Her earlier work on manumission (1971), done in collaboration with Schwartz (1974) and paralleled by Karasch (1987) on Rio de Janeiro and Kiernan (1976) on Paraty, is now being reexamined and modified in Brazil. Eisenberg (1981, 1987) has produced a study of manumission in nineteenth-century Campinas, and Carneiro da Cunha (1983) has examined the legal constraints on *libertos* (former slaves). In addition, Carneiro da Cunha (1985) has written a perceptive book on the place of freed Africans in Brazilian society and their return to Africa in the nineteenth century. Vidal Luna (1981, 1986) has examined the role of free people of color as slaveowners.

Free people of color have long fascinated scholars interested in the comparative history of race relations. Degler's (1971) emphasis on the "mulatto escape hatch" placed the role of free people of color at the heart of the different racial systems of Brazil and the United States. Interest in this subject is increasing in Brazil as part of a growing concern with continuing inequalities in Brazilian society. Concern with the rural and urban poor, the disabilities suffered by women, and the disadvantages of color in contemporary society has provoked new interest in the historical origins of these conditions. The burdens of color have received much attention and increasingly their origins are sought not so much in slavery itself but in the position of freed people in Brazilian society. Herbert Klein's (1969) overview of free people of color in Brazilian society defined the major issues. The now-classic work of Maria Sylvia de Carvalho Franco (1969) demonstrated how a study of the free population had to take slavery into account. This line of investigation has been followed by Mello e Souza (1982) and Eisenberg (1983). A work that unites slavery directly with the issue of gender is Silva Dias's (1984) study of women in nineteenth-century São Paulo. Giacomini (1988) also takes this approach. Lauderdale Graham (1988) examines domestic labor, slave and free and much of it female, in Rio de Janeiro. Studies like that of Bárbara Levy (1973) on urban Rio de Janeiro and Maria Yedda Linhares and Francisco C. Teixeira da Silva (1981) on agriculture have begun to remove slave studies from relative isolation and to tie them to broader social issues. That integration is also apparent in Viotti da Costa's (1985) general survey of nineteenth-century Brazil.

The movement for abolition has produced a distinct historiography meriting an extended discussion and upon which we can only touch here. The books by Toplin (1972) and Conrad (1972) have served as important milestones for subsequent scholarship. The synthetic articles by Graham (1966, 1970) defined the major approaches to the problem and suggested how Brazilian scholarship was moving from an interpretation that emphasized the personality and program of abolitionists and Dom Pedro II to more concern on the rise of a bourgeois mentality and a national economy antithetic to this archaic institution. Ricardo Salles (1990) has examined the role of blacks in the Paraguayan War and the effect of their participation on the attitudes of the Brazilian military. The debates over the nature and process of abolition have more recently been argued through detailed regional studies like Soares de Galliza on Paraíba (1979), Marchiori Bakos (1982) on Rio Grande do Sul, Marcos dos Santos (1980) on São Paulo, and Ferreira de Almieda (1977) on Espírito Santo. Solid economic studies like that of Eisenberg (1974), Jaime Reis (1974), and Galloway (1968) on Pernambuco have no parallels for other provinces; nor, to date, have there been any syntheses of the scope of Conrad (1972), although Reis de Queiroz (1981) has prepared a small volume summarizing the literature. Some attempt should be made toward new syntheses and detailed economic regional studies as the monographic literature expands.

The spurt of postemancipation studies on the transition from slave to free labor that have developed on the Caribbean and U.S. South was slow to develop in Brazil, except in those studies taking up the questions of immigration or demographic change, such as the work of José de Sousa Martins (1981), Eisenberg (1983), Leff and Klein (1974), and Stolcke (1986). This situation seems to be changing rapidly and a number of scholars are now at work on the immediate post-1888 period. That Brazil also moved from a monarchy to a republic in 1889 has led to an emphasis on political dimensions of the transition. Décio Saes (1985) has written a stimulating essay from that perspective. Ademir Gebara (1986) has addressed the question of labor supply after abolition, while Andrews (1988) has examined the impact of race of the labor market in São Paulo. A detailed study of the transformation of the land and labor market is provided by Mattos de Castro (1987). Viotti da Costa's (1985) general examination of the empire brings national politics and slavery together in a series of interpretative essays. What happened to the former slaves and how their lives were transformed remains to be studied and a number of scholars are at work on this problem, although research is complicated because most references to former slave status were eliminated shortly after abolition, thus making the tracing of former slaves particularly difficult in the existing documentation. A rich new line of research on the perception of former slaves and their acceptance as citizens has been opened by Marinho de Azevedo (1987) and Moritz Schwarcz (1987), both of whom demonstrate that a profound racist legacy continued after slavery.

The comparative perspective is now emerging in abolition and postemancipation studies like Blackburn's (1988) general history and Toplin's (1981) comparisons of the United States and Brazil. The essay by Scott (1988) and the companion article by Drescher (1988) indicate the direction of new studies while the work of Kolchin (1983) and Hahn (1990), which include comparisons with the end of serfdom in Russia or landholding power in Prussia, indicate how widely these comparisons will range. In a way, such works continue the trend begun by Freyre and Tannenbaum and push the chronological boundaries forward by emphasizing the similarity of processes in the creation and transformations of the modern world. Serious students of those processes can no longer ignore Brazilian history, nor can students of Brazil forget that its history is part of a larger story in which its experience with slavery should take a prominent place.

The considerable attention paid to slavery in Brazil has buried the old myth that the documents on slavery had been destroyed (Slenes 1983; Lacombe, Silva, and Barbosa 1988). Robert Conrad's (1983) compilation and translation of a variety of documents on Brazilian slavery is a model to be followed. Many archives and other institutions initiated cataloging and recovery projects in order to prepare guides to sources on slavery for the centenary of abolition (Arquivo Nacional 1988; Prefeitura Municipal do Salvador 1988?). New iconographic materials have been uncovered, such as the remarkable collection of slave photographs taken by Christiano, Jr. (Azevedo and Lissovsky 1988). The new studies have brought to light a rich harvest of materials ranging from parish registers to plantation accounts. Eduardo Silva (1984, 1986) has demonstrated the utility of private correspondence and planter manuals for an understanding of slavery from the planter point of view.

Historians must ultimately listen to the people who experienced slavery, to what they said and what they did. Planter views are easier to obtain than those of the slaves. Unlike the situation in the United States, where vast numbers of slave narratives exist and where government-sponsored collections of slave testimony were gathered and have subsequently been analyzed, slave and former slave writings or depositions are rare in Brazil. However, a few do exist (Schwartz 1979; Carneiro da Cunha 1984; Mott 1979; J. J.

Reis 1983). The extensive interview carried out in 1982 by Maestri Filho (1983) in a Curitiba hospital with Mariano Pereira dos Santos, an ex-slave, stands out as among the most interesting of these slave statements. Asked about the significance of abolition, he responded, "It's like I say, after liberation, *tamo na gloria* [we were in glory]!" But did he say exactly that? Márcia Campos Graf's (1988) interview with the same man reads quite differently and raises questions about the techniques and transcription of oral evidence. Recovering slave voices will not be an easy task or one any less free from the intellectual and political currents that have always infused the study of Brazilian slavery and made it a vibrant and challenging field of study and one central to an understanding of that nations' history and to the history of the Afro-American experience.

NOTES

1. Among the special issues of periodicals devoted to slavery were *Clio* (Universidade Federal de Pernambuco) 11 (1988); 12 (1989); "O protesto escravo" *Estudos Econômicos* 17–18 (1987–88); "Demografia de escravidão" *Estudos Econômicos* 17:2 (1987), passim; "Escravidão" *Revista do Departmento de História* (Universidade Federal de Minas Gerais) 6; *Luso-Brazilian Review* 25:1 (1988), passim; *Hispanic American Historical Review* 68:3 (1988), passim.

2. Keeping track of the rapidly growing bibliography on Brazilian slavery has become a major task in itself. The work has been facilitated by Robert Conrad, *Brazilian Slavery: An Annotated Research Bibliography* (Boston, 1977); Rizio Bruno Santana and Iraci del Nero da Costa, *A escravidão brasileira nos artigos de revistas (1976–85)* (São Paulo, 1985); and by the annual bibliographies on slavery compiled by Joseph Miller and published since 1980 in the journal *Slavery and Abolition*.

3. A good survey of the historiography of Brazilian slavery and of black life in Brazil is found in A. J. R. Russell-Wood, "Africans and Europeans: Historiography and Perceptions of Reality," in *The Black Man in Slavery and Freedom in Brazil* (London, 1982), 1–26.

4. I have briefly summarized this development in my foreword to Katia M. de Queirós Mattoso, *To Be a Slave in Brazil, 1550–1888*, trans. Arthur Goldhammer (New Brunswick, 1986), vii–xii.

5. I have not discussed here the parallel development of interest in race relations among social anthropologists that also emerged in the post–World War II era. The important work on race relations in Brazil sponsored by UNESCO and the subsequent publications of Charles Wagley, Marvin Harris, Harry Hutchinson, Thales de Azevedo, and others influenced a gen-

eration of scholarship in this area and played an important role in pointing historians toward new areas of investigation.

6. With few exceptions, I have not included the many valuable master's essays and doctoral theses produced in Brazilian universities because access to these is often difficult. A good guide to them is Carlos Humberto Corrêa, *Catálogo das dissertações e teses dos cursos de pós-graduação em história, 1973–1985* (Florianópolis, 1987). Readers should be aware that history theses produced in graduate programs in social sciences are not included in this volume.

7. The Portuguese language is rich in terms that in English might all be translated simply as "slavery." Other than *escravismo* and *escravidão*, the term *escravatura* has also been used by some authors, usually as a synonym for the former, but also as a term of description for an estate's slave force or community.

8. The works of Slenes and Carvalho de Mello are good examples of the limitations of using nationality as a criterion for evaluation of historical scholarship. While Slenes is North American born and Carvalho de Mello is a native of Brazil, both wrote doctoral dissertations in the United States and both now reside in Brazil. See Robert Slenes, "Demography and Economy of Brazilian Slavery" (Ph.D. diss., Stanford University, 1976); Pedro Carvalho de Mello, "Estimativa da longevidade de escravos no Brasil na segunda metade do século xix," *Estudos Econômicos* 13:1 (1983), 151–80.

9. The review article by Klein summarizes the recent work done on the demography of Minas Gerais and provides a useful listing of unpublished theses including those from the demography and social history program at the Universidade Federal do Paraná. See Herbert S. Klein, "The Population of Minas Gerais: New Research on Colonial Brazil," *Latin American Population History Newsletter* 4:1–2 (1984), 3–10.

WORKS CITED

Alden, Dauril
    1963   "The Population of Brazil in the Late Eighteenth Century. A Preliminary Survey." *Hispanic American Historical Review* 43:2, 173–205.
    1983   "Indian versus Black Slavery in the State of Maranhão during the Seventeenth and Eighteenth Centuries." *Bibliotheca Americana* 1:3, 91–142.
Alencastro, Luiz-Felipe de
    1979   "La traite négrière et l'unité nationale Brésilienne." *Revue Française d'Histoire d'Outre-Mer* 66: 244–45, 395–418.
    1984   "Prolétaires et esclaves: immigrés portugais et captifs africains à Rio de Janeiro, 1850–1872." *Cahiers du C.R.I.A.R.* (Université de Rouen) 4:119–56.

Almeida Barbosa, Waldemar de
  1972   *Negros e quilombos em Minas Gerais*. Belo Horizonte.
Alves Filho, Ivan
  1988   *Memorial dos Palmares*. Rio de Janeiro.
Amaral Lapa, José Roberto do, ed.
  1980   *Modos de produção e realidade brasileira*. Petrópolis.
  1982   *O antigo sistema colonial*. São Paulo.
Andrews, George Reid
  1988   "Black and White Workers: São Paulo, Brazil 1888–1928."
           In *The Abolition of Slavery and the Aftermath of
           Emancipation in Brazil*, ed. Rebecca Scott et al., Durham,
           N.C., 85–118.
Arquivo Nacional. Departamento da Imprensa Nacional
  1988   *Guia brasileiro de fontes para a história da África, da
           escravidão, e do negro na sociedade actual*. 2 vols.
           Brasília.
Aufderheide, Patricia Ann
  1976   "Order and Violence: Social Deviance and Social Control
           in Brazil, 1780–1840." Ph.D. diss., University of
           Minnesota.
Azevedo, Paulo César de, and Maurício Lissovsky, eds.
  1988   *Escravos brasileiros do século XIX na fotografia de
           Christiano Jr*. São Paulo.
Barros de Castro, António
  1977   "Escravos e senhores nos engenhos do Brasil." *Revista de
           Estudos Econômicos* 7:1, 177–220.
  1980   "A economia política, o capitalismo e a escravidão." In
           Modos de produção e realidade brasileira, ed. José Roberto
           de Amaral Lapa, Petrópolis, 67–108.
Barros dos Santos, Ana Maria
  1985   "Die Sklaverei in Brasilien und ihre Sozialen und
           Wirtschaftlichen Folgen." *Lateinamerika Studien* 20,
           Universität Erlangen-Nürnberg, Munich.
Bastide, Roger
  1960   *Les religions africaines du Brésil*. Paris.
  1973   *Estudos afro-brasileiros*. São Paulo.
—— and Florestan Fernandes.
  1971   *Brancos e negros em São Paulo: ensaio sociológico sobre
           aspectos da formação, manifestações atuais e efeitos do
           preconceito de cor na sociedade paulista*. São Paulo.
Beiguelman, Paula
  1967   *Formação política do Brasil*. 2 vols. São Paulo.
  1968   *A formacão do povo cafeeiro: aspectos políticos*. São Paulo.
Berrance de Castro, Jeanne
  1969   "O negro na guarda nacional." *Anais do Museu Paulista*
           23:149–72.

Bethell, Leslie
1970   *The Abolition of the Brazilian Slave Trade.* Cambridge.
Blackburn, Robin
1988   *The Overthrow of Colonial Slavery, 1776–1848.* London.
Borges Martins, Roberto
1980   *A economia escravista de Minas Gerais no século XIX.*
        Belo Horizonte.
1983   "Minas Gerais, século XIX: tráfico e apego à escravidão
        numa economia não-exportadora." *Revista de Estudos
        Econômicos* 13:1, 181–210.
Boschi, Caio César
1986   *Os leigos e o poder (Irmandades leigas e política
        colonizadora em Minas Gerais).* São Paulo.
Boxer, Charles R.
1963   *Race Relations in the Portuguese Empire, 1415–1825.*
        Oxford.
Campos Graf, Márcia Elisa de
1981   *Imprensa periódica e escravidão no Paraná.* Curitiba.
1986–87 "Entrevista com Mariano Pereira dos Santos, um exescravo
        de 122 anos." *Revista da Sociedade Brasileira de Pesquisa
        Histórica* 3:117–24.
Cano, Wilson and Francisco Vidal Luna
1985   "La reproducción natural de los esclavos en Minas Gerais."
        Revista Latinoamericana de Historia Económica y Social
        4:130–35.
Cardoso, Ciro Flamarion S.
1979   *Agricultura, escravidão, e capitalismo.* Petrópolis.
1982   *A Afro-América: a escravidão no novo mundo.* São Paulo.
1983   "Escravismo e dinâmica da população escrava nas
        Américas." *Revista de Estudos Econômicos* 13:1, 41–54.
1984   *Economia e sociedade em áreas coloniais periféricas:
        Guiana Francesa e Pará (1750–1817).* Rio de Janeiro.
1987   *Escravo ou camponês. O protocampesinato negro nas
        Américas.* Rio de Janeiro.
Cardoso, Fernando Henrique
1962   *Capitalismo e escravidão no Brasil meridional.* São Paulo.
Carneiro, Edison
1966   *O Quilombo dos Palmares.* 3d ed. Rio de Janeiro.
Carneiro da Cunha, Manuela
1983   "Sobre os silêncios da lei. Lei costumeira e positiva nas
        alforrias de escravos no Brasil do século XIX." *Cadernos
        IFCH Unicamp* no. 4. São Paulo.
1984   "Sobre a servidão voluntária: outro discurso. Escravidão e
        contrato no Brasil colonial." *Dédalo* 23:57–66.

1985   *Negros estrangeiros. Os escravos libertos e sua volta à África.* São Paulo.

Carreira, Antônio

1979   "Portuguese Research on the Slave Trade." In *The African Slave Trade from the Fifteenth to the Nineteenth Century.* Paris.

1983   *As companhias pombalinas de Grão-Pará e Maranhão e Pernambuco e Paraíba.* 2d ed. Lisbon.

Carvalho de Mello, Pedro

1978   "Aspectos econômicos da organização do trabalho da economia cafeeira do Rio de Janeiro, 1850–88." *Revista Brasileira de Economia* 32:1, 19–67.

1983   "Estimativa da longevidade de escravos no Brasil na segunda metade do século XIX." *Revista de Estudos Econômicos* 13:1, 151–80.

Carvalho Franco, Maria Silvia de

1969   *Homens livres na sociedade escravocrata.* São Paulo.

Chiavento, Julio José

1980   *O negro no Brasil: da senzala à guerra do Paraguai.* 2d ed. São Paulo.

Conrad, Robert Edgar

1972   *The Destruction of Brazilian Slavery 1850–1888.* Berkeley.

1983   *Children of God's Fire. A Documentary History of Black Slavery in Brazil.* Princeton.

1986   *World of Sorrow. The African Slave Trade to Brazil.* Baton Rouge.

Côrtes de Oliveira, Maria Inês

1979   "O liberto o seu mundo e os outros." Master's thesis from Salvador, Universidade Federal da Bahia.

Curtin, Philip D.

1969   *The Atlantic Slave Trade: A Census.* Madison.

Davis, David B.

1966   *The Problem of Slavery in Western Culture.* Ithaca.

1984   *Slavery and Human Progress.* New York.

Dean, Warren

1976   *Rio Claro. A Brazilian Plantation System, 1820–1920.* Stanford.

Degler, Carl

1971   *Neither Black nor White: Slavery and Race Relations in Brazil and the United States.* New York.

Dias Tavares, Luís Henrique

1967   "O processo das soluções brasileiras no exemplo da extinção do tráfico negreiro." *Revista de História* (São Paulo) 72:523–37.

1988   *Comércio proibido de escravos.* São Paulo.

Drescher, Seymour
1988   "Brazilian Abolition in Comparative Perspective." In *The Abolition of Slavery and the Aftermath of Emancipation in Brazil,* ed. Rebecca Scott et al., Durham, N.C., 23–54.

Eisenberg, Peter L.
1974   *The Sugar Industry of Pernambuco, 1840–1910.* Berkeley.
1981   "A carta de alforria e outras fontes para estudar a alforria no século XIX." *Memória da III Semana da História* (Universidade Estadual Paulista), 187–233.
1983   "Escravo e proletário na história do Brasil." *Revista de Estudos Econômicos* 13:1, 55–70.
1987   "Ficando livre: A alforria em Campinas no século XIX." *Estudos Econômicos* 17:2, 175–216.

Elbein dos Santos, Juana
1984   *Os Nàgô e a morte. Pàde, àsèsè e o Culto Égun na Bahia.* 3d ed. Trans. from French by the Universidade Federal da Bahia. Petrópolis.

Elkins, Stanley
1959   *Slavery: A Problem in American Institutional and Intellectual Life.* Chicago.

Ellis, Myriam
1973   "Escravos e assalariados na antiga pesca da baleia (Um capítulo esquecido da história do trabalho no Brasil colonial.)" *Anais do VI Simpósio Nacional dos de Professores Universitários de História: Trabalho Livre e Trabalho Escravo* 1:307–52.

Eltis, David
1987   *Economic Growth and the Ending of the Atlantic Slave Trade.* Oxford.

Ennes, Ernesto
1938   *As Guerras nos Palmares (Subsídios para a sua história).* Vol. 1. São Paulo.

Falcon, Francisco C. and Fernando A. Novais
1973   "A extinção da escravatura africana em Portugal no quadro da política econômica pombalina." *Anais do VI Simpósio Nacional dos Professores Universitários de História: Trabalho Livre e Trabalho Escravo* 1:405–31.

Fernandes, Florestan
1969   *The Negro in Brazilian Society.* Ed. Phyllis B. Eveleth; Trans. Jacqueline D. Skiles, A. Brunel, and Arthur Rothwell. New York.
1972   *O negro no mundo dos brancos.* São Paulo.

Ferreira de Almeida, Vilma Paraíso
1984   *Escravismo e trabalho. O Espírito Santo (1850–1888).* Rio de Janeiro.

Figueiredo, Ariosvaldo
  1984   *O Negro e a violência do branco (O negro em Sergipe)*.
          Rio de Janeiro.
Fragoso, João Luís and Manolo G. Florentino
  1987   "Marcelino, filho de Inocência crioula, neto de Joana
          Cabinda: um estudo sobré famílias escravas em Paraíba do
          Sul (1835–1872)." *Estudos Econômicos* 17:2, 151–74.
Freitas, Décio
  1976   *Insurreições escravas*. Porto Alegre: Editorial Movimento.
  1982   *Palmares: a guerra dos escravos*. 4th ed. Rio de Janeiro.
Freitas Brandão, Júlio de
  1973   "O escravo e o direito." *Anais do VI Simpósio Nacional
          dos Professores Universitários de História: Trabalho Livre
          e Trabalho Escravo* 1:255–84.
Freyre, Gilberto
  1933   *Casa grande e senzala*. Rio de Janeiro. (English version:
          The Masters and the Slaves. Trans. Samuel Putnam. New
          York, 1946.)
Gama Lima, Lana Lage
  1981   *Rebeldia negra e abolicionismo*. Rio de Janeiro.
Gebara, Ademir
  1986   *O mercado de trabalho livre no Brasil*. São Paulo.
Genovese, Eugene
  1971   *The World the Slaveowners Made*. New York.
  1979   *From Rebellion to Revolution: Afro-American Slave
          Revolts in the Making of the Modern World*. New York.
Giacomini, Sonia Maria
  1988   *Mulher e escrava*. Petrópolis.
Goldschmidt, Eliana
  1986–87 "A motivação matrimonial nos casamentos mistos de
          escravos." *Revista da SBPH* 3:1–16.
Gonçalves Salvador, José
  1981   *Os magnatas do tráfico negreiro*. São Paulo.
Gorender, Jacob
  1983   "Questionamentos sobre a teoria econômica do escravismo
          colonial." *Revista de Estudos Econômicos* 13:1, 7–40.
  1985   *O escravismo colonial*. 2d ed. São Paulo.
Goulart, José Alípio
  1971   *Da palmatória ao patíbulo (castigos de escravos no Brasil)*.
          Rio de Janeiro.
  1972   *Da fuga ao suicídio: aspectos da rebeldia dos escravos no
          Brasil*. Rio de Janeiro.
Goulart, Maurício
  1975   *A escravidão africana no Brasil: das origens à extinção do
          tráfico*. 3d ed. São Paulo.

Graham, Richard
1966 "Causes for the Abolition of Negro Slavery in Brazil: An Interpretative Essay. *Hispanic American Historical Review* 46:2, 123–37.
1970 "Brazilian Slavery Re-examined: A Review Article." *Journal of Social History* 3:4, 431–53.
1976 "Slave Families on a Rural Estate in Colonial Brazil." *Journal of Social History* 9:3, 382–402.
1981 "Slavery and Economic Development: Brazil and the United States South in the Nineteenth Century." *Comparative Studies in Society and History* 23:4, 620–55.

Gudeman, Stephen and Stuart B. Schwartz
1984 "Cleansing Original Sin: Godparentage and the Baptism of Slaves in Eighteenth Century Bahia." In *Kinship Ideology and Practice in Latin America,* ed. Raymond T. Smith. Chapel Hill, N.C.

Gutiérrez, Horácio
1985 "Posse de escravos no Paraná nas primeiras décadas do século XIX." Mimeo from the XIII National Symposium of History, ANPUH. Curitiba.
1986 "Casamentos nas senzalas. Paraná, 1800–1830." (1° seminário. Centenário da abolição do escravismo: Da época colonial à situaçao do negro na actualidade.) Instituto de Pesquisas Econômicas, São Paulo.

Hahn, Steven
1990 "Class and State in Postemancipation Societies: Southern Planters in Comparative Perspective." *American Historical Review* 95:1, 75–98.

Harris, Marvin
1964 *Patterns of Race in the Americas.* New York.

Hell, Jurgen
1986 *Sklavenmanufaktur und Sklavenemanzipation in Brasilien 1500–1888.* Berlin.

Holloway, Thomas H.
1989 "'A Healthy Terror': Police Repression of 'Capoeiras' in Nineteenth-Century Brazil." *Hispanic American Historical Review* 69:4.

Ianni, Octávio
1962 *As metamorfoses de escravo. Apogeou e crise da escravatura no Brasil meridional.* São Paulo.
1978 *Escravidão e racismo.* São Paulo.

Karasch, Mary C.
1987 *Slave Life in Rio de Janeiro, 1808–1850.* Princeton.

Kiernan, James
1976 "The Manumission of Slaves in Colonial Brazil: Paraty-1822." Ph.D. diss. New York University.

Kiple, Kenneth
  1989   "The Nutritional Link with Slave Infant and Child
          Mortality in Brazil." *Hispanic American Historical Review*
          69:4, 677–90.
Klein, Herbert S.
  1967   *Slavery in the Americas: A Comparative Study of Cuba
          and Virginia.* Chicago.
  1969   "The Colored Freedmen in Brazilian Slave Society."
          Journal of Social History 3:1, 30–52.
  1978   *The Middle Passage: Comparative Studies in the Atlantic
          Slave Trade.* Princeton.
  1987   "A demografia do tráfico atlântico de escravos para o
          Brasil." *Estudos Econômicos* 17:2, 129–50.
Kolchin, Peter
  1983   "Reevaluating the Antebellum Slave Community: A
          Comparative Perspective." *Journal of American History*
          70:3, 579–601 (1989), 637–76.
Kuznesof, Elizabeth Anne
  1986   *Household Economy and Urban Development. São Paulo,
          1765–1836.* Boulder, Colo.
Lacombe, Américo Jacobina, Eduardo Silva and Francisco de Assis
  Barbosa
  1988   *Rui Barbosa e a queima dos arquivos.* Rio de Janeiro.
Lara, Silvia Hunold
  1988   *Campos de violência. Escravos e senhores na capitania do
          Rio de Janeiro, 1750–1808.* Rio de Janeiro.
Latour da Veiga Pinto, Françoise, assisted by Antônio Carreira
  1979   "Portuguese Participation in the Slave Trade: Opposing
          Forces, Trends of Opinion within Portuguese Society,
          Effects on Portugal's Socioeconomic Development." In *The
          African Slave Trade from the Fifteenth to the Nineteenth
          Century.* Paris.
Lauderdale Graham, Sandra
  1988   *House and Street. The Domestic World of Servants and
          Masters in Nineteenth-Century Rio de Janeiro.* Cambridge.
Leff, Nathaniel H. and Herbert S. Klein
  1974   "O crescimento da população não européia antes do início
          do desenvolvimento: O Brasil do século XIX." *Anais de
          História* (Faculdade de Filosofia Ciências e Letras de Assis)
          6:51–70.
Levy, Bárbara
  1973   "Participação da população livre e escrava numa
          codificação sócio-profissional do Rio de Janeiro (1850–
          1870): alguns aspectos." *Anais do VI Simpósio Nacional
          dos Professores Universitários de História: Trabalho Livre
          e Trabalho Escravo* 1:639–58.

Libby, Douglas Cole
1984 Trabalho escravo e capital estrangeiro no Brasil. O caso de Morro Velho. Belo Horizonte.
1988 Transformação e trabalho em uma economia escravista. São Paulo.
Linhares, Maria Yedda and Francisco Carlos Teixeira da Silva.
1981 História da agricultura brasileira: combates e controvérsias. São Paulo.
Machado Monteiro, Helena
1987 Crime e escravidão. São Paulo.
MacLachlan, Colin M.
1973 "The Indian Labor Structure in the Portuguese Amazon, 1700–1800." In Colonial Roots of Modern Brazil, ed. Dauril Alden. Berkeley, 199–230.
1979 "Slavery, Ideology, and Institutional Change: The Impact of the Enlightenment on Slavery in Late Eighteenth-Century Maranhão." Journal of Latin American Studies 11:1, 1–17.
Maestri Filho, Mário José
1979 Quilombos e quilombolas em terras gaúchas. Porto Alegre: Escola Superior de Teologia São Lourenço de Brindes; Caixas do Sul: Universidade de Caixas do Sul.
1983 "É como eu digo: de agora, depois da libertação, 'tamo na glória!' Depoimento de Mariano Pereira dos Santos (ca. 1868–1982), ex-escravo, Hospital Erasto Goertner, Curitiba, Julho 1982." História: Questões & Debates (Curitiba) 4:6, 81–98.
1984 O escravo gaúcho: resistência e trabalho. São Paulo.
1984a O escravo do Rio Grande do Sul. Caixas do Sul.
Maeyama, Takashi
1981 "The Masters versus the Slaves under the Plantation Systems in Brazil: Some Preliminary Considerations." Latin American Studies University of Tsukuba, Japan 3:115–41.
Marchiori Bakos, Margaret
1982 Rio Grande do Sul: escravismo e abolição. Porto Alegre.
Marcílio, Maria Luiza
1968 La ville de São Paulo: peuplement et population. 1750–1850. Rouen.
1972 "Tendências e estruturas dos domicílios na capitania de São Paulo (1765–1828) segundo as listas nominativas de habitantes." Revista de Estudos Econômicos 2:6, 131–43.
1978 "The Price of Slaves in XIXth-Century Brazil: A Quantitative Analysis of the Registration of Slaves in Bahia." In Studi in Memoria di Federigo Melis, 5 vols. Rome. 5:83–97.

1986   *Caiçara: Terra e população.* São Paulo.
Marcos dos Santos, Ronaldo
1980   *Resistência e superação do escravismo na província de São Paulo (1885–1888).* São Paulo.
Marinho de Azevedo, Célia Maria
1987   *Onda négra, medo branco. O negro no imaginário das elites-século XIX.* Rio de Janeiro.
Martins Filho, Amilcar and Roberto B. Martins
1983   "Slavery in a Non-Export Economy: Nineteenth Century Minas Gerais Revisited." *Hispanic American Historical Society* 63:3, 537–69.
Mattos de Castro, Hebe Maria
1987   *Ao sul da história. Lavradores pobres na crise do trabalho escravo.* São Paulo.
Mattoso, Katia M. de Queirós
1971   "Propósito de cartas de alforria na Bahia, 1779–1850. *Anais de História* (Marília) 4:23–52.
1974   "Os escravos na Bahia no alvorecer do século XIX. (Estudo de um grupo social)." *Revista de História* 97:109–35.
1976   "Um estudo quantitativo de estrutura social: a cidade de Salvador, Bahia de Todos os Santos, no século XIX, primeiros resultados." *Estudos Históricos* (Faculdade de Filosofia, Ciências e Letras de Maríla, São Paulo) 15:7–28.
1978   "Inquisição: os cristãos novos da Bahia no século XVIII." *Revista dé Ciência e Cultura* 30:4, 415–27.
1979   *Testamentos de escravos libertos na Bahia no século XIX. Uma fonte para o estudo de mentalidades.* Bahia.
1986   *To Be a Slave in Brazil, 1550–1888.* Trans. from French by Arthur Goldhammer. New Brunswick.
1988   *Família e sociedade na Bahia do século XIX.* São Paulo.
Mauro, Frédéric
1983   *Le Portugal, Le Brésil et L'Atlantique au XVII siécle.* Paris (based on earlier version of 1960).
Medeiros dos Santos, Corcino
1978   "Relações de Angola com o Rio de Janeiro (1736–1808)." *Estudos Históricos* 12:7–68.
1980   *Relações comerciais do Rio de Janeiro com Lisboa (1763–1808).* Rio de Janeiro.
Mello e Souza, Laura de
1982   *Desclassificados do ouro. A pobreza mineira no século XVIII.* Rio de Janeiro.
1987   *O diabo e a terra de Santa Cruz.* São Paulo.
Menard, Russell and Stuart B. Schwartz
1990   "Transitions to African Slavery in the Americas." In *Slavery in the Americas*, ed. Wolfgang Binder. Erlangen-Nürnberg.

Mesquita Samara, Eni de
  1981   "Os agregados: uma tipologia ao fim do período colonial
            (1780–1830)." *Revista de Estudos Econômicos* 11:3, 159–68.
  1981a   "A estrutura da família paulista no começo do século
            XIX." *Boletim do Museu da Casa Brasileira* 4:29–38.
Metcalf, Alida C.
  1987   "Vida familiar dos escravos em São Paulo no século
            dezoito: o caso de Santana de Paranaíba." *Estudos
            Econômicos* 17:2, 229–43.
Mezan Algranti, Leila
  1988   *O feitor ausente. Escravidão urbana no Rio de Janeiro.* São
            Paulo.
  1988a   "Slave Crimes: The Use of Police Power to Control the
            Slave Population of Rio de Janeiro." *Luso-Brazilian Review*
            25:1, 27–48.
Miller, Joseph
  1988   *Way of Death. Merchant Capitalism and the Angolan
            Slave Trade 1730–1830.* Madison.
Monteiro, John
  1988   "Celeiro do Brasil: escravidão indígena e a agricultura
            paulista no século XVII." *História* 7:1–12.
  1988a   "From Indian to Slave: Forced Native Labour and Colonial
            Society in São Paulo during the Seventeenth Century."
            Slavery and Abolition 9:2, 105–27.
Moritz Schwarcz, Lilia
  1987   *Retrato em branco e negro.* São Paulo.
Mott, Luiz R. B.
  1973   "A propósito de três livros sobre o negro Brasileiro."
            Revista de História (São Paulo) 96:563–78.
  1974   "Brancos, pardos, pretos índios em Sergipe: 1825–1830."
            Anais de História 6:139–84.
  1976   "Estatísticas e estimativas da população livre e escrava de
            Sergipe del Rei de 1707 a 1888." *Mensário do Arquivo
            Nacional* 7:12, 19–21.
  1976a   "Pardos e pretos em Sergipe: 1774–1851." *Revista do
            Instituto de Estudos Brasileiros* 18:7–37.
  1979   "Uma escrava no Piauí escreve uma carta." *Mensário do
            Arquivo Nacional* 10:5, 7–9.
  1980   "Violência e repressão em Sergipe: notícias sobre revoltas
            de escravos (séc. XIX)." *Mensário do Arquivo Nacional,*
            11:5, 3–21.
  1985   *Piauí colonial: População, economia e sociedade.* Teresina:
            Projeto Petrônio Portella.
  1986   "O patrão não está: análise do absenteismo nas fazendas
            de gado do Piauí colonial." In *Brasil: História Econômica e
            Demográfica,* ed. Iraci del Nero da Costa. São Paulo. 29–
            36.

1986a   "Acontundá: raízes setecentistas do sincretismo religioso afro-brasileiro." *Revista do Museu Paulista* (New Series) 31:124–47.

1986b   *Sergipe del Rey. População, economia e sociedade.* Aracaju.

1987   "Uma santa africana no Brasil colonial." *D. O. Leitura.* São Paulo, 6 (62).

1988   *Escravidão, homossexualidade, e demonologia.* São Paulo.

Moura, Clóvis

1981   *Rebeliões da senzala. Quilombos insurreições guerrilhas.* 3d ed. São Paulo.

1983   *Brasil. Raízes do protesto negro.* São Paulo.

1987   *Quilombos. Resistência ao escravismo.* São Paulo.

1990   *As injustiças de Clio. O negro na historiografia brasileira.* Belo Horizonte.

Nero da Costa, Iraci del

1978   *Algumas características dos proprietários de escravos de Vila Rica.* (Universidade de São Paulo, Faculdade de Economia e Administração, Convênio IPE/FINEP, São Paulo.)

1983   "Nota sobre ciclo de vida e posse de escravos." *História: Questões & Debates* (Revista da Associação Paranaense de História, Curitiba) 4:6, 121–27.

—— and Horácio Gutiérrez

1984   "Nota sobre casamentos de escravos em São Paulo e no Paraná (1830)." *História: Questões & Debates* (Revista da Associação Paranaense de História, Curitiba) 5:9, 313–21.

Nina Rodrigues, Raymundo

1974   *Os africanos no Brasil.* 5th ed. São Paulo.

Nizza da Silva, Maria Beatriz

1980   "Casamentos de escravos na capitania de São Paulo." *Ciência e Cultura* 32:7, 816–21.

1983   "Escravidão e casamento no Brasil colonial." In *Estudos de História de Portugal*, 2 vols., 2:229–39. Lisboa.

1984   *Sistema de casamento no Brasil colonial.* São Paulo.

Novais, Fernando A.

1972   *Estrutura e dinâmica do sistema colonial.* Lisboa.

1979   *Portugal e Brasil na crise do antigo sistema colonial.* São Paulo.

Novinsky, Anita

1973   "Impedimento ao trabalho livre no período inquisitorial e as respostas da realidade brasileira." *Anais do VI Simpósio Nacional dos Professores Universitários de História : Trabalho Livre e Trabalho Escravo* 1:231–54.

Oliveira Portocarrero de Castro, Hélio

1973   "Viabilidade econômica da escravidão no Brasil, 1850–1888." *Revista Brasileira de Economia* 27:1, 43–67.

Oscar, João
1985   *Escravidão e engenhos. Campos; São João da Barra;*
            Macaé; São Fidélis. Rio de Janeiro.
Palacin, Luís
1973   "Trabalho escravo: produção e productividade nas minas de
            Goiás." *Anais do VI Simpósio Nacional dos Professores*
            Universitários de História: Trabalho Livre e Trabalho
            Escravo 1:433–48.
Pedreira, Pedro Tomás
1973   *Os quilombos brasileiros.* Salvador.
Pereira Toledo Machado, Maria Helena
1987   *Crime e escravidão. Trabalho, luta e resistência nas*
            lavouras paulistas 1830–1888. São Paulo.
Pessoa de Castro, Yeda
1980   *Os falares africanos na interação social do Brasil colonial.*
            Bahia.
Pinaud, João Luiz and Carlos Otávio de Andrade, et al.
1987   *Insurreição negra e justica.* Rio de Janeiro.
Pinheiro, Paulo Sérgio (coordinator)
1984   *Trabalho escravo, economia e sociedade.* Rio de Janeiro.
Pinto Venâncio, Renato
1986   *Ilegitimidade e concubinato no Brasil colonial.* Rio de
            Janeiro and São Paulo.
Postma, Johannes Menne
1990   *The Dutch in the Atlantic Slave Trade, 1600–1815.*
            Cambridge.
Prado, Jr., Caio
1942   *Formação do Brasil contemporâneo.* São Paulo.
Querino, Manuel
1938   *Costumes africanos no Brasil.* Rio de Janeiro.
Ramos, Artur
1951   *O negro brasileiro.* 3d ed. São Paulo.
1979   *As culturas negras no Novo Mundo.* 3d ed. São Paulo.
Ramos, Donald
1975   "Marriage and the Family in Colonial Vila Rica." *Hispanic*
            American Historical Review 55:2 (May), 200–225.
1975a   "City and Country: The Family in Minas Gerais, 1804–
            1838." *Journal of Family History* 3:4, 361–75.
1979   "Vila Rica: Profile of a Colonial Brazilian Urban Center."
            The Americas 35:4, 495–526.
Reis, Jaime
1974   "Abolition and the Economics of Slaveholding in North
            East Brazil." *Boletin de Estudios Latinoamericanos y del*
            Caribe 17:3–20.
Reis, João José
1983   "Poderemos brincar, folgar e cantar . . . : O protesto escravo
            nas Américas." *Afro-Ásia* 14:107–120.

1985 "O 'rol dos culpados': notas sobre um documento da rebelião de 1835." *Anais do Arquivo Público do Estado da Bahia* 48:109–18.

1986 *Rebelião escrava no Brasil. A história do levante dos Malês (1835)*. São Paulo.

1988 "Magia jeje na Bahia: A invasão do calundu do Pasto de Cachoeira, 1785." *Revista Brasileira de História* 8:16, 57–82.

Reis, João José and Eduardo Silva

1988 *Negociação e conflito. A resistência negra no Brasil escravista*. São Paulo.

Reis de Queiroz, Suely R.

1977 *Escravidão negra em São Paulo: um estudo das tensões provocadas pelo escravismo no século XIX*. Rio de Janeiro.

1981 *A abolição da escravidão*. São Paulo.

Ribeiro Júnior, José

1973 "Alguns aspectos do tráfico escravo para o Nordeste brasileiro no século XVIII." *Anais do VI Simpósio Nacional dos Professores Universitários de História : Trabalho Livre e Trabalho Escravo* 1:387–403.

Russell-Wood, A. J. R.

1968 *Fidalgos and Philanthropists. The Santa Casa da Misericórdia of Bahia, 1550–1755*. Berkeley.

1971 "Aspectos da vida social das irmandades leigas na Bahia colonial." In *O bi-centenário de um momento bahiano*, ed. Manoel de Aquino Barbosa. Salvador.

1974 "Black and Mulatto Brotherhoods in Colonial Brazil: A Study in Collective Behavior." *Hispanic American Historical Review* 54:4, 567–602.

1978 "Iberian Expansion and the Issue of Black Slavery: Changing Portuguese Attitudes, 1440–1770." *American Historical Review* 83:1, 16–44.

1982 *The Black Man in Slavery and Freedom in Colonial Brazil*. New York.

Saes, Décio

1985 *A formação do estado burguês no Brasil (1888–1891)*. Rio de Janeiro.

Salles, Ricardo

1990 *Guerra do Paraquai. Escravidão e cidadania na formação do exército*. Rio de Janeiro.

Salles, Vicente

1971 *O Negro no Pará sob o regime da escravidão*. Rio de Janeiro.

Scarano, Julita

1976 *Devoção e escravidão: a Irmandade de Nossa Senhora do Rosário dos Pretos no distrito Diamantino no século XVIII*. São Paulo.

Schwartz, Stuart B.
1974   "The Manumission of Slaves in Colonial Brazil: Bahia, 1684–1745." *Hispanic American Historical Review* 54:4, 603–35.
1978   "Indian Labor and New World Plantations: European Demands and Indian Responses in Northeastern Brazil." *American Historical Review* 83:3, 43–79.
1979   "Resistance and Accommodation in Eighteenth-Century Brazil: The Slave's View of Slavery." *Hispanic American Historical Review* 57:1, 69–81.
1985   *Sugar Plantations in the Formation of Brazilian Society. Bahia 1550–1835.* Cambridge.
Scott, Rebecca
1988   "Exploring the Meaning of Freedom: Postemancipation Societies in Comparative Perspective." In *The Abolition of Slavery and the Aftermath of Emancipation in Brazil,* ed. Rebecca Scott et al. Durham, N.C., 1–22.
Silva, Eduardo
1984   *Barões e escravidão. Tres gerações de fazendeiros e a crise da estrutura escravista.* Rio de Janeiro.
1986   *Memória sobre a fundação de uma fazenda na província do Rio de Janeiro.* Trans. by Fríncisco Peixoto de Lacerda, Barão do Paty do Alferes. Brasilia.
Silva, Marlene Rósa Nogueira
1988   *Negro na rua: a nova face da escravidão.* São Paulo.
Silva Dias, Maria Odila Leite da
1984   *Quotidiano e poder em São Paulo no século XIX.* São Paulo.
Slenes, Robert W.
1983   "O que Rui Barbosa não queimou: novas fontes para o estudo da escravidão no século XIX." *Revista de Estudos Econômicos* 13:1, 117–50.
1985   *Os múltiplos de porcos e diamantes: a economia escravista de Minas Gerais no século XIX.* Campinas: Cadernos IFCH, Unicamp.
1986   "Grandeza ou decadência? O mercado de escravos e a economia cafeeira da província do Rio de Janeiro, 1850–1888." In *Brasil: História Econômica e Demográfica,* ed. Iraci del Nero da Costa. São Paulo, 103–56.
Soares de Galliza, Diana
1979   *O declínio da escravidão na Paraíba, 1850–1888.* João Pessoa.
Sousa Andrade, Maria José
1988   *A mão de obra escrava em Salvador, 1811–1860.* São Paulo.

Sousa Martins, José de
   1981   *O cativeiro da terra.* 2d ed. São Paulo.

Souza e Silva, Joaquim Norberto de
   1986   *Investigações sobre os recenseamentos da população geral do império.* Facsimile ed. São Paulo.

Stein, Stanley J.
   1957   *Vassouras: A Brazilian Coffee County 1850–1900:* Cambridge, Mass.

Stolcke, Verena
   1986   *Cafeicultura: homens, mulheres, e capital (1850–1980).* São Paulo.

Tannenbaum, Frank
   1947   *Slave and Citizen.* New York.

Thornton, John
   1988   "On the Trail of Vodoo: African Christianity in Africa and the Americas." *The Americas* 55 (January): 261–78.

Titton, Gentil Avelino, OFM
   1973   "O Sínodo da Bahia (1707) e a escravatura." *Anais do VI Simpósio Nacional dos Professores Universitários de História: Trabalho Livre e Trabalho Escravo* 1:285–306.

Toplin, Robert
   1972   *The Abolition of Slavery in Brazil.* New York.
   1981   *Freedom and Prejudice.* Westport, Conn.

Vainfas, Ronaldo
   1986   *Ideologia e escravidão. Os letrados e a sociedade escravista no Brasil colonial.* Petrópolis.
   1989   *Trópico dos pecados.* Rio de Janeiro.

Vasconcelos Ferreira de Salles, Gilka
   1973   "O trabalhador escravo em Goiás nos séculos XVIII e XIX." *Anais do VI Simpósio Nacional dos Professores Universitários de História: Trabalho Livre e Trabalho Escravo* 1:599–638.
   1984   "A sociedade agrária em Goiás colonial." *Revista do ICHL* (Instituto de Ciências Humanas e Letras da Universidade Federal de Goiás) 4:1, 55–88.

Verger, Pierre
   1966   *O fumo da Bahia e o tráfico dos escravos do golfo de Benim.* Salvador.
   1968   *Flux et reflux de la traite des nègres entre le golfe de Bénin et Bahia de Todos os Santos du XVIIe au XIXe siécle.* Paris.
   1975   *Note sur le culte des Orisha et Vodoun à Bahia, la Baie de tous les saintes au Brésil et l'ancienne Côte des Esclaves en Afrique.* Dakar.
   1981   *Orixás.* Salvador.
   1985   *Lendas africanas dos Orixás.* Bahia.

Vidal Luna, Francisco
  1981   *Minas Gerais: escravos e senhores.* São Paulo.
  1986   "Estrutura da posse de escravos em Minas Gerais (1804)."
          In *Brasil: História Econômica e Demográfica,* ed. Iraci del
          Nero da Costa. São Paulo, 157–72.
————— and Iraci del Nero da Costa
  1979   "Algumas caraterísticas do contingente de cativos em
          Minas Gerais." *Anais do Museu Paulista* 29:79–97.
  1981   "Vila Rica: nota sobre casamentos de escravos (1727–
          1826)." *África* (Revista do Centro de Estudos Africanos da
          Universidade de São Paulo) 4:3–7.
  1982   *Minas colonial: economia e sociedade.* São Paulo.
  1982a   "Devassa nas Minas Gerais: observações sobre casos de
          concubinato." *Anais do Museu Paulista* 31:3–15.
  1983   "Posse de escravos em São Paulo no início do século XIX."
          Revista de Estudos Econômicos 13:1, 211–22.
Vilela Santos, Maria Januária
  1983   *A Balaiada e a insurreição de escravos no Maranhão.* São
          Paulo.
Viotti da Costa, Emília
  1966   *Da senzala à colônia.* São Paulo.
  1985   *The Brazilian Empire: Myths and Histories.* Chicago.
Wallerstein, Immanuel
  1974–80 *The Modern World System:* 2 vols. to date. New York
Wehling, Arno
  1973   "Aspectos do tráfico negreiro do Rio de Janeiro (1823–
          1830)." *Anais do VI Simpósio Nacional dos Professores de
          História: Trabalho Livre e Trabalho Escravo* 1:521–32.
Westphalen, Cecilia Maria
  1972   "A introdução de escravos novos no litoral paranaense."
          Revista de História (São Paulo) 89:139–54.

2 Sugar Plantation Labor and Slave Life

In the rush to document and portray the resourcefulness and resilience of the men and women who endured slavery and to demonstrate how various aspects of their life and culture were a creative response to the situation in which they lived, historians of the American slave regimes have been writing a new ethnography of slave cultures. Studies of slave religion, the arts, family, and the slave community, written with sympathy and conviction, have broadened and enriched our understanding of life under slavery, but at some cost. Slaves did not form a community like any other. The new studies have often pushed into the background the essential and distinctive fact of the slaves' lives that served as a backdrop to all their actions and constrained their lives as well as the decisions made by them and about them. Slaves were a labor force, and coerced work for others oriented virtually every aspect of their situation. To discuss slave life or culture without a recognition of this reality is an exercise in ethnographic fantasy.[1]

In this essay I wish to reintroduce work to a discussion of Brazilian slavery in order to establish a context in which slave life and aspirations developed. Of course, the nature of labor demands varied considerably in different slave regimes according to the kind of economic activity and the level of technology available. The variety of work requirements was a primary element that determined the nature of slave life by setting levels of owner expectation and ordering slave priorities. Simply put, those who worked on cattle ranches and lived in comparative isolation had different opportunities than those who labored in the gangs at the gold mines or those who cut sugar cane.

In a previous extensive study of the Brazilian colonial sugar regime as it existed in Bahia, I sought to demonstrate how the specific and peculiar nature of sugar production not only determined the structure and composition of the labor force but also influenced the conditions of work and life on the Brazilian sugar estates, or *engenhos.*[2] In this chapter, I return to that theme in order to draw the connections between work and slave life more sharply and to demonstrate that the nature of sugar production constrained owners and producers in a vast variety of ways. Work was the core of slavery and, by close attention to the specific requirements of the demands of sugar plantation agriculture within the context of Brazilian seignorial society, it is possible to examine the peculiar integration of labor and other aspects of the Brazilian slave life that made this society distinctive.[3]

Sugar, Work, and Slave Life

The Brazilian sugar regime in the seventeenth century, unlike its later Caribbean competitors, concentrated on the production of higher quality "clayed" sugar. Despite that specialization, in many ways it was representative of most new-world sugar plantations. With the exception of details and differences due to local conditions, sugar production in the colonial American regimes differed little from colony to colony, as the late seventeenth- and early eighteenth-century classics of Labat for the French Antilles, Ligon for Barbados, and Antonil for Brazil demonstrate.[4] To some extent, this situation arose because of conscious borrowing and imitation of the Portuguese model developed in Brazil by later English, Dutch, and French planters.[5]

Sugar was a distinctive crop: it called not only for good land and a particular climate but also for particularly heavy capital investment in buildings and equipment and a large labor force dedicated to continual and heavy activity during certain periods of the year. A sugar plantation, moreover, always needed a mill, or *engenho,* where the cane was processed. This combination of integrated agricultural and industrial activities on a rural property gave the sugar plantations their distinctive character and made them quite unlike most other agricultural units. Along with mining and shipbuilding, Europeans engaged in few activities more complex than sugar production in the early modern period.

Let us trace, then, the particular work requirements of the Brazilian sugar plantations as a basis for understanding how slaves were used and why certain opportunities for independent action and social advancement existed. In Bahia, the harvest (*safra*) lasted for about nine months and planting extended for two months beyond that, so crop-related labor continued for most of the year, thus making sugar production an ideal use of slave labor from the planters' point of view. Physical conditions on Bahian *engenhos* were extremely poor: lack of clothing, inadequate housing, poor nutrition, harsh discipline and cruel punishments. Above all, the labor requirements on sugar mills were particularly onerous. During the *safra* the mills operated through the night, and work sometimes continued for eighteen to twenty hours a day, with work organized in shifts within the mill. Exhausting labor, poor diet, and unpleasant and dangerous conditions combined to make sugar a particularly "bad" crop in all the new-world slave societies. Brazil was no exception.

These conditions and patterns in the trans-Atlantic slave trade contributed to an unhealthy demographic regime that in turn placed severe constraints on the options available to slaves. Bahian slaves suffered from high mortality and low fertility. Life expectancy at birth in the late eighteenth century was probably about twenty-three years in comparison to the thirty-five years calculated for U.S. slaves in 1850. The sex ratio in Bahia as a whole was about three men to every two women for most of the period (1600–1830), and on sugar estates sometimes 2:1. This imbalance originated in and was reinforced by the slave trade. Here was a population with an excess of men, a low percentage of children, and a high proportion of Africans. While there were periods such as that between 1750 and 1770 in which a downturn in the sugar industry and a resultant decrease in the slave trade tended to shift the ratio of Africans and *crioulos* and to improve the ratio of children to adults in the slave population, during most of the period (1600–1830) the overall patterns predominated. The annual rate of natural decline of this population was probably between 1.5 and 3 percent a year, and only the continued existence of an open slave trade allowed planters to expand or maintain their labor forces.

This demographic regime had a profound impact on planter perceptions and policies as well as on slave actions and reactions. Most planters, for example, saw no reason to stimulate stable families to promote a natural growth of the population. Since a slave could produce in fourteen to twenty-four months enough sugar to equal his or her value at purchase, as long as the trade remained open, planters believed that the risks and costs of raising *crioulos* (Brazilian-born black) children for fourteen years until they could become full workers was not worth the effort.[6] The policy was to use slaves to maximum production by keeping down costs and maintaining an intensive work schedule. For the planter to double his investment, an adult slave had only to live for five years under such conditions.

Planters, however, were moved by more than profit and loss. The model economic rationality was limited at times by a series of cultural and moral constraints codified in Portuguese law and in the teachings and precepts of the church. These also influenced slave life. For example, religious prohibitions against labor on the sabbath and on certain religious holidays was the chief cause of stoppage at the Bahian mills. About three-quarters of the days lost in the milling season resulted from stoppages for religious reasons. Slaves were allowed to use this "free" time for themselves, encouraged to form religious brotherhoods, and to participate in the cultural forms of the wider society.

But even if we lay aside the cultural constraints on the slave-owners' drive for profit, planters had another problem. Effective sugar production depended to some extent on slave cooperation. The complex operations of a mill were particularly susceptible to sabotage; a spark in the cane field, lime in a boiling pan, a cracked cogwheel at the mill itself could spell ruin. Moreover, sugar making demanded a series of skills and "arts," so that the problem was never simply the quantity and productivity of the labor force, but its quality and its cooperation as well.

Here we must return to the peculiar nature of sugar production. In a way the whole estate—field and factory—was an integrated series of processes in which considerable skill in timing and integrating the cutting, carting, milling, boiling, and drying had to be done based on experience and art. In the field, gang labor could be used, although it was common in cutting cane to assign daily quotas (*tarefas*) to teams of two people (usually a man and a woman), one to cut and the other to bind the cane into bundles. In the complex milling and boiling process other kinds of labor organization were used.

The mill and the boiling house were called by the Portuguese the *fábrica* (the word used today for factory) because of their industrial nature. Pressing the canes in the mill, clarifying the liquid in a series of cauldrons, skimming impurities, and pouring the liquid into molds that then crystallized into sugar were processes as old or older than the medieval Mediterranean world but was in some ways strikingly modern. The sugar-making process in the *fábrica* closely resembled the modern industrial assembly line. The pace of work was set by technology—the speed of the mill, the capacity of the kettles, and the temperature of the fires. The work was done in shifts and often measured in quotas. The labor was exhausting. "Sleepy as an *engenho* slave," was a common expression. The night-time scenes of boiling cauldrons, the whirring mill, and the sweating bodies caused more than one observer to evoke the image of hell. It was a glimpse of the industrial future that seared the vision of the preindustrial men who witnessed it.

This combination of traditional field practices with an industrial-style processing called for the establishment and integration of two different concepts of time and rhythms of work. The harvest cycle of planting, weeding, and cutting followed the natural rhythms of the season; and it was, in northeastern Brazil particularly, marked and limited by the rainy season (in Bahia from April to July), which brought an end to the harvest because it made transport of cane to the mill so difficult and because it changed the level of sucrose extracted from the cane. Within the mill and boiling house, however, the rhythm was not that of nature but that of a regulated, designed process. The work was not regulated by clocks (introduced rather late in the eighteenth century even in the Jesuit mills) but by capacity of the technology. Still, it was measured and assigned in quotas that paralleled agricultural task assignments.

The contrast here was, as Eugene Genovese has put it, "between peasant and factory cultures." All slave plantations had a tendency to push toward a modern work discipline, but sugar plantations, especially in their industrial sectors, represented the extreme case. Here, the contrast and potential conflicts between the rhythm of a traditional agricultural regime set within a supportive religious calendar that opposed a regulated and disciplined work regime were most apparent.[7] Leaving aside the question of African concepts of time and labor and their potential conflict with the plantation regime, there still remained the conflict between "peasant" and "worker" time and work rhythms.[8] Task and quota systems potentially served to integrate the two concepts of work time, setting field and mill operations on the same scale and allowing slaves the opportunity to return to the more natural and less-directed benefits of "peasant" time by successfully performing under the disciplined and measured work regime of "factory" time. The quota system presented slaves certain opportunities to be sure, but it also smoothed the operation of the plantation as a whole.

Similar advantages could also be gained by creating a hierarchy of workers. While physically exhausting and carefully regulated, the work in the mill was also socially differentiated. Specialized slaves—kettlemen, teachmen, carpenters, purgers, overseers, and sugar masters—created this social division that was both paralleled and reinforced by a hierarchy of color or racial categories as well. On one eighteenth-century plantation about three-quarters of the African and *crioulo* slaves were field hands, but only about half of the mulatto slaves worked in the fields. In contrast, although mulattoes only constituted about six percent of the total slave force, they occupied over twenty percent of the skilled, artisan, and managerial positions. While considerable attention has been devoted to the house slaves and those in skilled or managerial positions, in reality these made up less than twenty percent of the total slave force. Entry into these relatively few skilled and favored positions therefore was a desired privilege that could be controlled and manipulated by the slaveowners to extract cooperation and good service.[9]

Work in the cane fields was always slave, but in the *fábrica* slaves, freed, and free workers labored together, sometimes side by side. The relative proportions of these categories changed over time. From the seventeenth to the eighteenth century, slaveholders tended to replace white wage workers paid on a yearly basis with free and freed workers of color, a transition accompanied by a decline in the real wages of this class of workers. Moreover, planters increasingly used slaves in the skilled and managerial occupations within the mill, making this shift to reduce the cost of the considerable salaries that, in some cases, had made up as much as a third of the annual operating expenses of a mill. For the slaves, the opportunities that these skilled occupations offered served as incentives because the social differentiation of the sugar mill created the possibility of promotion within the labor force and within the plantation hierarchy. Eventually, with the introduction of more complex technology in the late eighteenth and nineteenth centuries, Brazilian planters complained of the ignorance of their slave and free colored workers who still treated sugar making as an art rather than a science; but in the short run the planters had benefited from the lower operational costs and the manipulation of work assignments that using these workers implied.

The use of slaves in managerial and skilled positions within the mill created a series of problems. While in the fields the amount of labor energy and its distribution was essential, the problem in the mill was the quality of labor. As in the modern factory, *engenho* workers were separated from the final product of their labor. Slaves did not make sugar, only the mill made sugar, while the workers repeated over and over the same limited task.[10] But this premature industrialization was conducted with slaves, and their use as technicians and artisans in a process that was easily sabotaged and that separated workers from the final product of their labor posed a seeming contradiction between slavery and industrial production.

The Whip, the Task, and the Hoe

The planters' answer to the dilemma of obtaining the quantity and quality of the labor needed was to find incentives that would elicit cooperation by offering at least a small window of hope. This is not to overlook the brutal use of force, especially in the field. Slavery always implied the whip or worse and the reality of punishment was ever-present, but unlike the situation in the field, I know of no reference to the use of the whip inside *fábrica*.[11] There, such physical production was counterproductive. While slaves might be given some unpleasant tasks (like stoking the furnaces) as punishment, most planters found other methods to assure cooperation and obtain the quality they demanded.

The *engenhos* created a series of positive and negative incentives not only within the sugar-making process but also extending outward into other aspects of society. Presents, rum, and extra rations or privileges were distributed, but even more important was diminution or a restructuring of work itself. The quota system was used not only in planting, cane cutting, and other field tasks but also within the mill itself (so many kettles of juice to tend, forms to fill, etc.), although in reality the pace of the mill really determined the speed of the process. Upon completion of the quota slaves were theoretically free to do whatever they desired; and the evidence is strong in Bahia and elsewhere in Brazil that slaves most desired to establish some degree of economic independence, which often meant to work on their own plots and gardens.[12] Using Sundays, religious holidays, and at times days set aside for self-maintenance, slaves could supplement their diet with their garden production, sell the surplus in local markets or back to the owner and keep the money earned either to buy other goods or to save for the eventual purchase of their freedom or that of a loved one.

The task system and its integration with slave desires for "free time," often to be devoted to small subsistence plots, provided slaves some social space, an opportunity to live better and, in some cases, a chance to participate directly in local markets. Then, too, such activity might ultimately gain the promise of freedom. The self-purchase of manumissions was relatively common in Bahia, and while it tended to be most characteristic of urban slavery, it was also found in the rural areas. Studies of Bahian manumission demonstrate that about half of all manumissions in Bahia in the period 1680–1750 were purchased, usually by the slaves themselves or by a member of the slave's family.[13] Bahia was not singular in this respect and similar patterns have been noted elsewhere in Brazil.

From the slaves' point of view, these opportunities may have seemed to be an "opening" or breach in the slave system. From the planters perspective, these were reasonable and effective responses to their labor needs. Malingering, recalcitrance, and sabotage were reduced because slaves had a reason to work efficiently and steadily to complete assigned tasks and gain time for themselves. Upkeep costs were reduced for the planters who could also calculate that after twenty years they might recapture all the slave's savings as well, in the form of a paid manumission. One planter manual in 1847 argued in favor of giving slaves their own gardens, "this links them to the land by the love of property. The slave who owns neither flees nor causes disorder."[14] This statement also implies some recognition of the positive force that stable families might have on slave production, and various ameliorationists urged promotion of slave families on both moral and economic grounds, especially in the nineteenth century.

Henry Koster, an Englishman who traveled and resided in Brazil between 1809 and 1815 and who managed a sugar estate in Pernambuco during that period, made some direct observations on the manner in which these aspects of slavery functioned. He noted that the Catholic religious calendar and custom provided a slave "many days of rest or time to work for his own profit" and that few masters violated this practice. The time thus afforded, enables the slave, "who is so inclined, to accumulate a sum of money." Since slaves were property, they could not own property under the law, but in practice slave ownership of property was widely recognized because it served the smooth operation of the slave system, and as Koster noted, "I believe there is no instance on record in which a master attempted to deprive his slave of these hard-earned gains." Most likely, Koster exaggerated, but his statement underlined the acceptance of the concept of slave property.[15]

Slaveowners were constrained both by custom and by slave resistance to accept the common practices. Violations did occur, but masters were often reluctant to face the criticism of public opinion by seizing a slave's property or by refusing an appeal for self-purchase. Koster also remarked on the difficulties encountered by masters who thought to act in this way. Slaves kept their money hidden or entrusted it to someone outside the master's control and they "would suffer any punishment rather than disclose the spot in which this wealth lies."[16] When they could, slaves put their money beyond the masters' reach. In the judicial inquiry following the Malê rebellion of Muslim slaves in Salvador in 1835, testimony from various participants indicated that freedmen in the city of Bahia kept trunks where slaves deposited their money and possessions for safekeeping.[17] If a master refused to allow a slave to buy his or her manumission, there was also the chance that the slave, especially if a *crioulo*, would take the money and use it to escape. Recognition of slave rights, therefore, resulted from considerations of morality and practicality.

Practical considerations might move a master to try to keep a skilled worker rather than allow the purchase of freedom. Koster reported the case of a slave who managed the boiling house of an *engenho* and who was such an excellent worker that the master refused to free him, even though the slave had accumulated money for his self-purchase. Forced to work in chains until his master's death, the slave finally bought his freedom from the widow. What is interesting here is the ability of this slave to use his position to accumulate money for his freedom and his expectations as a freedman. Koster added: "His trade of sugar-boiler renders him large profits yearly; and this injured man now lives in ease and comfort."[18]

While the task system, garden plots, and manumission all imply aspects of slave life that were to some extent goals outside the engenho regime, the acquisition of skills with the sugar-making process itself offered other incentives to slaves. Sugar masters, kettlemen, and foremen sometimes received rewards, wages, or even a percentage of their product as incentives. In the area of Campos (Rio de Janeiro) in 1790, a legal deposition reported that a slave who served as Sugar Master at any mill expected to earn between six and eight hundred *réis* per day as a minimum.[19]

Training for such a position was itself a reward. Mulattoes and crioulos were favored in skilled occupations or for the household tasks. They formed a privileged class of labor, working alongside freedmen. Their position was an example to other slaves of the rewards of cooperation. Skilled workers striving for manumission could hope for relatively secure employment after freedom, as the case mentioned by Koster suggests. In a particularly candid remark, the Jesuit administrator of an *engenho* wrote in 1623: "the mulattoes and crioulos are all very willing to work and all with hopes of manumission. God forgive whoever gave them this notion but, thanks to God I have them all in good service."[20]

The system of incentives was imperfect. Some slaves refused every blandishment and inducement to cooperate and resisted slavery in every way, but others sought to seek their advantage within the possibilities supplied by the *engenho* regime. The task system, slave gardens, the customary recognition of slave property (*peculium*), the hierarchy of skills and training, manumission, and even the general configuration of social distinctions in Brazilian society all served the ends of the slave regime and placed labor requirements at the core of the slave system and made the social relations of production its "inner secret." These were often interrelated in a direct way.[21] The social hierarchy of the *engenhos*—white owners and managers, Africans and blacks for the most part field hands, and some whites, some free, some freedmen and more mulattoes than proportionally in the population as skilled workers—reflected, reiterated, and reinforced the structure of Brazilian colonial society.

Slavery was a remarkably adaptive system and masters mixed force and incentives according to their personalities, local customs, regional and world economic conditions, and moral or cultural imperatives in a variety of combinations. The sugar planters' goal was to extract the most and the most-effective labor from the slaves. But to say that the system was adaptive is also to recognize the role that slaves themselves could have in it. Slaves were imaginative in manipulating the variations to suit their perception of advantage. What planters offered as incentives to serve their goals could be seen by slaves as an opportunity that might better their lives, and such incentives could take on an importance that the planters had not intended.

Both slaves and slaveowners could see the contradictions. Undoubtedly, the existence of opportunities within the work regime and an internal slave economy of self-provisioning worked to the masters' benefit. Slaves surely recognized this, but they could also see advantages for themselves. The struggle, then, was over the relative balance of advantage that work for the master, response to incentives, and work for themselves created. A certain amount of slave autonomy made the system operate more smoothly, but planters also realized that a slave tradition of self-reliance and autonomy was a potential danger to that system.[22]

The Peasant Breach

Up to this point, I have stressed the manner in which various advantages and opportunities offered to slaves served the labor regime of the sugar economy because in Brazil an extensive historiographical debate has developed about the so-called peasant breach in the slave system. In Brazil, scattered references are found regarding the existence of slave provision grounds and garden plots from the seventeenth to the nineteenth centuries.[23] While in part the debate over the "peasant breach" has centered on the significance that historians have ascribed to this feature of Brazilian slavery, the crucial issue is whether the existence of an "internal economy of slavery," which provided slaves some autonomy within the confines of the slave regime, represented their victory over a brutal coercive labor regime and a potential rupture of the slave system, or if it was allowed to exist principally because it served the interests of the masters.[24]

Almost certainly, the existence of slave property holding and a certain degree of autonomy resulted from a constant and shifting series of arrangements and negotiations that varied from region to region or even estate to estate over time. In northeastern Brazil some planters preferred to purchase most of the slaves' food, usually manioc flour, whale meat, or jerked salt beef. Others allowed slaves time to work on their own provision grounds. Most common was some combination of the two systems, serving the goals of the planters as well as responding to the desires of the slaves. An observer in 1837 suggested that the food provided to slaves was insufficient and that slaves preferred to grow their own even if that increased their labor burden.[25]

Henry Koster's comments submitted to Parliament in 1816 during the debates on the amelioration of slavery in the West Indies are most interesting in this regard.[26] Drawing on his Brazilian experience, Koster criticized statements made in Parliament claiming that because of the tropical climate one day's labor in Jamaica could provide as much food as twenty-five in Europe, and he ironically suggested that only witchcraft or *obeah* could provide the slaves with such an advantage over European peasants. He then turned to his firsthand Brazilian experience:

> Now I know that the Saturday of each week is not sufficient in Brazil for the slave to provide for the remaining six days of the week, unless he adds the gainings on Sundays and holidays, or unless his master's labor is done by task work, which may enable him to work

for an hour each day upon his own grounds. I have heard some plantation slaves, who supply themselves with food and do not labor by
task work, complain heavily of the Saturday not being sufficient. I
have likewise understood from many owners and managers, that they
did not consider it as affording competent time, unless the slave had
some trade and could labor for his master and be paid, or for some
other person, on his own days. . . . I cannot in anywise believe that
the labor of one day is sufficient to supply food for fourteen. If it is
so, this is a proof of the extreme avarice of men who will work their
dependents for so many hours in each day, when they might be
enriched by requiring so much less exertion from them.[27]

Koster's comment makes clear that a variety of arrangements
existed on the Brazilian plantations. Moreover, it underlines the
slaves' desire for more time for their own subsistence. Finally, it
also directly links the plantation task system to slave maintenance.
Koster viewed this arrangement, as in the long-run, more profitable
to the slaveowner than the unbridled working of the slaves on the
main plantation crop. How the slaves perceived this situation remains one of the most intractable questions to resolve. It is in this
regard that a singular statement made around 1790 by Brazilian
slaves from an *engenho* called Santana and the controversy that it
has engendered can be discussed.

The Slaves of Santana

In 1789 a group of slaves on Engenho Santana, a large plantation in Ilhéus, south of Bahia, killed their overseer, seized some
of the plantation's machinery, and ran off to form a settlement in
the forest. A number of military attempts to recapture them over
the course of the next few years proved unsuccessful, but the pressure finally moved the escaped slaves to enter into negotiations
with the owner of the mill. During this process, the fugitives drew
up a "treaty of peace" giving the conditions under which they would
agree to return to Santana and to slavery. The plantation owner
pretended to accept the terms, but then arrested the principal rebels
and sold them away, except for the leader, who was imprisoned for
many years in Salvador. (See Appendix A for a document describing
these events and Appendix B for the text of the Treaty.)

Such single estate revolts were not uncommon, but the proposed treaty was extraordinary. Given central place among the treaty's provisions were conditions relating to the nature of labor, the
quotas required in the task system, and to the slaves' access to

independent subsistence plots. This extraordinary document, one of the few in which Brazilian slaves spoke directly about the conditions of slavery, has provoked a considerable controversy about its precise meaning and to its applicability to slavery in general in Brazil. Therefore, before discussing its provisions, it will be useful to briefly set it into its specific context.

The Engenho Santana was located in Ilhéus, a region south of Bahia, and somewhat distant from the centers of political authority. The estate had been established in the sixteenth century by a governor and had been inherited by his daughter and later by her husband, the Count of Linhares. By 1573 Santana had 130 slaves, but, somewhat remote and isolated, it, like other Ilhéus mills, suffered from Indian attacks in the years between 1590 and 1601. By 1618 the Jesuit order had acquired Santana by bequest, and although its ownership was legally contested until the 1650s, the Jesuits remained in possession of the *engenho*.[28]

Under the Jesuits the *engenho* had an undistinguished financial history. Attempts at revitalizing it from its state of disrepair had begun to take effect by the 1630s and by the 1670s the mill had about 113 slaves, although productivity was only about ten metric tons a year.[29] Between 1730 and 1750 it yielded only a small annual profit of about 2 to 4 percent on the capital invested in its operations.[30] Sugar production continued low in the 1750s and the *engenho* turned also to timber extraction and some foodstuff production in these years. Despite its indebtedness and the difficulties of production, Engenho Santana was still a valuable asset when the government confiscated it from the Jesuits in 1759.[31]

Santana was bought sometime in the 1770s by Manoel da Silva Ferreira, who expanded its operations. By 1790, there were 300 slaves at Santana, and by the time two German scientists passed through the area in 1819, they could report about 260 slaves, who produced between 130 and 145 tons of sugar. The size of the slave force was exceptional for Bahian *engenhos*, which usually averaged between 80 and 120 slaves, and the level of productivity of roughly half a ton per slave was about as high as Brazilian mills attained in this period.[32]

The nature of Santana's slave force and its peculiarities have become an issue of debate among historians of slavery. As a Jesuit estate, its clerical administrators complained continually of the mill's isolation and the fact that it lacked dependent cane farmers and free skilled workers. By 1670, most of the sugar-making jobs at the mill were filled by slaves whose attitude made them "worse than galley slaves."[33] Jesuit administrators also complained of the bad habits of the slaves in general: They worked little and complained a great deal and were often described as slow to work, argumentative, and ready to take any advantage. Resident administrators complained of theft in the pantry, the storehouse, the mill, and in the fields.

Jesuit attitudes toward the Santana slaves do not seem very paternalistic. Father Pedro Teixeira on taking control of the mill in 1731 noted that he had received 178 slaves, which was to say, "the same as so many devils, thieves, and enemies." And he went on to describe them as the "worst indoctrinated thieves, and shameless persons (especially the women) that I have dealt with, lacking in their fear of God and in the service they owe to those who govern them."[34]

The family life of these slaves changed according to the convictions of the administrators. From 1704 to 1730 under Father Manoel da Figueiredo, who had serious reservations about the morals of slaves, conjugal and otherwise, marriages had not been promoted and virtually disallowed. The slaves had not been allowed to marry and the normally low fertility of Bahian slaves was made even worse by this policy. During the next twenty-five years an active policy promoting conjugal units within sanctioned marriages was followed by a series of Jesuit administrators. This produced a slave quarters characterized by a large proportion (80 percent) of double-headed household units and few solitaries or single-headed households. It also probably raised the fertility level slightly, although the evidence here is mixed.[35] By 1753, the family situation of the slaves seems relatively stable and by that time all of the slaves had acquired family names, a situation rare in Brazil.

How this population was transformed during the period of secular control after 1759 is still unclear. In the 1790s, a few African-born individuals remained among the slaves, but by 1828, the 222 slaves at Santana were, with the exception of one elderly woman, all Brazilian-born. This extraordinary situation was quite unlike that which obtained on most Bahian engenhos, where Africans predominated. Moreover, in contrast to most sugar mills, the sex ratio was well balanced with 109 males and 113 females.[36]

Finally, it appears that slaves at Santana had often grown some portion of their own food and that the cultivation of manioc had also been carried out by the plantation itself. One administrator complained in 1748 that his predecessor had stopped planting manioc because the slaves had often stolen from the fields but that manioc flour was needed "for the sick, and to supply the blacks who often are in need," and because "there is a good market for it in Bahia." In the 1750s, the *engenho* itself bought surplus manioc flour from the slaves at a price below its market value. The administrator in 1753 linked the family structure to slave subsistence when he complained that newly bought slaves were a liability because, "having no family, when they get ill, all the responsibility for their care falls on the administrator."[37] Inventories from 1752 to 1753 indicate that Santana planted some 39,200 *covas* of manioc to feed the slaves and the household. Contemporaries estimated that 500 *covas* were required to produce the ten bushels (*alquieres*) needed to feed a slave annually. Santana had 182 slaves in 1752 so that the *engenho* itself produced less than half of the yearly requirement. No wonder that at Santana's *casa da farinha*, where manioc was processed, two days a week were devoted to preparing flour from manioc that the slaves themselves brought in.[38]

The sexually imbalanced and heavily African nature of the Bahian slave force has been seen as a major contributing factor in the intense degree of slave resistance in the period from 1807 to 1835.[39] Santana, with its large size, apparent familial stability, balanced sex ratio, and Brazilian-born slaves, proved no less restive. The slaves of Santana revolted at least three times in this period— 1789–93, 1821–24, and again in 1828.[40] The basis of their resistance seems to have rested not on African ethnic solidarities but rather on shared goals, specific objections to those who ran the estate for the absentee owners, and on their dissatisfaction with particular aspects of the work regime.

With the specific situation of Santana in mind, let us return to the "Treaty of Peace," offered by the fugitives of 1789. (See the Appendix.) This group, led by a *cabra* (mulatto) named Gregório Luís, submitted a series of nineteen demands or articles that listed their major concerns. The list is just as revealing in what it contains as what it omits. Thirteen of the demands dealt directly with work requirements: quotas in various tasks, minimum number of workers to be assigned to particular jobs, and specific tasks like working in a swampy cane field or gathering shellfish, which the rebels refused to do. The rebels asked, for example, for a 30 percent reduction in the number of canes required as a daily quota for a cane cutter. They also required that the quota for women in manioc cultivation be set 20 percent lower than that of men.[41]

Most interesting from the point of view of slave autonomy are the paragraphs relating to one aspect of it, subsistence. First, the fugitives asked for Fridays and Saturdays free from plantation crop labor so that these days, and Sundays, to which they were already entitled, could be devoted to working on their own plots. They sought the right to plant rice and to cut timber wherever they wished. They also asked that canoes and nets be provided to them, enabling them to supplement their subsistence. That their expectations went beyond subsistence, however, was underlined by their request that the owner build a large boat so that when their goods were sent to Salvador they would not have to pay freight costs. In other words, they hoped to sell their surplus in the market of Salvador. Along with their desire to "play, relax, and sing without needing permission," the demands relating to their time and labor indicate a strong impulse toward autonomous labor and economic opportunity.

The owner might have been able to accept the abridged form of servitude that these demands implied, but certain other provisions of the treaty were particularly revolutionary and totally unacceptable. The rebels demanded the right to approve the appointment of their overseers. Moreover, they wished to remain in control of the *engenho*'s equipment, the means of sugar production. Little wonder that the owner feigned acceptance of the proposals, but took the first opportunity to arrest the leaders and have them imprisoned or sold to far-off Maranhão.

For the reasons cited above Santana was not a typical Brazilian plantation, but the question remains of whether the demands of its rebellious slaves represented a series of desiderata pointing out the direction of the hopes and goals of other Brazilian slaves.[42] The rebelliousness of Santana's slaves indicates that African ethnic solidarity was not the only motivation in slave attempts to strike out against slavery. Perhaps one might even speak of a "creole" program that sought more autonomy and independence within slavery, except that there is also evidence of Africans in Rio de Janeiro and Salvador who sought some autonomy within the system by accumulating money, working on their own, and forming self-help associations.[43] Evidence is beginning to accumulate not only in Brazil but in many slave regimes that such autonomy and an internal slave economy were integral aspects of slavery, offering certain definite advantages to the slaves and yet manipulated for advantage by the masters.[44]

Finally, it should be noted that the documentation concerning Santana and a number of other references to slave marketing of their own produce date from the last decades of the eighteenth and early nineteenth centuries. In Brazil this period was one of considerable urban growth, an expanding export economy, and an increase in slave imports, as well as a general rise in the population. All of these factors contributed to the growth of an internal market for foodstuffs in Brazil and made the right to provision grounds and access to the market particularly attractive to slaves. The expansion of subsistence crop production was noticeable in this period in many regions of Brazil. While slaves had usually benefited from control of their own food resources, there had probably never been as much advantage in that control or in access to the market as there was at this time. There had also probably never been as much need for such activity. The boom in world demand for sugar and other plantation crops in this period had made the cultivation of foodstuffs even less attractive to planters who were willing to shift this burden on to the slaves themselves. It would seem that the internal dynamic of slave aspirations and hopes was no less tied to the economic possibilities of the slave system than were those of the masters.

NOTES

1. The same point is discussed and documented by Peter Kolchin, "Reevaluating the Antebellum Slave Community: A Comparative Perspective," *Journal of American History* 70:3 (Dec. 1983), 579–601.

2. Stuart B. Schwartz, *Sugar Plantations in the Formation of Brazilian Society* (Cambridge, 1985). The following paper draws heavily on materials presented in this book and attempts to summarize arguments and data presented there, and then to incorporate these with new materials available on the question of slave autonomy.

3. I have emphasized the specificity of sugar labor requirements to the workings of colonial society in "Segredos internos: trabalho escravo e vida escrava no Brasil," *História: Questões e Debates* 3 (June 1983), 45–61. See also Philip D. Morgan, "Task and Gang Systems: The Organization of Labor on New World Plantations," in *Work and Labor in Early America*, ed. Stephen Innes, (Chapel Hill, N.C. 1988), 189–220.

4. André João Antonil, *Cultura e opulência do Brasil por suas drogas e minas*, ed. Andre Mansuy, (Paris, 1965), originally published in 1711; Richard Ligon, *A True and Exact History of the Island of Barbados* (London, 1657); Jean Baptiste Labat, *Nouveau voyage aux iles de l'Amerique* (The Hague, 1724), original edition of 1696.

5. Ligon noted that early planters on Barbados turned to northeastern Brazil to perfect the sugar-making process. This transfer of knowledge is

discussed in David Watts, *The West Indies: Patterns of Development, Culture, and Environmental Change since 1492* (Cambridge, 1988), 178–84.

6. There were exceptions to this strategy especially on ecclesiastical properties. Some, but not all, of the Jesuit *engenho* administrators argued on moral and economic grounds for the promotion of stable families, the raising of slave children, and improved physical conditions for slaves. The Benedictine Order seems to have consistently followed an "ameliorationist" policy and by the nineteenth century a number of "progressive" planters also urged such practices. See my discussion in *Sugar Plantations*, 355–57; Stuart B. Schwartz, "The Plantations of St. Benedict: The Benedictine Sugar Mills of Colonial Brazil," *The Americas* 39:1 (July 1982), 55–86.

7. Eugene Genovese, *Roll, Jordan, Roll: The World the Slaves Made.* (New York, 1976), 284, 291–94. This point was noted in Ligia Bellini, "O Compromisso impossivel," Universidade Federal da Bahia (ms., 1987).

8. On the conflict between European and African concepts of time and work see Keletso E. Atkins, "Kafir Time: Preindustrial Temporal Concepts and Labour Discipline in Nineteenth-Century Colonial Natal," *Journal of African History* 29:2 (1988), 229–44. See also the discussions of changing concepts of time in Jacques Le Goff, *Time, Work, and Culture in the Middle Ages* (Chicago, 1980); and E. P. Thompson, "Time, Work-discipline and Industrial Capitalism," *Past and Present* 38 (1967), 56–97.

9. One slave tried to protect his work status in the courts. Joaquim, a slave of Francisco de Sousa in the city of Salvador who worked as the carrier of a sedan chair, petitioned to have the courts intervene to prevent his owner from sending him to work as a field hand outside the city. His petition failed. See APB, Ouvidoria geral do civel 1,97,178 (Bahia, 24 Oct. 1780).

10. This point is made by Antônio Barros de Castro, "Escravos e senhores nos engenhos do Brasil" (Ph.D. diss., Universidade Estadual de Campinas, 1974).

11. On the importance of physical coercion within the Brazilian slave regime see Silvia Hunold Lara, *Campos da Violência* (São Paulo, 1988), 57–113. The extent to which a psychopathic master could make life a living hell is made clear by the Bahian case of the wealthy and powerful Garcia Davila Pereira de Aragão, whose abuses of his slaves were denounced to the Inquisition. See Luiz R. B. Mott, "Terror na Casa da Torre: tortura de escravos na Bahia colonial," in *Escravidão e invenção da liberdade* ed., João José Reis (São Paulo, 1988), 17–32.

12. Ciro Flamarion S. Cardoso, *Agricultura escravidão e capitalismo* (Petrópolis, 1979), 133–54, provides a brief summary of the question and compares Brazil to the Caribbean, where he finds many parallels.

13. Stuart B. Schwartz, "The Manumission of Slaves in Colonial Brazil: Bahia, 1680–1745," *HAHR* 54:4 (Nov. 1974), 603–35, demonstrates that the percentage of paid manumissions changed over time and reached over 50 percent by the 1740s. A summary of the various quantitative studies

of manumission in Brazil forms part of Peter Eisenberg's study of manumission in Campinas. See "Ficando livre: As alforrias em Campinas no século xix," *Estudos Econômicos* 17:2 (1987), 175–216.

14. Francisco Peixoto de Lacerda Werneck, *Memória sobre a fundação de uma fazenda na provincia do Rio de Janeiro*, ed. Eduardo Silva (Brasília, 1985), 33–41, 63–64. See also Eduardo Silva, "A função ideológica da brecha camponesa," *Anais. IV Reunião da Sociedade Brasileira de Pesquisa Histórica* (São Paulo, 1985), 191-95. A number of essays on the theme are presented in João José Reis and Eduardo Silva, *Negociação e conflito* (São Paulo, 1989).

15. Henry Koster, *Travels in Brazil*, 2 vols. 2d ed. (Philadelphia, 1817), 192. Various wills and inventories of Bahian planters sometimes noted slave property and even slaves owned by other slaves. To date there is no study in depth on Brazil similar to Roderick A. McDonald, "Goods and Chattels: The Economy of Slaves on Sugar Plantations in Jamaica and Louisiana" (Ph.D. diss., University of Kansas, 1981).

16. Koster, *Travels*, II, 192.

17. João José Reis, *Rebelião escrava no Brasil* (São Paulo, 1986).

18. Koster, *Travels*, II, 192–93n.

19. Hunold Lara, *Campos da Violência*, 186.

20. Father Matias (?) to Father Estevão da Costa (Bahia, 3 Oct. 1623), ANTT, CSJ, maço 70, n.89.

21. Lara, *Campos da Violência*, 208–10 presents a discussion of the sources and notes a case from 1773 in which an elderly slave purchased his freedom by providing agricultural products. Other cases she presents from Campos indicate recognition of slave property holding and the use of presents and rights to subsistence plots as rewards.

22. These themes have been addressed by Ira Berlin and Philip D. Morgan in their introduction to *The Slaves' Economy: Independent Production by Slaves in the Americas*, special issue of *Slavery and Abolition* (In press).

23. See the discussion in Cardoso, *Escravo ou camponês?* 91–125.

24. The issue is discussed by Ciro Flamarion S. Cardoso, "The Peasant Breach in the Slave System: New Developments in Brazil," *Luso-Brazilian Review* 25:1 (Summer 1988), 49–58, and more extensively in his *Escravo ou camponês. O proto-campesinato negro nas Américas* (São Paulo, 1987). See also Antônio Barros de Castro, "A economia política, o capitalismo e a escravidão," in *Modos de produção e realidade brasileira*, ed. José Roberto de Amaral Lapa (Petrópolis, 1980), 67–107. Eduardo Silva has addressed another aspect in "A função ideológica da 'brecha camponesa,'" in João José Reis and Eduardo Silva, *Negociação e conflito* (São Paulo, 1989), 22–31.

25. Federico Leopoldo C. Burlamaqui, *Memoria analytica acerca do commercio d'escravos e acerca da escravidão domestica* (Rio de Janeiro, 1837), 79.

26. Henry Koster, "On the Amelioration of Slavery," in *The Pam-*

phleteer 8:16 (London, 1816), 305–36. A new edition of this long-forgotten article rediscovered by Manuela Carneiro da Cunha is in press in the journal *Slavery and Abolition.*

27. Ibid., 329.

28. I have summarized the complex legal history of the Santana and Sergipe do Conde sugar mills in *Sugar Plantations,* 489–97.

29. Dauril Alden, "Sugar Planters by Necessity, Not Choice: The Role of the Jesuits in the Cane Sugar Industry of Colonial Brazil, 1601–1759," in *The Church and Society in Latin America,* ed. Jeffrey A. Cole (New Orleans, 1984), 139–72.

30. "Conta de tudo o que esta igreja tem recibido pertencente ao Engenho de Santana . . . 1730–1750, ANTT, CSJ, maço 54, n.22. See the fuller discussion in *Sugar plantations,* 227.

31. Alden, "Sugar Planters by Necessity," 140–45.

32. The plantation was acquired in the nineteenth century by Felisberto Brant Pontes, Marquês de Barbacena a conservative spokesman for the planter class and an advocate of close control of the slaves. See João José Reis, "Resistencia escrava em Ilhéus: Um documento inédito," *Anais do Arquivo do Estado da Bahia,* 44 (1979), 285–97. See also the discussion in Schwartz, *Sugar Plantations,* 484–85.

33. Padre Felipe Franco (Santana, 15 March 1671), ANTT, CSJ, maço 70, n.383; Padre Pedro Teixeira to Colegio de Santo Antão (Santana, 11 Nov. 1731), maço 15, n.26.

34. ANTT, CSJ, maço 15, n.24.

35. The age of first-birth for women seems to have dropped from 20.5 years to 18.6, but the number of children per woman seems to have dropped between 1731 and 1753. See *Sugar Plantations,* 394–402.

36. Inventário, Marques de Barbacena, APB, judiciaria, maço 2738 (1828). My thanks to João José Reis for providing me a copy of this document.

37. Jerónimo da Gama, "Informe do estado pasado e presente do Engenho de S. Ana." ANTT, CSJ, maço 54, n.51.

38. Ibid; Inventário feito por P. João Cortes, ANTT, CSJ, maço 54, doc. 52 (1752). The calculations for annual manioc consumption were made by José da Silva Lisboa in 1781. See *ABNRJ,* 32 (1910): 494–506. See chapter 3 for a more detailed discussion.

39. João José Reis, "Slave Resistance in Brazil, Bahia, 1807–1835," *Luso Brazilian Review* 25:1 (Summer 1988), 111–44.

40. Reis, "Resistencia escrava em Ilhéus," 288–91.

41. I have published the treaty and a related document along with a discussion in Stuart B. Schwartz, "Resistance and Accommodation in Eighteenth Century Brazil: The Slaves' View of Slavery," *HAHR* 57:1 (1977), 69–81.

42. Jacob Gorender, "Questionôamentos sobre a teoria econômica do escravismo colonial," *Estudos Econômicos* 13:1 (1983), 8–39. Gorender basing himself on Koster's comments in *Travels in Brazil* concerning Benedictine estates argues that conditions on Santana, a former Jesuit plantation

represents a peculiar set of conditions associated with the ameliorationist practices on ecclesiastical estates. It would seem that the Benedictines did institute a series of positive measures to promote stable families, slave initiative, and a certain degree of autonomy among their slaves. See Schwartz, "The Plantations of St. Benedict: The Benedictine Sugar Mills of Colonial Brazil," *The Americas* 39:1 (July 1982), 1–22. The evidence for these practices is far less clear for the Jesuits, and as the documentation from Santana itself indicates, Jesuit application of such principles varied considerably according to the beliefs of individual administrators. In any case, by the time of the 1789 rebellion, Santana had been in secular hands for thirty years. See the comments on Gorender's position in Cardoso, *Escravo ou camponês*, 116–25.

43. Mary C. Karash, *Slave Life in Rio de Janeiro, 1808–1850* (Princeton, 1987), 298–301, 335–44. Reis, *Rebelião escrava*, 216–34.

44. Berlin and Morgan, Ibid.

APPENDIXES: Documents Relating to the Fugitives of Engenho Santana

APPENDIX A

Arquivo Público do Estado
da Bahia: Seção histórica
Cartas ao Govêrno, 207

Illustrious and most Excellent Sir

The Supplicant Gregório Luís, a *cabra* finds himself a prisoner in the jail of this High Court where he was sent by his master, Captain Manoel da Silva Ferreira, resident on his Engenho called Santana in the district of the Town of Ilhéus; there coming at the same time with him, as I remember, some fifteen or sixteen other slaves. These were sent to the merchant José da Silva Maia, his commercial agent, so that he could sell them in Maranhão while the Supplicant came with the recommendation that he be held in prison while the Court of that district prepared the charges so that he could be given exemplary punishment. Taking a preliminary investigation of the Supplicant, I have determined the following facts. The above men-

tioned Manoel da Silva Ferreira being master and owner of the aforesaid
engenho with three hundred slaves, including some of the Mina nation
discovered the majority of them in rebellion refusing to recognize their
subordination to their master. And, the principal leader of this disorder
was the Supplicant who began to incite among them the partisan spirit
against their master and against the Sugar Master. The Supplicant was able
with a few of his followers to kill the latter and until now none know
where they buried him. Taking control of part of the *engenho*'s equipment,
they fled to the forest refusing not only to give their service or to obey
their master, but even placing him in fear that they would cruelly take his
life. For this reason the *engenho* has remained inactive for two years with
such notable damage that its decadence is dated from that time forward,
and, moreover, these damages added to the danger that the rest of the slaves
might follow the terrible example of those in rebellion. Thus the majority
of the slaves persisted divided into errant and vagabond bands throughout
the territory of the *engenho*, so absolute and fearless that the consternation
and fright of their master increased in consideration that he might one
day fall Victim to some disaster. Matters being in this situation, the rebels
sent emissaries to their Master with a proposal of capitulation contained
in the enclosed copy [see Document II] to which he showed them that he
acceded: some came and others remained. The Supplicant as the most
astute was able to extort from him a letter of Manumission which was
granted at the time without the intention that it have any validity, at the
same time he [the Supplicant] sought the District Judge who entering the
engenho with eighty-five armed men sought out the house of his Master:
The latter who could not now confide in the principal leaders of that
uprising took advantage of a stratagem of sending the Supplicant Gregório
and fifteen others with a false letter to the Captain major of the militia,
João da Silva Santos, who was in the Vila of Belmonte, telling them that
they would receive from him some cattle and manioc flour for the *engenho*.
Arriving at the said Vila all were taken prisoner with handcuffs despite
the great resistance that they made almost to the point of much bloodshed.
They were finally conducted to the jail of this High Court as I have said,
that is, the Supplicant as the prime mover to be held until his charges
were seen and the others with orders to the aforementioned merchant to
be sold to Maranhão as they were.

Twice there has been required from this court an order to be sent
the investigation or any other charges against the Supplicant and until now
they have not arrived.

I must also tell Your Excellency that the Master of the said Engenho
has on repeated occasions recommended with the greatest insistence that
the Supplicant not be released from prison except by a sentence that exiles
him far away because if he is freed he will unfailingly return to the *engenho*
to incite new disorders, that may be irreparable.

That which is reported here seems to me enough to give Your Excellency a sufficient idea concerning the Supplicant and the reasons for

his imprisonment. God Protect Your Excellency. Bahia 22 of January of 1806.

The Desembargador Ouvidor geral do Crime

Claudio José Pereira da Costa

APPENDIX B

Treaty Proposed to Manoel da Silva Ferreira
by His Slaves during the Time that They
Remained in Revolt

My Lord, we want peace and we do not want war; if My Lord also wants our peace it must be in this manner, if he wishes to agree to that which we want.

In each week you must give us the days of Friday and Saturday to work for ourselves not subtracting any of these because they are Saint's days.

To enable us to live you must give us casting nets and canoes.[1]

You are not to oblige us to fish in the tidal pools nor to gather shellfish, and when you wish to gather shellfish send your Mina blacks.

For your sustenance have a fishing launch and decked canoes, and when you wish to eat shellfish send your Mina blacks.

Make a large boat so that when it goes to Bahia we can place our cargoes aboard and not pay freightage.

In the planting of manioc we wish the men to have a daily quota of two and one-half hands and the women, two hands.[2]

The daily quota of manioc flour must be of five level *alqueires*, placing enough harvesters so that these can serve to hang up the baskets.[3]

The daily quota of sugarcane must be of five hands rather than six and of ten canes in each bundle.[4]

On the boat you must put four poles, and one for the rudder, and the one at the rudder works hard for us.

The wood that is sawed with a hand saw must have three men below and one above.[5]

The measure of firewood must be as was practiced here, for each measure a woodcutter and a woman as the wood carrier.[6]

The present oversees we do not want, choose others with our approval.

At the milling rollers there must be four women to feed in the cane, two pulleys, and a *carcanha*.[7]

At each cauldron there must be one who tends the fire and in each series of kettles the same, and on Saturday there must be without fail work stoppage in the mill.

The sailors who go in the launch beside the baize shirt that they are given must also have a jacket of baize and all the necessary clothing.

We will go to work the canefield of Jabirú this time and then it must remain as pasture for we cannot cut cane in a swamp.

We shall be able to plant our rice wherever we wish, and in any marsh, without asking permission for this, and each person can cut jacaranda or any other wood without having to account for this.

Accepting all the above articles and allowing us to remain always in possession of the hardware, we are ready to serve you before because we do not wish to continue the bad customs of the other *engenhos*.

We shall be able to play, relax and sing any time we wish without your hinderance nor will permission be needed.

NOTES

1. The *tarrafa,* or casting net, is still widely used along the coast of Northeast Brazil. It is presently about 170 inches in length with a 480-inch circular bottom that is weighted. See Shepard Forman, *The Raft Fishermen* (Bloomington, 1970), 58–59.

2. Daily quotas (*tarefas*) were measured in "hands," as a mnemonic device. While it is possible to establish the quantity of a *tarefa* of sugar cane, it has been impossible to do so for manioc. See note 4, below.

3. The *alqueire* is a dry measure equal to 36.27 liters or approximately one English bushel. The reference to baskets (*tipitís*) are to the long tubular baskets used to squeeze the moistened manioc flour in order to extract the natural poisons found in it.

4. In Bahia the traditional hand of cane was 5 fingers each composed of 10 bundles with 12 canes per bundle. Thus a hand equaled 600 canes. The treaty seeks a reduction in the number of hands and the number of canes in a bundle. The Santana fugitives wanted a daily quota of 2,500 canes ($5 \times 5 \times 10 \times 10$) instead of the former 3,600 canes ($6 \times 5 \times 10 \times 12$). In other words, they sought a quota reduction of 30 percent.

5. The reference here is apparently to the ripsaw that was widely used in colonial Brazil. There is a good pictorial representation of its use by slaves in Jean Baptiste Debret, *Viagem Pitoresca e Histórica ao Brasil,* 2d ed., 3 vols. in 2 (São Paulo, 1949). The occupation of sawyer (*serrador*) was commonly listed for sugar plantation slaves since building and repairing the mill called for much carpentry.

6. Some idea of the quota of firewood required of slaves is provided by Antonil. He reported that the daily requirement was a pile of firewood 7 *palmos* (*palmo* = nine inches) high by 8 *palmos* deep of 63 inches by

72 inches. This was the equivalent of one cartload. See Antonil, *Cultura e Opulencia*, 200.

7. *Moedeiras* were the women who fed the cane through the milling rollers. The juice squeezed from the cane was collected in a large vat (*parol*) and was then taken out by buckets on a hoist (*guinda*) and poured into the cauldrons for boiling. The women employed in this task were called *guindadeiras*. *Carcanha* or *calcanha* was the woman who kept the lamps lit and removed skimmings from the kettle.

3 Peasants and Slavery: Feeding Brazil in the Late Colonial Period

Brazil was a great colonial enterprise, characterized for over three hundred years by plantations, mines, and an export economy. Slavery was the predominant labor form in Brazil, but always on the margins of the export economy and increasingly over time, there existed a population of rural workers and householders who constituted a peasantry. Traditionally, Brazilian historiography has naturally concentrated on the export economy and slavery, but by doing so, it has left unstudied the internal development of the colony and the social relations of production in the nonslave sectors of the economy, especially among this peasantry.

The relationship between the export and internal economies and between slavery and other forms of labor organization remains to be explored. Models for analyzing these relationships have been developed for the plantation colonies of the Caribbean, but in a place as large and as ecologically diverse as Brazil, such models have not proven particularly helpful. Historians must reconstruct the specific historical processes in which the relations between slavery and peasantry were formed.

Study of that relationship is complicated by the past research agenda and assumptions of economic history. Studies of the Third World in general and Latin America in particular have long emphasized the export orientation of these regions and the negative impact of colonial economies and especially plantation systems on economic growth and social relations. Much of what is called Dependency theory takes as its point of departure a vision in which these colonial economies are characterized by plantation or mining enclaves with few links to, and no positive effects on, the internal growth of their surrounding regions; a sharp distinction between export-oriented, often slave-based plantations and a more "natural" indigenous peasant sector; and a continually unequal relationship of exchange between colony and metropolis.[1]

Modern economists recognize that agriculture has several functions during the process of economic development and that among these are providing an adequate food supply and earning foreign exchange.[2] In Brazilian historiography, export and subsistence agriculture, like their parallel productive forms of slave plantation and peasant household, have been viewed as dichotomies—metaphors for slavery and freedom, dependence and autonomy, feudalism and capitalism. While we now have a relatively well-rounded view of Brazilian slavery, the free rural small-holders have remained marginal in studies of the Brazilian past, subject to widely different interpretations and labels. In this chapter I suggest that historically in Brazil, peasant and slave production, or more exactly, provisioning and export agriculture, were intimately related in a complex, multidimensional, and historically changing relationship.[3] They were, in effect, two faces of the same coin.

Peasants and the Colonial Economy

Peasantry in Brazil came from no precolonial heritage, traced its lineage to no fallen civilization, and bore no collective folk memory of a glorious past. It was, instead, a "reconstituted" peasantry, a direct result of the colonial economy and slavery that emerged at the edges of the slave economy, and then grew in importance alongside it. In the colony from its inception, this free rural population of small farmers, tenants, and dependents remained for the most part faceless and even unnamed. The word "peasant" (campones) was rarely used to refer to them and was replaced instead by a variety of terms describing variations in tenure, dependence, or rusticity (matuto, caipira, etc.). Rarely given an active role in Brazilian history, the peasantry was seen as a "telluric" population, fixed upon the countryside, to be cataloged by observers like the flora and fauna, and forced to watch as history passed them by.[4]

It may be theoretically confusing to lump cash tenants, sharecroppers, and small holders within the same category, but if we view peasantry as a process and a set of relationships that includes the domestic mode of production, a reduced distinction between household and economy, and productive activities shaped or determined to a considerable degree by powerful outsiders, then I believe that the term "peasantry" is a useful category.[5] I suggest that the definitional problem is even more complex than we have imagined, because during the late colonial era many sectors of this peasantry were increasingly drawn toward commercial agriculture and toward the use of slaves as they began to play an important role in the development of the internal economy of Brazil.

Within the context of a colonial export economy the peasantry had long been defined as the providers of food. The crucial role of feeding the cities, mining towns, and plantations belonged to the free rural population, but the bread of every day varied regionally. Brazil could roughly be divided into two zones: the country of manioc (cassava) and the country of maize, since these two staples formed the basis of diet in most places. Both cultigens were grown throughout the colony, but manioc was the prefered food of the North and Northeast, where it was prepared as a coarse flour and made into a variety of breads, meals, and puddings. Manioc's outstanding resistance to drought and its ability to thrive in poor soils made it particularly adaptable to areas of the Northeast, where sugar was not cultivated.[6] These features and the fact that manioc does poorly in river bottom land—the prime location for sugar—made the two crops regionally compatible. Moreover, the relative ease of manioc cultivation and its enormous caloric yield per unit (over 3 times that of maize) gave it a privileged place among the peasantry despite its notable lack of protein.[7] In Bahia at the close of the colonial era the ratio of manioc to maize in the common diet was approximately ten to one.[8]

As one moved southward the ratio changed. A 1778 census of the captaincy of Rio de Janeiro demonstrated that manioc was still predominant in that region, but by ratios of only three or four to one.[9] In the uplands of Minas Gerais, maize was increasingly important where it was often prepared as *fuba,* a kind of porridge. But it was really in the mixed farming regions from São Paulo southward that maize and wheat were the prefered crops.

The relationship between these food crops and export staples was always a complex one in Brazil. In the last decades of the eighteenth century, the Brazilian economy experienced a rapid expansion led by an agricultural renaissance. The roots of this resurgence could be partly traced to the earlier reforms of the Marquis of Pombal and their continuation by a series of reformist ministers much influenced by physiocratic ideas. Little doubt exists that international conflicts in the period from 1774 to 1815, which disrupted

France and England's access to their traditional sources of colonial products, created new opportunities for Brazil. The disruption of the British tobacco trade caused by the American Revolution, the destruction of plantation agriculture in St. Domingue after the slave rebellion of 1792, and Anglo-French maritime warfare throughout much of this period all contributed to the resurgence of Brazilian trade. Increased exports were led by the traditional Brazilian products—sugar, tobacco, and hides—but these were now accompanied by such products as cacao, cotton, coffee, and indigo, which had until this period never been important articles of export.[10]

The Brazilian agricultural renaissance increased Brazil's position of dominance in the Portuguese imperial economy. By 1800, Brazilian products made up over 60 percent of Portuguese exports to Europe, North Africa, and North America, and gave Portugal a favorable trade balance with its major partners by the early nineteenth century. At the same time, however, this situation accompanied by an ever greater Brazilian contraband trade with England, which lowered the demand for Portuguese manufactures, created a balance of payments deficit for Portugal with its Brazilian colony.[11]

The outlines of Brazil's agricultural renaissance are now relatively well known. Clearly, Brazil's growth in this period rested squarely on its export sector, which in turn was made possible by an intensification and expansion of the colony's principal labor form. Slavery, in fact, expanded at the end of the colonial period. Slave imports to the traditional markets of Bahia, Rio de Janeiro, and Recife reached new heights. Other regions such as Maranhão, São Paulo, Paraná, and Rio Grande do Sul, none of which had previously been characterized by export economies and a predominance of slave labor, were pulled into the expanding export trade and a growing dependence on slavery.

Behind the expansion of Brazil's export slave-based economy in the late colonial period remains the complex and less-known story of the growth of the internal economy, and through regional development and integration, the beginnings of a national market. Accompanying this process and central to it was the growth of a free rural population whose orientation toward these internal markets made the simultaneous intensification of slave-produced export crops possible. In short, two parallel developments, the expansion of slave-based export agriculture and the growth of a free rural "peasantry" took place at roughly the same time. There was some novelty in this. While slave-produced exports had been the basis of Brazil's economic existence since the mid-sixteenth century and there was nothing surprising in their expansion, the colony in 1780 was not what it had been a century before. Important transformations had taken place in the size, composition, and distribution of the population; in the colony's economic infrastructure; and in the texture of social relations. Some of these changes were already in motion before the 1780s, but it is clear that the emergence of a free rural population and the development of a national market in foodstuffs after that date facilitated the new export expansion.

Both peasants and slaves were increasing in the period. In this chapter, I demonstrate how and why this happened by concentrating on the internal economy and on food production, especially of manioc flour, that basic Brazilian staple. This is not an easy task. At present some questions about this topic cannot be answered. We have no adequate measure of how much surplus was available from peasant production, therefore it is virtually impossible to calculate the degree and pace at which the peasant economy became commercialized. While it is apparent that small-scale producers responded to new opportunities to feed distant markets, it is impossible to gauge either the attitudinal or the economic changes that such actions demanded. Nor can we weigh the benefits against the increased risks of dependence on these markets. These gaps only underline the fact that many questions about the internal organization of the late colonial economy have remained not only unanswered but also unasked because of the predominant historiographical emphasis on the export sector. Here, I suggest ways in which the export and subsistence functions of agriculture interacted and examine, in a limited way, the effects this relationship had on social developments during a crucial period in Brazilian history.

The Context of Population

The late colonial period in Brazil was characterized by population growth. The reasons for this and the rate of increase varied from captaincy to captaincy, but the process was general. The best estimates for population in the colony indicate a growth from about 1.5 million inhabitants around 1776 to over 2 million by 1800 and perhaps 3.5 million by 1819.[12] These figures suggest rapid annual rates of growth of 1.2 percent between the first two dates to about 3 percent for the period 1800 to 1819. Some portion of this increase was due to the twenty to forty thousand new slaves imported from Africa each year during the period of the agricultural boom, a level of import that exceeded the mortality rate among slaves. Much of

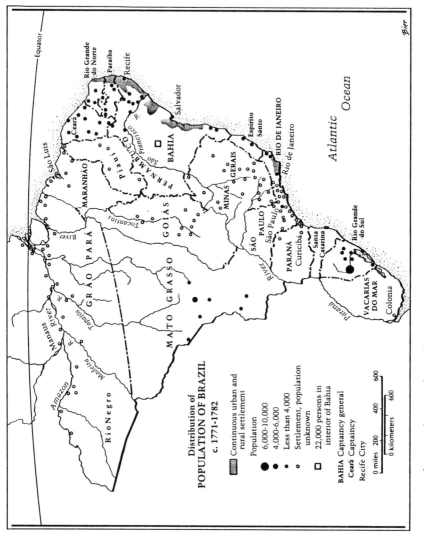

Figure 1. The Population of Brazil toward the End of the Eighteenth Century.
Source: Dauril Alden, *Royal Government in Colonial Brazil* (Berkely: University of California Press, 1963).

the increase also seems to have been the result of a natural increase of free persons, especially the free colored population. Free people of color seem to have demonstrated consistently higher birth and lower death rates than the slave population, although their mortality rates were usually less positive than those of the whites.[13] Then too, manumission practices, which tended to favor mulattoes, children, and women, also contributed to the growth of this group.[14] The overall demographic statistics indicate clearly that the free coloreds were the most rapidly growing segment of the population. In Bahia, Goiás, Pernambuco, and Minas Gerais *pardos* made up 30 percent or more of the population and in the colony as a whole they made up just under that figure (27.8). When added to the slave population, the colored population totaled two-thirds of the colonial Brazilian population.[15] The Brazilian population of the late colonial period was predominantly black, mulatto, and *mestiço,* and it was growing at a rapid pace due primarily to forced immigration (slaves) and natural increase (free coloreds).

The increase of the latter was particularly noticeable in the development of a colonial peasantry. A free rural population had always existed in the colony, but the middle years of the eighteenth century seem to have been particularly important for its formation. The reasons for this process have never been studied in depth, but certainly include both economic and demographic factors. The contraction of the export sector in the period from 1730 to 1760, which led perhaps to a turn to subsistence agriculture; the growth of the mining and population centers of Minas Gerais, which created a demand for provisions; the cumulative effects of manumission, which contributed to the enlargement of a free colored population; and the natural growth of that population all contributed.

By the 1760s, when regional censuses became relatively common, it was clear that a large free rural population existed in many parts of the colony. We can refer to this population as a peasantry, although they were defined or categorized by a variety of terms depending on their relationship to the land, to those who owned land, and to the market. The composition and situation of the peasantry varied from region to region. In São Paulo many were freeholders involved in subsistence agriculture. In Minas Gerais, the decline of the mining economy after 1750 had led to the development of mixed agriculture. In the Northeast, there were many small owners in the interior and also large numbers of dependent *moradores* and *agregados* who labored on the lands of others. Landlessness and poverty characterized much of the northeastern free rural population. But in the Northeast as elsewhere in the colony, considerable variation existed within the peasant sector in terms of income and property ownership.

While perhaps 80 percent of Brazil's population still resided in rural areas in 1800, the growth of the major coastal cities and the development of other urban centers was another feature of the late colonial period. Over sixty new towns were founded between 1780 and 1819. Cities like Salvador and Rio de Janeiro grew rapidly. Rio, already a major port by 1800, led the way after the arrival of the Portuguese court in 1808. With an annual growth rate of 2.8 percent, by 1821 it had almost 80,000 inhabitants. In 1800 Salvador had at least 50,000 inhabitants and by 1820 perhaps twice that number. Recife's population grew from 18,000 in 1782 to 34,000 by 1822, an annual rate of 2.3 percent. By the turn of the century, São Paulo and São Luís each had over 20,000 inhabitants. Natural growth, the influx of slaves, and cityward migration all contributed to this urbanization. To a large extent created by the export economy, these urban centers formed internal markets that demanded supplies from the rural economy and from the international and colonial trades.[16]

The fundamental aspect of Brazilian society and economy was its continuing dependence on slavery. Because of the deadly demography of Brazilian slavery characterized by low fertility and high mortality levels and a resulting natural rate of decline, the Brazilian slave regime was particularly dependent on the Atlantic slave trade. Replacement of the existing slave force or expansion depended primarily on it, and, to a lesser extent, on the intercaptaincy movement of slaves. Available statistics, although incomplete and inconsistent, demonstrate a pattern in which Brazilian slave imports from Africa decreased during the middle decades of the eighteenth century as the export economy declined.

The resurgence of Brazilian agriculture resulted in an expansion of the slave trade, especially after 1780 and continuing until the 1830s. In this pattern, Brazil accompanied the general expansion of slave-based agriculture in the Atlantic economies during this period.[17] In Brazil, the scale and intensity of expansion varied from captaincy to captaincy, but the process was general. We can use some representative examples here. Estimates for Bahia, the colony's major exporter of sugar and tobacco, show an increase from about 20,000 arriving Africans in the period 1786–90 to 34,000 for the following five-year period, reaching a level of almost 10,000 slaves a year from 1826 to 1830.[18] Imports to cotton-exporting São Luis de Maranhão demonstrate a similar pattern growing from an average of 1,120 a year (1780–84) to 1,830 (1785–90) and slipping back somewhat to 1,662 in the following quinquennium.[19]

Tracing the importation of slaves to southern Brazil is more difficult. The captaincy of Rio de Janeiro was itself a centerpiece of the agricultural renaissance and its port also served as the major point of entry for slaves sent to Minas Gerais and the south. Estimates for its trade with Angola show a rise of imported Africans from 6 to 7,000 a year in the 1770s to over 10,000 a year in the decade after 1795. With a steady increase in the proportion of slaves from East Africa (Mozambique), Rio de Janeiro became the major slaving port, so that by the 1820s it was receiving over 30,000 Africans a year.[20] Even in the cattle and wheat producing southern captaincy of Rio Grande do Sao Pedro (later Rio Grande do Sul) the slave population grew markedly, so that between 1780 and 1802 the proportion of blacks and mulattoes increased from 29 to 41 percent of all inhabitants.[21] By 1814, over 20,000 slaves and 5,000 freedmen lived among the roughly 70,000 inhabitants of the captaincy. In short, slave imports to northern Brazil remained relatively stable from 1780 to 1830, but imports increased rapidly in southern Brazil. Historian David Eltis has provided estimates for slave imports to Brazil indicating that the southern captaincies received almost 300,000 Africans in the decade of 1821–30, a rate that would later increase with the rise of coffee agriculture in southern Brazil.

While data on slave importation is discontinuous and sometimes confusing, it generally underlines the significant expansion of Brazil's slave labor force in the late colonial and Joanine periods. The economic transformation of Brazil in this period was, at the first level, made possible by an expansion of Brazil's traditional form of labor, and despite over two and a half centuries of experience with this institution, little effort was made to ameliorate the conditions resulting in the deadly demography of Brazilian slavery.

The traditional practice of importing an excess of men to women at a rate of about 3:2 seems to have continued. Rio Grande do São Pedro in 1802, for example, had 8,187 slave men and only 4,271 slave women. (sex ratio of 192) By 1838, the city of Rio de Janeiro had 22,192 male slaves and 14,945 females. Even in Minas Gerais, where the decline of mining in the period had lessened the demand for new slaves, the sexual imbalance in favor of men continued, especially at the older ages. This imbalance with its negative effects on fertility and nuptiality was exacerbated in plantation areas. In Bahia, sugar *engenhos* sometimes had a dramatic imbalance with

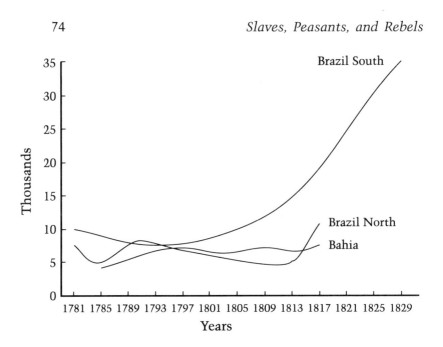

Figure 2. Slave Imports to Brazil
Source: David Eltis, *Economic Growth and the Ending of the Transatlantic Slave Trade* (Oxford, 1987), 43.

sex ratios of two men to every woman. The same pattern could be seen in Pernambuco. On 51 *engenhos* in Serinhaem in 1788, 68 percent of the slaves (2,569/3,801) were males; a sex ratio of 209 males to every 100 females. All of these figures point in the same direction. Brazilian slaveowners were anxious to have immediate returns from their investment in slave labor and few were interested in improving nutrition or in fostering procreation as means of strengthening and expanding the labor force. This may have been very rational behavior from the point of view of men and women who had borrowed heavily in order to seize the opportunities provided by the new demand for Brazilian products and who were faced with mortgage payments, but the overall effect on the slave population was a continuation of the conditions that made Brazilian slavery so dependent on the slave trade.[22]

Given these basic economic and demographic features of the late colonial period, the simultaneous growth of both the slave and the peasant sectors of the labor force was not an anomaly.[23] The "peasant sector" provided a basis of provisioning that allowed for an expansion of slave-based export agriculture and for the growth of the urban centers. Second, once that expansion was under way, small- and medium-scale farming for internal markets continued to feed the cities, support the export sector and allow planters the luxury of practices that gave slight attention to subsistence agriculture. Finally, some of the earnings in the production of foodstuffs for local markets may have been used to finance the expansion of slavery as profits were used to purchase slaves to increase food production or as profits from food production were moved into other activities such as coffee plantations. Thus, rather than a dichotomy between archaic peasant and dynamic export production, these two sectors became intimately related. What is noticeable in the late colonial era is the progressive capitalization of subsistence agriculture evidenced by the increasing use of slaves for food production, even by small peasant producers.

Regional Response: Provisioning in Southern Brazil

To examine the relationship between the export economy and the production of foodstuffs for consumption in Brazil, let us turn to two dynamic captaincies. Rio de Janeiro and Bahia with their respective capitals, the cities of Rio and Salvador, provided markets and capital for the rural economy. Both of these areas had been linked to the export economy long before the mid-eighteenth century, but both experienced rapid expansion in the period after 1780.

Considerable evidence suggests that the growth of Rio de Janeiro as an urban center and the expansion and diversification of export agriculture in its hinterland served as a motive force for the development of an internal market in provisions in southern Brazil. This growth in turn stimulated the development of an infrastructure of improved roads, port facilities, and coastal shipping (*cabotagem*) that made the provisioning of the Rio market feasible and profitable.[24] The principal regions supplying the city and export sector of Rio de Janeiro—Minas Gerais, São Paulo, and the South (Rio Grande, Santa Catarina, Paraná)—responded to the new opportunities differently, dependent on their previous economic bases and social organization. Rio Grande, for example, increased livestock and grain production based on large family farms, while in Minas mixed farming using slaves no longer needed in the moribund mining industry was common. In general the market attracted increased production of foodstuffs and a penetration of commercial agriculture in the countryside marked by the presence of slave labor.

In the mid-eighteenth century, the peasantry of São Paulo, the *caipira paulista,* lived mostly on isolated, small-scale subsistence farms, largely divorced from the market.[25] São Paulo had provided some provisions, cattle, and mules to Minas Gerais during the mining boom of the early eighteenth century, but the opening of the "New Road" (Caminho novo) from Rio to Minas Gerais in 1733 and then the stagnation of the mines had brought a decline in this commercial agriculture. In the 1760s, over half of the captaincy's population was listed as unpropertied. The majority of this predominantly rural population lived by itinerant slash and burn agriculture, dispersed on small plots (*sítios volantes*) and producing only enough for their own consumption.[26] In 1766 the captain-general, the Morgado de Matheus, lamented that the subsistence orientation of the populace left so little corn in the marketplace that it was impossible to find two hundred *alquieres,* an amount that in Portugal any poor parish priest could place at sale.[27] The town council of São Paulo also voiced similar complaints, ascribing the shortages to the sloth of the small farmers. However, the constraints of subsistence production, and not indolence, lay at the heart of the matter.[28] Limited markets and minimal opportunities for capital accumulation provided few chances, little to stimulate investment, techological innovation, land improvement or growth. Rural São Paulo indeed seemed an isolated and poor backwoods region.

The situation of the captaincy changed markedly in the 1770s when, under the urging of a series of activist governors and with the cooperation of resident merchants, sugar production began to create an export activity. This agriculture stimulated the development of an infrastructure such as an improved and expanded road system stretching from the port at Santos to the sugar-producing regions of the interior.

Between 1780 and 1830, São Paulo developed an active export sector based first on sugar and then on coffee.[29] Much recent historiography has concentrated on the ways in which the transformation of the paulista economy brought about changes in the structure and organization of the family or residential units, demographic features of the population, and the distribution of land and slaves.[30] While it is clear that export agriculture had such effects, these were not limited only to these areas directly involved in exports or plantation agriculture.

The commercialization of agriculture drew in the subsistence sector as well. Humble but landowning farmers in places like Atibaia, in the periphery of the city of São Paulo, provided food to the city on a continual, if irregular, basis.[31] Areas such as Areias, Taubaté, and Guaratinguetá contained, a rural class with small holdings and a few slaves who marketed their produce locally. Investment in slaves, in fact, was a common feature among those agriculturalists who owned property.[32] In Santana de Paranaíba, a region that began to grow sugar after 1770, a certain category of small-scale slaveholders developed considerably. By 1798, they comprised over 80 percent of the slaveowners of the region and controlled about 30 percent of the slaves.[33] Whether they should be thought of as "poor planters" or as wealthy peasants is a conceptual problem that need not distract us at this point. In Paranaíba and elsewhere in the captaincy, agriculturists in both the export and internal sectors were increasingly drawn into the market economy in a variety of ways.

Whatever the impulse given by exports like sugar, it is clear that the commercialization of agriculture and its subsequent effects on land values and familial structures resulted to a large extent from new market demands within the colony itself. Here, the growth of the cities São Paulo and especially of Rio de Janeiro and the expansion of the export sectors of these regions created a series of linkages with broad effects on the nonexport sectors. The urban demand for meat, coupled with an expanding plantation production in need of transport facilities and provisions for its slave workers, created new opportunities for livestock and food production and stimulated the development of an infrastructure of roads and way stations for the mule trains (*tropas*) and cattle drives that met these needs.

São Paulo became a major producer and a conduit for livestock. A government collection post had been established at Sorocaba on the road from the South and in its register the progress of livestock production can be traced. From an annual average of about 5,000 head per annum, which passed through the register from 1750–80, the number doubled to almost 10,000 between 1780 and 1820. By the early 1820s almost 30,000 head of mules, horses, and cattle paid the government impost each year.[34]

The demand for livestock created new centers of production. The Southern frontier of São Paulo, the "quinta comarca," which comprises the present day state of Paraná, contained excellent pasturage in the "campos gerais Curitibanos." Curitiba developed as an important center, a place where the livestock were wintered before being driven northward to the fair at Sorocaba on the edge of the good pasture lands. The residents of Curitiba often bought stock farther south in Rio Grande do Sul and then after wintering them in Paraná resold them. Cattle and mules provided their own transport and could be moved with only a few drovers, but roads and a series of way stations developed on the major routes. Expansion of occupied areas increased as the "campos de Guarapuava" and the "campos de Palmas" were opened and new ranches created. Some great fortunes were made in the process like that of João da Silva Machado (later Baron of Antonina), who opened the west of Paraná and of Antônio da Silva Prado (later Baron of Iguape), who held the contract for tax collection at Sorocaba and was a great cattle merchant in his own right.[35] Alongside these fortunes were hundreds of smaller cattle *fazendas* and even more numerous agricultural *sítios*. Many of these produced a surplus of corn, beans, tobacco, rice, and wheat that was either sold regionally or shipped to São Paulo and Rio de Janeiro from the port of Paranaguá.[36] Sitios, especially those along the major roads, also supplied the cattle raising *fazendas* and the wintering points (*invernadas*), thus creating a web of relations from the markets in Rio de Janeiro to the small scale farming in the south.[37]

The increasing commercialization of the economy of the region can be seen in various ways. Between 1798 and 1830, the size of the slave population increased by about one-third.[38] Between 1820 and 1838, the number of merchants in Curitiba quadrupled. Paraná became an integral part of the colonial economy as a supplier to the internal markets linked to the export trade. Although we have no way of knowing whether the number of small farmers increased in this period, the proportion of peasant producers being drawn toward the marketplace is suggested by the increasing flow of foodstuffs to regional markets.

The impact of the export sector's growth on the internal economy and the formation of a national market was nowhere more apparent than in Brazil's southernmost region, Rio Grande do Sul. Although Portugal had intermitently maintained an outpost on the River Plate from the 1680s, and the region had played a strategic role in Portuguese imperial considerations in the middle years of the eighteenth century, occupation of the region was spotty and the small population was thinly scattered over an immense territory. Military outposts with their garrisons served as the basis of settlements, and the Portuguese crown sponsored colonization with Azorean couples who were sent to farm wheat. However, the majority of the population made a living by rustling, smuggling goods and harvesting the virtually feral cattle herds. By the mid-eighteenth century, drives of mules and cattle were being sent northward along the Caminho de Viamao to Curitiba and then Sorocaba, but the real growth of Rio Grande took place after 1780 with the increased demand for its products in the urban centers and the export-producing plantations.

The statistics of production and export, although sometimes contradictory and often incomplete, outline the process of Rio Grande's growth. From 1750 to 1780, the region sent about 5,000 mules a year to São Paulo, but between 1780 and 1800 that number increased to 10,000 per annum and then doubled again to 20,000 from 1800 to 1826.[39] The total number of animals of all types grew at a rate of 25 to 40 percent a year despite culling, slaughter, and sales, so that the value of the total herd (*rebanho*) increased from 340 thousand milréis in 1780 to 960 thousand milréis by 1787.[40] Along with live animals, Rio Grande began to export dried salted meat, jerky, or *charque*. Producers set up the first factory in 1780 shortly after a devastating drought in northeastern Brazil had decimated herds there and driven up the price of dried meat. Producers in Rio Grande siezed this opportunity and production grew rapidly, stimulated by another drought in the Northeast (1791–93) and then by abolition of the royal salt monopoly in 1801, which had long made the costs of salting meat prohibitive. The expanding plantation zones and the growing urban populations of Rio de Janeiro, Bahia, and Pernambuco became major consumers of Rio Grande *charque*.

Finally, Rio Grande also became a grain exporter. Wheat and wheat flour were shipped in large quantities to a number of Brazilian ports, but principally to Rio de Janeiro. In 1787 Rio Grande produced over 105,000 arrobas of wheat, of which Rio de Janeiro received 85,000 and some of the remainder went to other ports.[41] Clearly, this was commercial farming. The Azorean couples who had been established as small-scale farmer colonists provided a basis for this agricultural expansion. Land was easy to acquire and units were relatively large. In 1787, of the 841 properties in Rio Grande do Sul, less than 10 percent were smaller than two hundred hectares and over 50 percent were between 200 and 5,000 hectares.[42]

Despite an antique historiography emphasizing the "freedom of the pampa" it is also now well established that from the outset slaves were present in the military outposts and were used in agriculture and ranching in Rio Grande. In 1780, approximately one-third of the region's population of 17,923 was black, and that proportion increased. By 1814, almost 40 percent of the population was of African or Afro-Brazilian origin.[43] Slaves were employed princi-

pally in commercial wheat production and then after 1780 in the
charqueadas, where the cattle were slaughtered and the dried meat
prepared. The commercialization of colonial provisioning created a
demand for labor that was satisfied in the traditional Brazilian manner—by the use of African and Afro-Brazilian slaves.

The difficulty of separating the export sector from the internal
market is apparent in the case of the commerce between Rio Grande
do Sul and Rio de Janeiro. By 1803, over half of the ships that called
at Rio de Janeiro had embarked from Rio Grande (134 out of 218),
and large quantities of grain, *charque,* hides, and other pastoral or
agricultural products were unloaded in Rio de Janeiro throughout
the period.[44] The populace of Rio consumed a portion of these
commodities, but an even greater amount was exported to Portugal
and to Angola. In a sense, for the producers in Rio Grande do Sul
it made no difference where their products were ultimately consumed. This captaincy was integrated into the Brazilian colony by
an active coastal trade that supplied the markets of Rio de Janeiro,
Bahia, and other ports. The sugar planters of Bahia and Pernambuco
came to depend on the "noxious salt meat of Rio Grande" to feed
their slaves, and the Rio Grande producers oriented themselves
toward the internal markets made possible by Brazil's urban and
export sectors.[45]

In the case of Minas Gerais, we can see the effects of the
creation of an expanding internal market on the growth of the
regional economy and the commercialization of subsistence agriculture. The economy of Minas Gerais had entered a period of
extended decline as the production of gold and diamonds declined
after the mid-eighteenth century. The mining centers contracted
and the number of mines and washings decreased as the population
moved to small-scale subsistence farming and ranching. By 1810,
fewer than 10 percent of the captaincy's approximately 150,000
slaves still worked in mining. The slave population, in fact, declined
from about 190,000 in 1786 to 148,000 in 1808, the majority of them
in rural occupations.[46] While some of these slaves were employed
in export-oriented agriculture such as sugar, cotton, and the nascent
coffee plantations, by the beginning of the nineteenth century, most
slaves probably labored in the production of provisions for the Rio
de Janeiro market. The slave population of Minas Gerais began to
grow again in the early nineteenth century and the region continued
to be a major importer of Africans in the slave trade.

The economy of Minas Gerais responded to the expanding
internal markets of the late colonial era. The old roads across the

Mantiqueira range, formerly serving to transport the gold of Minas Gerais to the port of Rio de Janeiro, became the routes by which cattle, hogs, dried meat, cheese, tobacco, and some cotton cloth reached the Corte. By 1818, over 56 percent of the value of goods shipped from Minas was in commodities for internal consumption.[47] Large mule *tropas* traversed these roads and the owners of large provision farms and of mule teams made common cause with Rio merchants to secure adequate roads, bridges, and ports.

Minas Gerais in the late colonial period presents what to some scholars seems an anomaly: an area of vigorous economic growth with a large slave population based on the continuous importation of new slaves from Africa but seemingly separated from the export sector. The mixed economy of Minas and the "self-sufficiency" of its *fazendas* noted by various travelers has led some authors to argue that Minas was a virtually autarchic region with a growing economy based on its own internal consumption.[48] While these authors are correct in pointing out the nonplantation nature of Minas slaveholding, they miss the point that mineiro slaveowners were still producing for a market and that the small-scale mixed agriculture proved profitable enough to generate incomes that made the purchase of additional slaves feasible. Rather than operating in a self-contained economy, the mineiro producers seem to have been profoundly and continuously dependent on the international slave trade. The local and regional markets available to their products provided the resources that financed the continuation and expansion of this slave-based economy.

The type of labor in Minas Gerais was never in doubt. During the mid-eighteenth century the free population had grown by natural increase and might have provided a labor force to meet the oportunities of the late colonial expansion. The availability of free land, however, and the ease with which sufficient food could be grown made this population unavailable as regular agricultural workers. They preferred to live on their *roças* as independent "peasants," using household production to fulfill their needs.[49] Some, in fact, were attracted to the provisioning market and became slave-owners as well. In the late colonial era, it was simply more profitable to depend on the international slave trade than to enforce land policies or social measures that would create a nonslave agricultural labor force.

The transition to small-scale (but slave-produced) provisioning agriculture in Minas Gerais presented few difficulties. Slaveholding in Minas Gerais even during the great mining boom had always been on a small scale, characterized by (1) a low-level concentration of slave property, (2) over 70 percent of owners with fewer than five slaves, and (3) between a quarter and a half of the slaves held in units of this size.[50] The concentration on agriculture oriented toward the market did not call for any marked change in the traditional regional patterns of slaveholding. The key to the expansion of slavery was not an export crop, but simply a market profitable enough to sustain returns that made the purchase of additional laborers worthwhile.

Planter and Slave Responses: The "Peasant Breach"

In the export sector itself, both slaves and masters also responded to the export boom in ways that affected the plantation system and the colony's internal market. With strong prices for Brazilian exports in the international market, planters demonstrated a marked reluctance to grow provisions for their own labor force and preferred instead either to purchase what was needed or to encourage the slaves to grow their own food. In the mid-eighteenth century planters calculated that it was necessary to provide one *alqueire* (bushel) of manioc flour per slave each forty days, or roughly nine to ten bushels a year. This quota was not hard to produce. José da Silva Lisboa estimated that even the most ordinary land would yield 20 *alqueires* for every thousand *covas* (holes) planted and that a slave could plant one hundred *covas* a day. Thus, in ten days of planting and ten days of harvesting a slave could produce twice the amount needed for his own subsistence.[51] Still, many planters preferred to buy provisions and thus when costs were cut, slave rations often suffered first.

Scattered evidence indicates the planter strategy of buying provisions. In Bahia, the purchase of food for slaves usually constituted between 20 and 30 percent of a sugar plantation's annual operating expenses. Even so, observers from the sixteenth to the nineteenth century noted that slaves in this region were poorly fed. Some figures from Pernambuco are revealing in this regard. On fifty-one *engenhos* in the parish of Serinhaem in 1788 there were 3,801 slaves, but these *engenhos* produced only 11,105 *alqueires* of manioc or less than three *alqueires* per slave. Thus, almost two-thirds of the food requirement had to be satisfied by purchase or by slaves growing their own food. The sugar- and rum-producing district of São Gonçalo (Rio de Janeiro) in this period had a population of about 5,900 but grew only 13,800 *alqueires* of manioc or less than 2 *alqueires* per person.[52] This pattern can be seen in many export producing regions. It made the plantations dependent on food suppliers and thus made planters and especially slaves vulnerable. It provided a strong incentive to slaves to seek opportunities to grow some portion of their provisions and to have access to a marketable commodity.

The practice of slaves producing their own food has engendered an intense historical and ideological debate, much of which revolves around the social relations of slave food production and the degree of autonomy in which slaves could determine the labor inputs, crop selection, and marketing of surplus. Whether this activity constituted a "peasant breach" in the slave system or was simply a continuation of the slave mode of production is the matter in debate.[53] Slaves, even when they produced their own food, were not peasants because the level of coercion and the limitations on their decisions were generally in excess of the conditions under which peasants operated. Still, the "peasant breach" was a step toward more independence and as such it was recognized by the slaves as an improvement in their lives as the tendency toward peasantry in the postemancipation Caribbean suggests.

In the debate over the "peasant breach" in Brazil, neither side has given much attention to changes over time. The "Brazil system" of providing slaves to grow their own crops had existed from the seventeenth century at least but was probably practiced more intensely in some places and times than in others. Much of the evidence of slave food production comes, in fact, from the later eighteenth and nineteenth centuries. Given the strong market for export crops in the late colonial period, it is not difficult to see why planters would favor devoting as much land as possible to these. At the same time, slaves could perceive the advantage of supplementing their diet and of marketing the surplus, especially at a time when urban demand for provisions was high. Some slaves at least produced enough to supply their own needs and sell the remainder in local markets, while other plantations and the towns became consumers of these commodities.

Price series of basic food commodities from both Rio de Janeiro and Salvador indicate that demand was high. The price for manioc in Salvador rose from 1770 to 1800, slipped somewhat in the 1810s and then rose again to the mid-1820s. Food prices in Rio de Janeiro demonstrated a similar pattern.[54] If there were a time when slaves might profit from a marketing of their surplus, the late colonial era was that time.

Slave food production had positive benefits for both slaves and masters. Planter manuals made it clear that social control was also a consideration. As some Vassouras coffee planters later put it in 1854, "the slave who owns neither flees nor causes disorders."[55] Moreover, allowing slaves some free time for this purpose provided an incentive within the regular work routine and thus reduced supervisory problems. From the slave point of view the ability to earn some money in order to buy clothing or other goods, or perhaps to eventually purchase manumission, was a desired advantage. While slaves might be cheated of these funds, it was a custom to respect their integrity because the utility of providing slaves with a goal was so important for the maintenance of discipline and control.[56]

The expanding slave force of the period thus formed both a market for and a supplier of provisions. Whether a particular plantation or region was a net consumer or provider of foodstuffs varied according to specific circumstances. Also, it is impossible to calculate the proportion of slave-grown provisions that were consumed by the growers themselves or reached the market, or to know what percentage of provisions that reached local markets were produced by slaves on their own. Still, it is clear that the internal market created some opportunities that the slaves themselves were anxious to seize. When, as we saw in Chapter 1, a group of recalcitrant slaves in Ilhéus in 1789 demanded time to grow their own food and a means of transporting it to market in Salvador, they were demonstrating by their goals the penetration of commercial agriculture into the heart of the slave system.

Bahia: Peasant Responses and the Tensions between Food and Exports

In those captaincies like Bahia, which had a strong export sector, the tension between food production and export agriculture was an old and continuing problem, exacerbated especially during periods of export expansion. As early as the mid-seventeenth century the problem of food shortage in plantation zones had emerged. In Pernambuco, Maurits of Nassau, Governor of Dutch Brazil, had ordered in 1638 the planting of at least five hundred *covas* of manioc for each slave owned in order to avoid shortages.[57] In Bahia, governors beginning in the mid-seventeenth century had limited the planting of sugar and tobacco to certain regions in the Recôncavo in order to thereby insure that other areas would produce foodstuffs to feed the plantation population and the city of Salvador.[58]

The people and the garrison of Salvador came to depend heavily on the regions of Bahia's southern coast (Boipeba, Cairú, Camamú, and Ilhéus) for their supply of manioc flour, and it became susceptible to manipulation of supply by growers and merchants. As one governor put it in 1670, "always in every administration there has been hunger and the excessive price of flour in this market (*praça*).[59] This led in 1688 to a legal requirement that every sugar and tobacco planter in the Recôncavo cultivate five hundred covas for each slave owned.[60] This legislation was repeated in 1701 at which time a new requirement forced merchants in the slave trade to maintain manioc farms to supply their ships. Both planters and ship owners found ways to circumvent the legislation, prefering to purchase foodstuffs rather than raise them.[61] Behind this legislation was a belief that about one-third the flour produced from five hundred covas would provide enough sustenance for an individual so that the remaining two-thirds could be marketed. If this calculation is accurate, then Silva Lisboas's later estimates of production of ten *alqueires* per thousand *covas* are indeed a minimum yield based on poor soil. Better lands might be able to yield up to thirty alqueires per thousand covas.

The conflicting yet interdependent demands of export agriculture and the slave trade with those of the urban population as well as the food needs of the population as a whole, created social and economic effects of long-term significance in the colony. Clearly, in areas where the cultivation of export crops was possible, foodcrop production, with its lower returns to investment, was avoided. Subsistence agriculture became both socially and economically despised. Certainly, sugar planters wanted little part of it. The famous statement of Manoel Ferreira da Câmara in 1807 that he would cultivate no manioc, in order to avoid the absurdity of "renouncing the best agriculture in the world for the worst," underlined this feeling.[62] Data derived from plantation lists for Pernambuco and Sergipe de El-Rey in the 1780s indicates that many sugar planters grew no manioc or very little to feed their slaves.[63] Royal governors and municipal councils struggled throughout the eighteenth century to impose the forced production of foodstuffs on sugar and tobacco planters and slave shippers, and to create zones exclusivly devoted to food production.[64]

In Bahia, the regionalization of food production was made possible by designation of those parishes with sandy soils (*areias*) or of lighter rainfall as zones for manioc production.[65] This was resisted in various ways, and from time to time the crown had to intervene to prohibit tobacco cultivation or cattle raising, but eventually the southern Recôncavo (Jaguaripe, Maragogipe) and the south coast of the captaincy became the principal sources of foodstuffs for the city of Salvador and for the areas of sugar cultivation. The reluctance of export producers in the Recôncavo to plant manioc and the regionalization of its cultivation made Salvador and the Recôncavo particularly susceptible to the manipulation of supply and price. As early as 1706, the governor of Bahia accused producers of conspiring (fazendo entre sy convensão de não venderem") to raise the price of flour.[66] Similar complaints and government intervention continued throughout the eighteenth century.

The contraction of the export economy in the 1760s combined with a growth of the rural peasantry had increased the supply of food and had lowered the price enough, so that by 1770, the slave shippers could petition to be excused from their obligation to maintain *roças*, arguing that the roles of merchant and planter were incompatible. The Count of Povolide, governor at that time, disagreed, but pointed out that the merchants had always avoided "this easiest of all agricultures only because of of the sloth which in this country abounds." He pointed out that shortages still occurred.[67]

The shortages long experienced by the the slave merchants became a general problem as the economic recovery and export expansion of the late colonial period made the problem of food supply acute. By the early 1780s, price fluctuations and shortages moved the government to action. In 1785, the municipal council of Salvador ordered that all potential farmers should grow manioc and to this end it ordered an inventory of all manioc production.[68] These lists served as a basis for the operation of a public granary, the *celeiro público*, created in 1785 as a means of insuring the city's supply.[69] The *celeiro* represented a governmental attempt to stabilize and control food sales in Salvador. All manioc flour, beans, rice, and maize sold in the city had to be sold to the *celeiro*, which then charged a tax of twenty *réis* per alqueire for the service it provided. While the *celeiro* centralized the market, producers objected to its control and found innumerable ways to circumvent it. Manioc flour purchases averaged three hundred thousand alqueires between 1785 and 1812 (see table 1). But at a rate of consumption of ten alqueires per year, this amount would have provided only about 40 to 60 percent of the needs of Salvador's population of between fifty to eighty thousand inhabitants. The

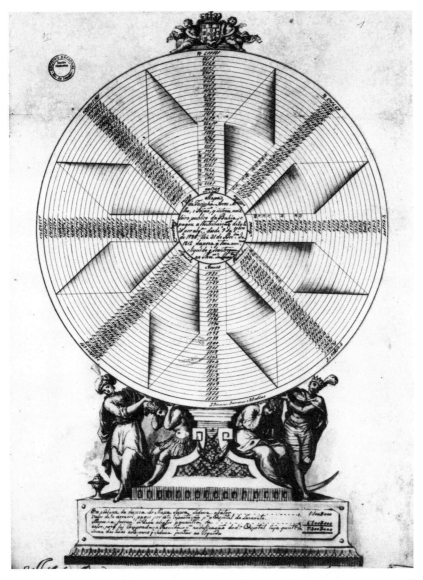

Figure 3. The Art of Bureaucracy. An elaborate illustration recording all foods entering the *Celeiro Público* from 1785 to 1812 and its operating expenses.

Sources: Arquivo Nacional do Rio de Janeiro, Mesa da Inspeção.

complaints of manioc farmers were echoed by intellectuals of a laissez faire persuasion. While the *celeiro público* did prevent serious shortage in the city, it could not stave off the continued upward trend of commodity prices.

As the export surge intensified, the problem of food supply in the captaincy worsened. Cultivators, attracted by high prices for sugar and tobacco, either abandoned food production or moved from areas restricted to that agriculture. The royal judge (*ouvidor*)

Table 1. Food Purchases in the *Celeiro Público* of Salvador and Sugar Exports, 1785–1812

Year	Farinha	Arroz	Milho	Feijão	Sugar Arrobas
1785	83,949	6,003	8,522	1,973	
1786	221,078	13,056	20,099	7,449	
1787	230,000	18,169	24,539	7,675	
1788	289,809	10,520	23,020	7,774	
1789	269,992	7,247	23,340	5,856	
1790	274,636	7,645	22,298	11,629	
1791	289,648	11,157	10,581	6,745	
1792	365,378	9,538	11,819	3,505	
1793	257,502	10,087	12,621	5,513	
1794	237,180	7,245	14,397	6,474	
1795	282,244	7,416	21,418	5,967	
1796	300,922	10,049	19,376	4,235	1,165,426
1797	289,187	7,077	19,497	7,954	423,956
1798	278,149	8,263	25,716	11,772	758,848
1799	288,011	10,248	24,006	6,375	679,484
1800	281,155	7,574	21,806	8,135	608,299
1801	279,908	5,610	23,091	5,299	989,024
1802	362,218	6,186	17,296	5,546	605,210
1803	302,031	9,641	25,797	6,472	906,448
1804	296,406	6,354	21,656	4,858	653,049
1805	287,181	17,407	21,216	3,376	908,764
1806	347,083	29,721	27,244	5,484	893,144
1807	391,807	38,108	23,056	7,104	953,377
1808	248,751	32,202	30,150	6,370	101,947
1809	293,313	20,620	35,155	7,142	464,478
1810	311,376	17,485	33,898	5,656	267,724
1811	363,671	23,363	28,046	6,712	53,163
1812	327,071	45,797	29,860	8,173	

Sources: Jobson de Andrade, O Comercio Colonial; AMRJ, Codice 623, pacote 1.

of Ilhéus, noting the "damnable indolence of the farmers" who had disobeyed royal orders and planted sugar cane, ordered them to return to manioc production in 1780.[70] In 1786, the government sought to stop *engenho* construction in Porto Seguro on lands reserved for foodstuffs.[71] By the 1790s, Dom Fernando José de Portugal, was reporting on the large-scale abandonment of manioc cultivation and a shift of capital and slaves to sugar, cotton, and tobacco, the effects of which could also be seen in the hunger and poverty of the small interior towns as well.[72]

Hunger, high prices, and shortages of flour in Bahia were to some extent a result of the colonial system and the existence of alternate markets. Manioc flour was also an export commodity and some had always been sent to the African coast. In 1796, Minister Dom Rodrigo de Sousa Coutinho had ordered the Governor of Bahia to increase manioc production in order to supply flour to Portugal to alleviate the bread shortage in the metropolis. The governor found this idea impractical and noted at the time that Bahia could not even feed itself without food imports from other captaincies.[73] By the 1810s, enough manioc flour was sent to Europe to cause further complaints.[74] While price of manioc flour lessened in this decade, drought, government regulations, the attractions of export agriculture, and manipulation of food stocks by speculators created a situation that led to a weakening supply. The Câmara of Santo Amaro wrote in 1817 that the population was on the point of starvation due to the lack of flour.[75] Reforms were suggested, but there seems little doubt that the material conditions and real income of the majority of the free population worsened during the period of the export boom, and that this situation was made most apparent in the price and availability of foodstuffs in the cities.[76]

For the producers of manioc the problem centered on risks. Manioc could be produced for self-consumption with few tools, on relatively marginal lands, and with low labor inputs. This husbandry was so easy that anyone attempting to produce for the market was faced with very weak prices in "good years." In the "bad years" of flood or drought when the prices rose, marginal producers not only had little to sell, but sometimes failed to feed themselves. The purchase of slaves to increase production, therefore, called on an outlay of capital and was predicated on the expectation of years that were neither "too good" nor "too bad." Unable to control the vagaries of the weather, producers, not surprisingly, attempted to hold manioc supplies back and thus manipulate the market to the dismay of Salvador's residents and local administrators.

The copious official correspondence, generated by the problem of food supply and the existence of census materials and lists of manioc producers, provides a basis for understanding the organization of manioc production. Manioc farming was a poor man's agriculture, often organized as peasant production. Although a few self-sufficient "subsistence" farmers were involved in this husbandry, the production of foodstuffs for the market by small farmers characterized the Bahian market.

Significant regional differences in the structure of manioc production are apparent. In table 2, I present the manioc production of three areas that supplied Salvador. The parishes of Sergipe de El-Rey, which also produced some sugar, produced enough manioc to market about one-quarter to one-third of the yield. The regions of Cairú and Maragogipe were clearly fully devoted to provisioning for the Bahian market. Using a conservative yield ratio of twenty *alqueires* per thousand *covas*, it is clear that these regions were capable of producing twice their subsistence needs and that a large proportion of production was marketed. Noticeable here is the penetration of this small-scale production by slave labor. In a list of manioc producers in Cairú prepared in 1786 there were 188 people listed, 169 of whom owned slaves.[77] These slaveowners held on an average of 4.3 slaves and only four owned fifteen or more. It was only "the most humble of those farmers . . . who work only with their own efforts (*braço*) without the aid of any captive," in the words of the *ouvidor* of Ilhéus.[78] In 1817, there were some 2,500 slaveowners and 11,500 slaves in the manioc-producing parishes of Maragogipe and Jaguaripe. The mean number of slaves per owner was 4.5 and the concentration of ownership was low (Gini coefficient of .38 to .45). These figures indicate a widespread ownership of slaves and their use in food production. The prevalence of slaves in this agriculture raises serious questions about the characterization of peasantry in Brazil.

The information from Sergipe de El-Rey, contained in table 2, underlines the continuing tension between manioc growing and the production of export crops. In this region, which produced both sugar and manioc and upon which Salvador depended for some of its manioc supply, food production fell below requirements. Even if we calculate higher yields at twice the expected minimum, local needs were barely met because a number of sugar producers

Table 2. Subsistence and Surplus in Manioc Production, Bahia and Sergipe de El-Rey

	Growers (1)	Covas (000) (2)	Slaves	Total Pop. (1)×45+(3) (4)	Alqueires (2)×20 (5)	Subsistence Need (4)×10 alq. (6)	Marketable Surplus (5)−(6) alq. (7)	Surplus as Percent of Production (8)
Maragogipe (1780)	402	2,640	(1,809)[1]	3,618	52,800	36,180	16,620	31
Cairú (1785)	188	884	635	1,481	17,680	14,810	2,870	16
São Cristóvão (Sergipe) (1786)	138	325	373	994	6,500	9,940	6,310	−53
Ribeira da Vasabarris[2] (1785)	165	389	788	1,530	7,780	15,305	4,150	−96

[1]Number of slaves based on an 1817 slave census at 4.5 per owner. See Schwartz, Sugar Plantations, 443.
[2]There were eight engenhos with 204 slaves that grew no manioc.
Sources: BNRJ, I-31,30,51; APB, Cartas ao governo, 188.

planted little or no manioc for their workers. Here, the conflict between export crop and food requirements were put into stark focus as planters made the decision to buy rather than plant manioc or to leave slaves to fend for themselves.

At this point it is impossible to determine the typicality of the Bahian situation, but figures from that captaincy suggest some futures lines of investigation and hypotheses to be tested. First, considerable evidence from Bahia, Minas Gerais, and São Paulo indicates the employment of small-scale farming and food production with the use of slave labor. One is tempted to argue that slavery was becoming a more widely diffused institution in the late colonial period than it had ever been. Second, "peasant" producers with access to the growing markets in cities and in the plantation sector appear to have responded by increasing production, and manioc cultivation lent itself to expansion with increases primarily in labor inputs. Rather than an avoidance of the market economy, small farmers and even slaves, when they could—as in the case of Engenho Santana examined in chapter 2—actively sought to expand production.[79] Data from Bahia indicates that a large portion of "peasant" production could be marketed. Surely, this proportion varied widely in time and place, but the penetration of commercial relations into peasant production seems clear. Finally, the creation of a provisions market as a result of export-led growth raises serious questions about the enclave nature of the plantation economies and should lead to a further examination of the internal linkages within the colonial economy.

The experience of late colonial and early national Brazil demonstrates the continuing power of slavery to determine all aspects of the economy and to penetrate into sectors not previously characterized by slave labor. Accompanying this penetration, of course, were the concommitant social relations of a slave regime. Small-scale peasant production and slave-based agriculture were no longer two distinct alternatives, but rather two related processes in which the tendency for slavery to expand predominated. Even as Brazil sought to balance the production of food for consumption at home with its export agriculture, the question of slavery remained unchallenged. Frei Vicente do Salvador, Brazil's first historian, had said in the seventeenth century that, Brazil was such a wonderful land, "it could support itself even if all its ports were closed."[80] At the end of the colonial era, and especially after 1808 when the level of Brazilian exports began to increase, the real question, in fact, was whether Brazil could feed itself with its ports open. It did so by expanding the use of slaves.

NOTES

1. George Beckford, *Persistent Poverty* (Oxford, 1972), is a classic example. See also Lloyd Best, "Outlines of a Model of Pure Plantation Economy," *Social and Economic Studies* 17 (Sept. 1968): 283–324. A discussion of this literature and a more favorable view of the plantation economy is presented in Edgar Graham and Ingrid Floering, *The Modern Plantation in the Third World*, (New York, 1984). A critique of this literature based on a particular case is Trevor Sudama, "The Model of the Plantation Economy: The Case of Trinidad and Tobago, *Latin American Perspectives* 6:1 (Winter 1979), 65–83.

2. See Fernando B. Homen de Mello, "Export Agriculture and the Problem of Food Production," *Brazilian Economic Studies*, (Instituto de Planajamento Econômico e Social, n.7, 1983), 1–20. The question is an old one. See also the classic by Sebastião Ferreira Soares, *Notas estatísticas sobre a produção agrícola e carestia dos gêneros alimenticios no império do Brasil*, (Rio de Janeiro, 1860).

3. The secondary role assigned to "peasant" or small-scale agriculture can be seen from different viewpoints in Alberto Passos Guimarães, *Quatro séculos de latifundio*, 4th ed. (Rio de Janeiro, 1977), 105–66; and Jacob Gorender, *O escravismo colonial*, 2d. ed. (São Paulo, 1985), 285–99. For comparison, see Douglas McCalla, "The Internal Economy of Upper Canada: New Evidence on Agricultural Marketing before 1850," *Agricultural History* 59:3 (July, 1985), 397–416; Jeremy Atack and Fred Bateman, "Self-Sufficiency and the Marketable Surplus in the Rural North, 1860," *Agricultural History* 58:3 (July 1984), 296–313.

4. Terms such as *agregado, morador, cafuso, matuto,* and *sitiante* have all been used. See my comments in "Perspectives of Brazilian Peasantry," *Peasant Studies* 5:4 (1976),11–20.

5. John Duncan Powell, "On Defining Peasants and Peasant Society," *Peasant Studies Newsletter* 1:3 (1972), 94–99.

6. On the properties of manioc see Anna Curtenius Roosevelt, *Parmana. Prehistoric Maize and Manioc Cultivation along the Amazon and Orinoco* (New York, 1980), 118–37. See also William S. Saint, Jr., *The Social Organization of Crop Production: Cassava, Tobacco, and Citrus in Bahia, Brazil* (Cornell University: Latin American Studies Program Dissertation Series, 1977), 49–65.

7. Roosevelt, *Parmana*, 124. Roosevelt cites a 1959 study on Brazil

in which manioc produced 14.2 million calories per hectare, maize 4.4, rice 3.9, and sweet potatoes and yams 7.5 million.

8. My estimate of the ratio is based on purchases of the public granary of Salvador. See table 1.

9. Reports of food crop production in the agricultural census of 1778 taken under the Marquis of Lavradio indicate that manioc still predominated in the captaincy of Rio de Janeiro. See *RIHGB* 76:1 (1913), 289–360.

10. Dauril Alden, "Late Colonial Brazil, *CHLA* 2:602–22, provides the best summary of the agricultural renaissance and careful compilations of the export figures. J. H. Galloway, "Agricultural Reform and the Enlightenment in Late Colonial Brazil, *Agricultural History* 53:4 (Oct. 1979), 763–79 discusses the ideological climate of the period. See also Leopoldo Jobim, *Reforma agraria no Brasil colônia* (São Paulo, 1983) in which he examines the attitudes of the reformers on land reform. I have dealt with the impact of the boom in Bahia in *Sugar Plantations and the Formation of Brazilian Society,* (Cambridge, 1985), 415–38.

11. Fernando A. Novais, *Portugal e Brasil na crise do antigo sistema colonial* (São Paulo, 1979) and José Jobson de A. Arruda, *O Brasil no comércio colonial* (São Paulo, 1980) are essential reading on the export economy and Brazil's role in the Portuguese colonial system.

12. For the year 1819 I have used the estimates of Alden, "Late Colonial Brazil," 602–10; and of Maria Luiza Marcílio, "The Population of Colonial Brazil," *CHLA*, 37–66.

13. The demographic features of the free colored population have received less attention than those of the slaves. While this segment of the population was obviously growing rapidly, the exact causes and dynamic of that growth remain unclear. The best summary of the problem is still Herbert Klein, "Nineteenth-Century Brazil," in *Neither Slave Nor Free*, eds. David W. Cohen and Jack P. Greene (Baltimore, 1972), 309–34, which includes some basic population statistics. Unfortunately, A. J. R. Russell-Wood, "Colonial Brazil," 84–133 in the same volume does not contain similar data from before 1808, although using qualitative materials he is able to present an excellent analysis of their position in society. See also a further elaboration of this theme in A. J. R. Russell-Wood, *The Black Man in Slavery and Freedom in Colonial Brazil* (New York, 1982). Much more work on a regional basis is needed, such as that of Katia M. de Queirós Mattoso on Bahia. For a summary of her findings see *To Be a Slave in Brazil*, trans. from French edition of 1979 by Arthur Goldhammer (New Brunswick, 1986).

14. On manumission practices and patterns there are now in-depth studies of Bahia, Paraty, Campinas, and Rio de Janeiro. All indicate a favoring of mulattoes, young children, and of women in the manumission process. No one has yet calculated the impact of manumission on the differential demographic rates of slaves and the free colored population. See Stuart B. Schwartz, "The Manumission of Slaves in Colonial Brazil, Bahia, 1684–1746," *HAHR* 54:4 (1970), 313–33; Katia M. de Queirós Mattoso,

"A propósito de cartas de alforria na Bahia, 1779–1850," *Anais da História* (Marilia) 4 (1972), 23–52; James Patrick Kiernan, "The Manumission of Slaves in Colonial Brazil: Paraty, 1789–1822" (Ph.D. diss., New York University, 1976); Peter L. Eisenberg, "Ficando livre: As alforrias em Campinas no século xix," *Estudos Econômicos* 17:2 (1987), 175–216. On Rio de Janeiro, Mary Karash, *Slave Life in Rio de Janeiro* (Princeton, 1986) contains data on manumission.

15. Alden, "Late Colonial Brazil," 607.

16. On the urban system of colonial Brazil see Richard M. Morse, "Brazil's Urban Development: Colony and Empire," in *From Colony to Nation*, ed. A. J. R. Russell-Wood (Baltimore, 1974), 155–84. Figures for Recife are taken from Bainbridge Cowell, Jr., "Cityward Migration in the Nineteenth Century: The Case of Recife, Brazil," *Journal of Latin American Studies and World Affairs* 17:1 (1975), 43–63.

17. David Eltis, *Economic Growth and the Ending of the Atlantic Slave Trade* (New York, 1987), 47–62.

18. See the discussion of sources in Schwartz, *Sugar Plantations*, 338–345. Cf. David Eltis, *Economic Growth and the Ending of the Slave Trade* (Oxford, 1987), table A.1, 243.

19. Colin M. MacLachlan, "African Slave Trade and Economic Development in Amazonia," in *Slavery and Race Relations in Latin America*, ed. Robert B. Toplin (Westport, Conn., 197), 112–45.

20. Corcino Medeiros dos Santos, "Relações de Angola com o Rio de Janeiro (1736–1808)," *Estudos Históricos* 12 (1978), 7–68; Herbert S. Klein, *The Middle Passage* (Princeton, 1978), 54. See also Joseph Miller, *Way of Death: Merchant Capitalism and the Angolan Slave Trade, 1730–1830* (Madison, 1989), 445–531.

21. Corcino Medeiros dos Santos, *Economia e sociedade no Rio Grande do Sul (século xviii)* (São Paulo, 1984), 32–34.

22. Fernando Henrique Cardoso, *Capitalismo e escravidão no Brasil meridional* (São Paulo, 1962), 42; Mary C. Karasch, "Slave Life in Rio de Janeiro, 1808–1850," (Princeton, 1988), 29; Donald Ramos, "Vila Rica: Profile of a Colonial Urban Center," *The Americas* 35:4 (April 1974), 495–526. Schwartz, *Sugar Plantations*, 350–70; IHGAP, Mapa geral da vila de Seranhaem (1788), estante A, gaveta 5.

23. The interest in small-scale subsistence and foodstuff agriculture in colonial Brazil is a recent development. Important work has been done by Maria Yedda Linhares and Francisco Carlos Teixeira da Silva, *História da agricultura brasileira* (São Paulo, 1981), 107–60; Maria Yedda Linhares, "Subsistencia e sistemas agrários na colónia: uma discussão," *Estudos Econômicos* 13 (1983),745–62; Ciro Flamarion S. Cardoso, *Agricultura, escravidão e capitalismo*, (Petrópolis, 1979); José Roberto do Amaral Lapa, *O antigo sistema colonial*, (São Paulo, 1982), especially "O mercado interno colonial," 38–65; Eullia Maria Lahmeyer Lobo, *História poltico-administrativa da agricultura brasileira, 1808–1889* (financed by the Ministry of Agriculture but published without reference to place or date of publication). Especially

useful from a theoretical viewpoint is Ana Célia Castro, et al., *Evolução recente e situção atual da agricultura brasileira* (Brasília, 1979). Substantial monographic studies are now appearing. Gilka Vasconcelos Ferreira de Salles, "A sociedade agrária em Goiás colonial," *Revista do ICHL* 4:1 (1984), 55–88, is an example. By far the most detailed and careful study of the relationship between export and subsistence agriculture and its effects on land and labor markets is Hebe Maria da Costa Mattos Gomes de Castro, "A margem da história (Homens livres pobres e pequena produção na crise do trabalho escravo)," Master's thesis, Universidade Federal Fluminense, 1985).

24. A detailed study of the sources of supply for Rio de Janeiro is found in Larissa Virginia Brown, "Internal Commerce in a Colonial Economy: Rio de Janeiro and its Hinterland, 1790–1822" (Ph.D. diss., University of Virginia, 1986). An important source of information is Eulalia Maria Lahmeyer Lobo, *História do Rio de Janeiro,* 2 vols. (Rio de Janeiro, 1978).

25. There is now a considerable literature on the economic transformation of eighteenth-century São Paulo and its social results. An essential starting point is Alice P. Canabrava, "Uma economia de decadência: Os níveis de riqueza na capitania de São Paulo, 1765/67," *Revista Brasileira de Economia* 26:4 (1972), 95–123; and her "A repartição da terra na capitania de São Paulo, 1818," *Estudos Econômicos,* 2:6 (1972), 77–130. The unfortunately still-unpublished work of Maria Luiza Marcílio, "Crescimento demografico e evolução agrária paulista, 1700–1836" (thesis of Livre Docencia, University of São Paulo, 1974) is a provocative analysis of the process. An example of her findings is found in Luís Lisanti Filho and Maria Luiza Marcílio, "Estrutura demografica, social, e economica da vila de Lages, 1798–1808," *Estudos Históricos* (Marília), 8 (1969), 9–52. Also important is Elizabeth Anne Kuznesof, *Household Economy and Urban Development. São Paulo, 1765–1836,* Dellplain Latin American Series, n.18 (Boulder, 1986), which concentrates on family structure and production. Oscar Holme, "Ubatuba: de uma agricultura de subsistência para uma agricultura comercial" (Ph.D. diss., University of São Paulo, 1971) and Luís Lisanti Filho, "Comércio e capitalismo. O Brasil e a Europa entre of fim do século xviii e o íncio do século xix (o exemplo de tres vilas paulistas—Campinas, Itú, e Porto Feliz, 1798–1828/9" (Ph.D. diss., University of São Paulo, 1962) are important unpublished studies of the process. See also the recent study of Alida C. Metcalf, "Family and Frontier in Colonial Brazil: Santana de Paranaíba, 1580–1822" (University of California, in press, 1992).

26. Canabrava, "Uma economia," 103–4.

27. Cited in Kuznesof, *Household Economy,* 25–26.

28. Canabrava, "Uma economia," 121. Cf. John J. McCusker and Russell R. Menard, *The Economy of British America, 1607–1789* (Chapel Hill, N.C., 1985), 295–309.

29. The fundamental study on the reborn paulista sugar industry is Maria Thereza Schorer Petrone, *A lavoura canavieira em São Paulo* (São Paulo, 1968).

30. Other than the works cited above in note 25, see, for example, Eni de Mesquita Samara, "Os agregados: Uma tipologia ao fim do período colonial (1780–1830)," *Estudos Econômicos* 11:3 (1981), 159–68; Maria Luiza Marcílio, "Tendências e estruturas dos domicílios na capitania de São Paulo (1765–1828) segundo as listas nominativas de habitantes," *Estudos Econômicos* 2:6 (1972), 131–43; Alida C. Metcalf, "Recursos e estruturas familiares no século xviii, em Ubatuba, Brasil," *Estudos Econômicos* 13:special edition (1983), 771–86. This line of investigation owes much to the pioneering work of Lucilia Hermann published first in 1948 and recently republished as *Evolução da estrutura social de Guaratinguetá num período de trezentos anos,* (São Paulo, 1986).

31. Comments on Atibaia, the "granary of São Paulo," are found in Kusnesof, "Household Economy," 111.

32. Emilio Willems, "Social Differentiation in Colonial Brazil," *Comparative Studies in Society and History* 12:1 (1970), 31–49.

33. Alida C. Metcalf, "Families of Planters, Peasants, and Slaves: Strategies for Survival in Santana de Paranaíba, Brazil, 1720–1820" (Ph.D. diss., University of Texas, 1983).

34. Maria Thereza Schorer Petrone, *O Barão de Iguape* (São Paulo, 1976), 20–24.

35. Ibid., 18–20.

36. Ibid. On the port of Paranaguá the work of Cecilia Maria Westphalen is essential. See, for example, "O porto de Paranaguá e as fluctuações da economia ocidental no século xix," *Boletim do Departamento de História do Universidade Federal do Paraná* 20 (1973). By the end of the eighteenth century, Paranaguá also served as an exchange point for goods from Europe and northeastern Brazil headed for the Rio de La Plata.

37. Marina Lourdes Ritter, *As sesmarias do Paraná no século xviii* (Curitiba, 1980), 197–207.

38. In 1798, Paraná had a total population of 20,999 of which 4,273 were slaves. By 1830, the total population had risen to 36,701 of which 6,260 were slaves. See Iraci del Nero da Costa and Horácio Gutiérrez, *Paraná: Mapas de habitantes 1798–1830* (São Paulo, 1985), 18, 156.

39. Medeiros dos Santos, *Economia e sociedade do Rio Grande,* 75.

40. Ibid., 82–84.

41. Rudolph William Bauss, "Rio de Janeiro: The Rise of Late Colonial Brazil's Dominant Emporium, 1777–1808" (Ph.D. diss., Tulane University, 1977), 133–35, 183–84. See also the figures in Brown, "Internal Commerce," 434. Some of the Rio Grande grain shipments included reexports from Santa Catarina, which itself was becoming a supplier of the food markets in Rio de Janeiro and the Northeast. See Laura Machado Hübner, *O comércio da cidade do Desterro no século xix* (Florianópolis, 1981), 43–63.

42. Corcino Medeiros dos Santos, "Distribuição e uso da terra no Rio Grande do Sul no século xviii," in *A Propriedade rural. Anais do VII Simpósio dos Profesores Universitários de História* 3 vols. (São Paulo, 1976), 2:371–90.

43. The classic study of the use of slaves in the economy of Rio Grande do Sul is Fernando Henrique Cardoso, *Capitalismo e escravidão no Brasil meridional* (São Paulo, 1962). On social customs see, Joseph Hörmeyer, *O Rio Grande do Sul de 1850* (Porto Alegre, 1986), 64–83.

44. Jobson de A. Arruda, *O Brasil*, 159.

45. The observation was made in 1800 by Marco Antônio de Sousa in *Memoria sobre a capitania de Serzipe* 2d. ed. (Aracaju, 1944), and is cited in Schwartz, *Sugar Plantations*, 139.

46. Amilcar Martins Filho and Roberto B. Martins, "Slavery in a Non-Export Economy: Nineteenth-Century Minas Gerais Revisited," *HAHR* 63:3 (August, 1983), 537–69. See also Roberto Borges Martins, "A Economia escravista de Minas Gerais no século xix" (Belo Horizonte, 1980), Centro de Desenvolvimento e planejamento regional, Universidade Federal de Minas Gerais, n.10.

47. Alcir Lenharo, *As tropas de moderação* (São Paulo, 1979), 79. In 1818–19, Minas exported goods worth 1,620,285$. Of this total 913,650$ was allotted for the internal market. The quantities are somewhat deceptive because the market for Brazilian cotton in those years was very good and the large amount of cotton produced which raised the proportion of export values was, in fact, an extraordinary situation.

48. This is the central point of Martins Filho and Martins, "Slavery in a Non-Export Economy," 537–38. The reader should consult the critiques of this thesis by Robert Slenes, Warren Dean, Stanley Engerman and Eugene Genovese published at the same time in *HAHR* 63:3 (1983), 569–90. See also the demographic critique in Wilson Cano and Francisco Vidal Luna, "La reproducción natural de los esclavos em Minas Gerais," *HISLA* 4 (1985), 130–35. The issue is also perceptively discussed in Douglas Cole Libby, *Transformação e trabalho em uma economia escravista* (São Paulo, 1988), 38–61.

49. On the development of mixed agriculture, see Lawrence J. Nielsen, "Of Gentry, Peasants, and Slaves: Rural Society in Sabar and its Hinterland" (Ph.D. diss., University of California, Davis, 1975).

50. "Estrutura da posse de escravos," in *Minas colonial: economia e sociedade,* ed. Francisco Vidal Luna and Iraci del Nero da Costa (São Paulo, 1982), 31–56; Francisco Vidal Luna, *Minas Gerais: escravos e senhores* (São Paulo, 1981).

51. AHU, Bahia pap. avul. caixa 61 (1751). Silva Lisboa's estimates were made in a letter to Dr. Domingos Vandelli in 1781. See *ABNR* 32 (1910), 494–507. The letter is discussed in Thales de Azevedo, *Povoamento da cidade do Salvador,* 2d. ed. (Salvador, 1969), 239. Manioc had various advantages as a slave crop. It has no fixed harvest season, although it is still often planted in July, "the month of Santana," traditionally a month when the sugar harvest was over. Manioc can be left in the ground for long periods of time before it rots. See Saint, *The Social Organization,* 54–55; Mario Hiraoka and Shozo Yamamoto, "Changing Agricultural Land Use in the

Agreste of Northeast Brazil," *Latin American Studies* (University of Tsukuba, Japan), 2 (1981), 81–117.

52. "Mappa geral da Vila de Serinhaem (1788)," IHGAP, Estante A, gaveta 5. In addition to the manioc produced on the fifty-one plantations, ten *engenhos* also listed a small production of rice, but none yielded over forty bushels in that year. On São Gonçalo, see ANTT, Mss. do Brasil, codice 4, f.291.

53. See chapter 2. Key writings in the debate on the peasant breach are Ciro Flamarion S. Cardoso, "A brecha camponesa no sistema escravista," in *Agricultura, escravismo, e capitalismo* (Petrópolis, 1979), 133–54; Antônio Barros de Castro, "A economia política, o capitalismo e a escravidão," in *Modos de produção e realidade brasileira*, ed. José Roberto de Amaral Lapa (Petrópolis, 1980), 67–108; Jacob Gorender, "Questionamentos sobre a teoria econômica do escravismo colonial," *Estudos Econômicos* 13:1 (1983), 7–40; Stuart B. Schwartz," Resistance and Accomodation in Eighteenth-Century Brazil: The Slaves' View of Slavery," *HAHR* 57:1 (Feb. 1977), 68–81.

54. See the discussion in Schwartz, *Sugar Plantations*, 435–36, The starting points for commodity price series in this period are Harold B. Johnson, "A Preliminary Inquiry into Money, Prices, and Wages in Rio de Janeiro, 1763–1823," in *Colonial Roots of Modern Brazil*, ed. Dauril Alden (Berkeley, 1973), 231–84; Katia M. de Queirós Mattoso, "Sociedade e conjuntura na Bahia nos anos de luta da independencia," *Universitas* 15–16 (1973), 5–26.

55. This comment is cited by Eduardo Silva in "A função ideólogica da 'brecha camponesá," in Reis and Silva, *Negociação e conflito*, 22–31. See also his *Barões e escravidão* (Rio de Janeiro, 1984), especially the section: "A carestia dos generos: como sustentar a bicharada," 159–70.

56. Henry Koster, *Travels in Brazil*, 2d ed., 2 vols. (Philadelphia, 1817), II, 194, 226–28. Koster points out that in Pernambuco the tradition of a slave *peculium* was generally respected.

57. José Antônio Gonsalves de Mello, *Tempo dos flamengos*, 2d ed. (Recife, 1978), 150; Evaldo Cabral de Mello, *Olinda restaurada* (São Paulo, 1975), 192. The problem of manioc versus sugar is discussed in Gileno de Carli, "Geografia econômica e social da canna de açúcar no Brasil," *Brasil Açúcareiro* 10:1 (1937), 24–41; 10:2 (1937), 200–226.

58. *Bando* (5 Feb. 1639) BI, Cartas do Conde de Torre, Livro 2, n.3; *Bando* (28 May 1654), APB, ord. reg. 59, f.70–71. The Conde de Atougia lifted old prohibition on tobacco planting in Cachoeira and Inhambupe because the manioc flour produced in these regions did not go to Salvador.

59. *Bando* (24 April 1670) Governor Alexandre de Sousa Freire. ACS, 125.5 Provisões.

60. The *câmara* of Salvador sought this legislation because of shortages and high prices. Its proposal was forwarded to Lisbon in 1687 by Governor Matias da Cunha who also reported that many sugar plantations

(*engenhos*) planted no manioc and others who had lands for such plantings, rented these out. Cf. ACB, III, (14 July 1686), 32–33; Da Cunha to Conselho Ultramarino (9 Aug. 1687), AHU, Bahia pap. av. caixa 15.

61. ACS, Provisões reais 25.2, f.131v.–132; 27.2, f.137–38. The law requiring slave shippers to maintain manioc farms was a source of conflict between the *câmara* of Salvador and the merchants of the city. Not only did slavers prefer to buy manioc rather than produce it, but in 1729 it was estimated that over 6,000 *alqueires* were used in the Mina trade alone. See AHU, Bahia pap. avul. caixa 90 lst series uncat. (27 July 1729); caixa 45, lst series uncat. (21 May 1731); APB, Cartas do Senado 132, f.160. Complaints against the merchants continued through the eighteenth century. See that of 6 November 1754 in *ABNRJ* 31 (1909), 90. docs. 1, 351; 1, 352.

62. See the discussion in Azevedo, *Povoamento*, 265–99.

63. APB, Cartas ao govêrno 188.

64. In 1693 the grazing of horses and cattle in Cachoeira and Maragogipe was limited in order to protect manioc farming (ACS, 124.1 Provisões). In 1706 when the residents of Maragogipe, Capanema, and Cachoeira sought to have the prohibition on tobacco planting lifted, the Governor supplied the crown with a negative opinion, arguing that this would lead to an abandonment of manioc farming. (APB, Ord. reg. 7, n.511, 511A; ACS 124.7 Provisoes, fs. 60–61).

65. I have discussed the agricultural geography of the Recôncavo in *Sugar Plantations*, 75–97.

66. Vasco Cezar de Meneses to crown (25 May 1706), APB, Ord. reg. 7, n.511A; AHU, Bahia pap. avul. caixa 57 lst series uncat. (15 March 1750).

67. Conde de Povolide to Conselho Ultramarino (1771), APB, Ord. reg. 72; *ABNRJ* 32 (1910), 258, doc. 8458.

68. The first of these I have seen is from Jaguaripe and dates from 1780-81. See APB, Cartas ao governo 188; Oficio do capitão mor das ordenanzas de Jaguaripe . . . (30 Nov. 1781) remette as relações dos lavradores empregados na plantação da mandioca," BNRJ, I-31,30,52. See also BNRJ II-34, 5, 28 on that region. Six lists of 1785–86 from the area of Sergipe de El-Rey are found in APB, Cartas ao governo 188. The 1786 list from Cairú is in BNRJ, I-31,30,51.

69. See the discussion in Katia M. de Queirós Mattoso, *Bahia: A Cidade do Salvador e seu mercado no século xix* (São Paulo, 1978), 252–55.

70. Provisão, Ouvidoria de Ilhéus (1780), APB, Cartas ao governo 181.

71. Dom Rodrigo José de Meneses to Ouvidor of Porto Seguro (22 Nov. 1786), APB, Cartas ao governo 188.

72. Gonçalo Francisco Monteiro *ouvidor* of Ilhéus wrote to the governor in Bahia of the hunger in his area because "of the lack of agriculture and manioc planting." The decline in manioc production resulted in a loss in the royal tithe contact to half its former level. See APB, Cartas ao governo 198 (27 Jan. 1796). See also APB, Cartas do governo a S. Mgde. 1794–97, f.230. A similar process appears to have taken place in Pernambuco. In the

semiarid *agreste* small farmers were shifting to cotton and abandoning manioc thereby causing shortages. See José Ribeiro Júnior, "Trabalho e fome numa economia colonial," *História*, 2 (1983), 15–20.

73. Dom Fernando José de Portugal to Dom Rodrigo de Sousa Coutinho (31 Dec. 1796), *ABNRJ* 34 (1913), 405–6. doc. 16.779.

74. Vicente de Sá Portella, capitão mor of Santa Luzia do Rio Real in Sergipe de El-Rey complained to the governor of Bahia that shortages in Bahia were due to export to Europe and to Pernambuco. He estimated that his region produced two hundred thousand *alqueires* a year. In 1812 it had sent forty thousand to Salvador. See APB, Cartas ao govêrno 238.

75. Juiz de fora of Santo Amaro, José Bonifacio de Araujo e Azambuja (8 June 1817), APB, Cartas ao govêrno 241.

76. José de Sá e Bettencourt, "Memoria sobre a lavoura de mandioca no têrmo da Vila de Camamu e a plantação de algodão." APB, Cartas ao governo clx, f.499–511.

77. BNRJ, I-31,30,51.

78. Bartolomeu Siqueira Lima, ouvidor interino de Ilhéus (19 Oct. 1795), APB, Cartas ao govêrno 209.

79. See above pp.

80. Frei Vicente do Salvador, *História do Brasil*, 4th ed. (São Paulo, 1965), book I, chap. 11, 83.

4 Rethinking Palmares: Slave Resistance in Colonial Brazil

Colonial Brazil, based as it was on the coerced labor of Indians and Africans, was continually threatened by various forms of resistance to the fundamental institution of slavery.[1] Throughout the Americas wherever slavery was a basic institution, slave resistance, the fear of slave revolt, and the problem of fugitive slaves plagued colonists and colonial administrators. This resistance took a number of forms and was expressed in a variety of ways. Day to day recalcitrance, slow downs, and sabotage were probably the most common forms of resistance, while self-destruction through suicide, infanticide, or overt attempts at vengeance were the most extreme in a personal sense. In Brazil, the most dramatic examples of collective action were a number of slave revolts that took place in Bahia in the early nineteenth century, but actions like the Malê rebellion of 1835 were truly extraordinary events.[2] By far, the most common form of slave resistance in colonial Brazil was flight, and a characteristic problem of the Brazilian slave regime was the continual and widespread existence of fugitive communities called variously *mocambos, ladeiras, magotes,* or *quilombos*.

There was a time when Brazilian historiography ignored this aspect of Brazil's past, but work during the past half century, especially on the great fugitive community of Palmares, has considerably changed this situation.[3] Still, in many ways, the topic of slave flight and resistance in Brazil has been treated as a deceptively simple one, and analyses of it have often been based on a limited set of questions to which common sense answers have been made: Why did slaves flee? To escape slavery. Where were runaway communities located? Far from possible white retaliation. Why did fugitives attack white society? To liberate their fellows and because they hated slavery. Was there class solidarity among slaves? Of course. What kind of societies did fugitives create? More or less egalitarian ones based on African traditions. Noticeably missing from the study of marronage in Brazil has been concern with some of the issues that have preoccupied students of this phenomenon in other American slave societies or solid evidence that would illumine some of the more intractable questions about ethnic solidarities, political goals, and strategies, as well as variations in form. For example, distinctions between the *petite marronage* of slaves who absented themselves for short periods and those who fled to escape slavery altogether has rarely been made in Brazilian historiography.[4] Maroon intentions have preoccupied much writing in Jamaica and Haiti, but not in Brazil, except for the case of Palmares. To what extent did escaped slaves organize a resistance that consciously aimed at overthrowing or at least attacking slave society rather than seeking their personal freedom is a question that has remained without answer in Brazil, even though such an answer would provide a measure of the "revolutionary" nature of escaped slave communities.[5] To some extent these questions are difficult to answer because of a lack of appropriate documentation, but a close reading of local sources and the use of ethnohistorical techniques may begin to offer a few tentative answers to some of the central questions of fugitive communities in Brazilian slave society.

In this chapter, I examine aspects of fugitive communities in three major areas of colonial Brazil: the plantation zone of Bahia; the mining district of Minas Gerais; and the inaccessible frontier of Alagoas, site of Palmares, the largest fugitive community. The goal here is to find patterns in the origins, creation, internal organization, and destruction of these fugitive communities in order to better understand the slave regime and the way in which Africans and Afro-Brazilians responded to it.

Bahia: A Plantation World

Runaway communities flourished in almost all areas of the captaincy of Bahia, although in some regions the problem was unusually acute. The geography and ecology of much of the Bahian littoral aided escape, and the result was a large number of fugitives and *mocambos*. A report by an unnamed Jesuit written in 1619 outlined the problem and its perception by white society:

this people has the custom of fleeing to the woods and joining in hideouts where they live by attacks on the settlers, stealing livestock and ruining crops and cane fields which results in much damage and many losses beyond that of loosing [sic] their daily labor. And many of these (escapees) live for many years in the forest never returning and living in these mocambos which are places or villages that they have made deep in the forest. And from here they set out to make their assaults, robbing and stealing and often killing many, and in these attacks they seek to carry off their male and female relatives to live with them like gentiles.[6]

The frequency of *mocambo* formation and the extent of their geographical location within the captaincy is underscored by the following table that spans over two centuries.

Certain characteristics of the captaincy of Bahia contributed to slave flight and the formation of runaway communities. A major terminus of the Atlantic slave trade and a major plantation zone throughout its history, Bahia had always maintained a large servile population, which by the end of the colonial era constituted about one-third of the total population. However, in plantation zones, slaves often made up over 60 percent of the inhabitants. Conditions on the *engenhos* were physically exhausting and treatment in terms of food and housing was poor. Sometimes slaves had to deal with particularly cruel or sadistic masters, but even beyond these the general concept of slave management disregarded the long-term benefits of "good" treatment and emphasized the extraction of as much labor with as little cost as possible.[7] Slaves also lived with limited familial opportunities. Patterns in the Atlantic slave trade and a planter preference for young adult males over women resulted in a chronic sexual imbalance. These problems made for a population that had less to lose by flight or other forms of resistance, at least in the view of observers in nineteenth-century Brazil who advocated stable families and a balanced sex ratio among the slaves as a means of control.[8] However, these "progressive" ideas were not shared by the slaveowners of colonial Bahia. Flight and *mocambos* remained a feature of Bahian slavery throughout its history.

While the sugar-growing parishes of the Bahian Recôncavo contained the largest number and highest percentage of slaves, the region of Bahia experiencing the greatest incidence of *mocambo* formation was the southern towns of Cairú, Camamú, and Ilhéus. These towns and their surrounding districts were devoted for the most part to the production of manioc, the basic subsistence crop of Brazil. The work requirements were less than those of the sugar

Table 3. Partial List of Bahian Mocambos

Date	Type	Name	Locale	Size/ Comments	Sources
1614			sertão		1
1629			Rio Vermelho		2
1632	*mocambo*				3
1636			Itapicuru	40+	4
1640	*mocambo*		Rio Real		5
1655			Jeremobão		6
1666	*mocambo*	Irará	Inhambupe		7
1666–67	*mocambo*		Torre		8
1667	*mocambo*		Jaguaripe		9
1681–91	*mocambo*	Acaranquanha	Serra de Jacobina	60+	10
1687	*mocambo*		Rio Real, Inhambupe		11
1692			Camamú	mulatto leader	12
1699	*mocambo*		Cairú		13
1705			Jacuipe		14
1706			Jaguaripe		15
1713	mocambo		Maragogipe		16
1714	*mocambo*		"campos de Cachoeira"		17
1722	*mocambo*		Cairú	400	18
1723	*mocambo*	Quiricós		"grande"	19
1726	*mocambo*	Camisão		"old"	20
1733	*mocambo*		Canaveíras	"grande"	21
1734	*mocambo*		Santo Amaro, Nazaré		22
1735			Jacobina		23
1736	*mocambo*		Rio das Contãs		4
1744–64	*quilombo*	Buraco de Tatú	Itapuã	61+	25
1745			Santo Amaro		26
1789		Santana	Ilhéus		27
1791	*quilombo*	Matas do Concavo	Jacuipe		28
1796	*quilombo*		Serra de Orobó		29
1801	*quilombo*		Jacobina		30
1807	*mocambo, quilombo*	"cabula"	suburbios	"innumerable"	31

Date	Type	Name	Locale	Size/ Comments	Sources
1807	*quilombo*	Rio das Contas	Ilhéus		32
1809	*quilombo*		Cachoeira	"grande"	33
1825	*mocambo*		Itaparica	muitos	34
1826	*quilombo*	Urubá	suburbias	50 +	35

Sources:

1. Leite, *História de companhia de Je-sús no Brasil*, 10 vols. (Lisbon, 1938–50), 5: 265.
2. Moura, *Rebeliões*, 75.
3. ACS, 1:213.
4. ACS, 1:310–11, 329.
5. ACS, 1:
6. Pedreira, *Os Quilombos*, 78.
7. *Documentos do Arquivo Nacional*, 27, 25.
8. *DH*, 11:385–86.
9. *DH*, 8:301–2.
10. ACS, 124.1.
11. ACS, 124.1.
12. Ignácio Accioli de Cerqueira e Silva, *Memórias históricas e políticas da Província da Bahia*, ed. Braz do Amaral, 6 vols. (Bahia, 1925), 2:142.
13. APB, CdG 150, f. 144v.
14. Pedreira, *Os Quilombos*, 83–84.
15. Ibid.
16. Ibid., 86–88.
17. Ibid., 91–92.
18. AHU, Bahia, p.a. 27.
19. *DH*, 45,
20. Pedreira, *Os Quilombos*, 101–2.
21. *DH*, 75, 106, 133, 138.
22. *DH*, 75, 298; 76, 20–21.
23. *DH*, 76, 81.
24. *DH*, 76, 335.
25. AHU, Bahia, cat. 6,456.
26. BNRJ, II-34,6,32.
27. APB, CaG,
28. APB, OR 86, f. 242–45.
29. Ibid.
30. Pedreira, *Os Quilombos*, 123–24.
31. BNRJ, I, 31,27,1: AHU, Bahia, cat. 29.815.
32. APB, Cdo G ao SMgd. 177.
33. APB, Cao G ao, 218.
34. BNRJ, II-33,26,35.
35. Pedreira, *Os Quilombos*, 141–43.

plantations and slaves lived in smaller units in this region. While the predominance of slaves in the population found in the sugar-growing areas was absent, the proportion of slaves in the population of this southern zone still reached between 40 and 60 percent. Relatively good conditions in terms of work requirements, diet, and physical well-being as well as a large proportion of slaves in the population have been postulated in other situations as factors that stimulated slave resistance.[9] In this case, however, the frontier nature of this region and its unstable military conditions was the most important contributing factor to successful slave escapes. Cairú and Camamú were constantly threatened by attack from hostile Aimoré Indians. This fact and the distance from military aid coming from Salvador made suppression of slave *mocambos* difficult. Attacks by Indians or, *gentio barbaro* (savage gentiles), and *mocambo* depredations were linked in the mind of the colonists, and various measures were taken to suppress both. Expeditions to eliminate these threats set out in 1663, 1692, 1697, and 1723, but the frequency

of repetition indicates a lack of success. Black and mulatto freedmen, "tame" Indians, and black militia units from Bahia were all
used in these expeditions, but a major innovation was the use of
Indian fighters and backwoodsmen (*bandeirantes*) from São Paulo.[10]
This tactic, initiated in the 1670s by Governor Afonso Furtado do
Castro do Rio Mendonça, had some success, and "Paulista" contin-
gents were subsequently employed elsewhere in the Northeast for
similar operations, the most notable being the destruction of the
great *quilombo* of Palmares in 1684–85.[11]

While the *mocambos* of southern Bahia never reached the size
or extent of Palmares, the threat they posed was no less real. One
mocambo was reported in 1723 to have over four hundred inhabitants, but size alone was not the sole determinant of *mocambo*
danger in this region.[12] In another instance in 1692, a group of
fugitives led by five mulatto "captains" began to sack the farmlands
near Camamu and threatened to seize the town itself. Not only
was southern Bahia disrupted, but the Recôncavo was also thrown
into turmoil as word of these events reached the slave quarters of
the *engenhos* and planters feared a similar outbreak. A Portuguese
military expedition in 1692 finally destroyed this *mocambo* by lay-
ing siege to the stockaded village. The final battle cry of the defenders: "Death to the whites and long live liberty."[13]

The fear that towns like Cairú and Camamú, far from the
centers of governmental authority, might actually be seized was
not wholly exaggerated. In 1767, the interim captain of Sergipe de
El-Rey reported continual depredations by armed bands of fugitives,
adding that in the time of his predecessor an armed band of escaped
slaves had marched into town at nine in the morning with flags,
drums, and crowns on their heads and demanded that the royal
official grant them letters of manumission. The official had sounded
the alarm but the absence of troops allowed the fugitives to escape
unharmed.[14]

Such audacity also underlined a basic reality. The majority of
Bahian *mocambos* were located relatively close to population centers or to the surrounding plantations. Whereas Palmares flourished
in the remote interior of Alagoas and other fugitive communities
also existed in remote regions, the vast majority of the Bahian
mocambos and those elsewhere in Brazil remained close to towns
and farms, although often in inaccessible locations. In fact, some
of the towns within the present-day urban network of Salvador
originated as runaway communities.

The reasons for this pattern of fugitive settlement are varied.

Certainly, until the eighteenth century, hostile Indians constituted an effective barrier to black as well as white penetration of many regions. Most importantly, the internal economy of the *mocambos* made proximity to settled areas a prerequisite for success. Rather than a return to African pastoral or agricultural pursuits, *mocambo* economies were often parasitic, based on highway theft, cattle rustling, raiding, and extortion. These activities might be combined with agriculture as well, but rarely did *mocambos* become wholly self-sufficient and completely isolated from the colonial society that generated, and at the same time feared them.

The depredations of escaped slaves led colonial officials to consider *mocambo* fugitives along with highwaymen to be common criminals, thus subject to regular criminal penalties. However, the actions of fugitive slaves were more than simple crimes because they implied, and were sometimes overtly directed as, an attack on the existing social order. In a very real sense *mocambo* depredations foreshadowed the social banditry, or *cangaço*, of postcolonial Brazil. The *mocambo* represented an expression of social protest in a slave society.

Anti-*Mocambo* Measures

Colonists and royal officials developed a number of measures to deal with *mocambo* formation and activity. One tactic was to apprehend fugitives before they could join together in bands. As early as 1612, Alexandre de Moura, captain of Pernambuco, petitioned the crown for the creation of a *capitão de campo* (bush captain) in each of the eight parishes of that captaincy, who with the aid of twenty Indians would hunt down escaped slaves.[15] It is uncertain exactly when these officers were introduced to Bahia but by 1625 the town council of Salvador had set the scale of rewards for these slave hunters. The *capitão do campo*, or *capitão do mato* as the office came to be called, worked on a commission basis, receiving a reward for each fugitive captured. This system was formalized in 1676.[16] The *câmara* (town council) of Salvador fixed the price of reward in accordance with the distance involved. By 1637, these rewards were extended to anyone capturing a fugitive, not just to the bush captains. As we shall see, a similar system was adopted in Minas Gerais and elsewhere in Brazil. The bush captain became a ubiquitous aspect of rural Brazil.[17]

The system was not without difficulties. To claim the prescribed rewards, overzealous bush captains were not above arresting

slaves who were merely on errands. Slaveowners sometimes showed
a marked reluctance to pay the fee for old or infirm slaves who
were no longer useful. On a number of occasions, a backlog of
elderly unclaimed fugitives in the municipal jail of Salvador forced
the town council to auction the prisoners to the public in order to
pay for expenses. The position of bush captain often attracted somewhat marginal individuals, former slaves and colored freedmen, who
were resented by the slaveowners and hated by the slaves.[18] Still,
the bush captains provided a relatively effective means of appre-
hending individual fugitives, although controlling the problems of
slave revolt or the activities of already formed *mocambos* was usually beyond their capacities.

A second and still unstudied method of slave control and capture in Brazil was the calculated use of Indians as slave catchers
and as a counterforce to *mocambos* and possible slave revolts. In
the sixteenth century, sugar planters and absentee donataries sought
to bring Indians from the interior to serve as a defense force against
possible slave uprisings as well as a buffer against still unreduced
tribes of the backlands.[19] In the seventeenth century, colonists in
Bahia tried unsuccessfully to have Indian villages located near their
farms. The Jesuits objected, fearing colonist exploitation of Indians
as laborers; the clerics, however, recognized that Indian allies were
the "walls and bulwarks" of the colony. As early as 1614, Indians
from the Jesuit mission village of São João were used to destroy a
mocambo. Probably the most explicit statement of the usefulness
of Indian allies against a restive slave population was made in 1633
by Duarte Gomes de Silveira, a colonist in Paraíba who wrote:
"There is no doubt that without Indians in Brazil there can be no
Negroes of Guinea, or better said, there can be no Brazil, for without
them [Negroes] nothing can be done and they are ten times more
numerous than the whites; and if today it is costly to dominate
them with the Indians whom they greatly fear . . . what will happen
without Indians? The next day they will revolt and it is a great risk
to resist domestic enemies."[20]

Indian irregulars led by Portuguese officers or captains were
consistently and successfully employed against *mocambos* throughout colonial Brazil. The destruction of virtually every *mocambo*
from Palmares to the much smaller hideouts of Bahia, Rio de Janeiro, and Goias depended to a large extent on Indian troops and
auxiliaries.

Paradoxically, there are also many references to the incorpo-
ration of African and Afro-Brazilian slaves into Indian villages and

of Indian inhabitants in fugitive communities. Portuguese authorities feared the disruptive and potentially dangerous nature of such
contacts. In 1706, the crown ordered that blacks, mixed bloods, and
slaves be prevented from penetrating the interior, where they might
join with hostile Indian groups. Despite such measures, Afro-Indian
cooperation against both the Portuguese and the Dutch in Brazil
was common. In Bahia, a famous example of Afro-Indian collaboration is provided by the long-lived syncretic messianic religion
called *Santidade*, which flourished in the southern areas of the
captaincy in the late sixteenth century among Indian groups. By
1613, it was reported that escaped slaves had joined the movement
and were participating in its raids and even stealing slaves from
Salvador. As late as 1627, despite punitive expeditions, Santidade
adherents were still launching attacks.[21]

This leads us to the still-ignored problem of Afro-Indian contacts and social relations. Despite Portuguese attempts to turn the
Indians into allies against potential slave resistance, a number of
factors drew African slaves and Indians together. For the runaways
and unreduced Indian tribes there was the common goal of opposition to the European-imposed slave regime. Within captivity too
Indians and Africans were often in intimate and common contact.
Indians continued to comprise a large, although decreasing percentage of the plantation labor force in the period 1580–1650, and
marriages between blacks and Indians were not uncommon. Some
observers, like the Jesuit Father Belchior Cordeiro, felt that African
slaves became more tractable when brought into contact with Christian Indians, but whatever the policy, Indian-African contacts did
take place. Indians remained throughout the colonial era both the
best potential allies and the most effective opponents of slave
fugitives.[22]

The primary tactic employed against *mocambos* was simply
to destroy them and to kill or reenslave their inhabitants. Portuguese opposition to the fugitive communities can be easily explained. *Mocambo* raids and thefts endangered towns, disrupted
production, and cut lines of communication and travel.[23] Moreover,
a *mocambo* either by its raids or by its attraction drew other slaves
from captivity. Many observers noted the effects of *mocambos* on
the slave quarters and one report of 1692 noted that "no settler
will have his slaves secure" so long as *mocambos* persisted.[24] *Mocambos* posed a threat to the economic and social fabric of this
slave regime.

For most colonial officials accomodation with *mocambos* and white inhabitants was simply unthinkable. Unlike Jamaica, where a treaty was finally concluded with the runaway maroons, similar tactics were harshly rebuked when suggested in Brazil. In 1640 Viceroy Jorge de Mascarenhas, Marquis of Montalvão, suggested as a wartime measure that a peace mission of a Jesuit linguist and Henrique Dias, leader of a pro-Portuguese black regiment, be sent to a certain *mocambo*. The mission would offer freedom to runaways if they would serve in the black regiment and if they agreed to harbor no new fugitives. His suggestion met with a stern rebuff from the planter-dominated *câmara* of Salvador, which stated: "Under no circumstances is it proper to attempt reconciliation nor to give way to slaves who might be conciliated in this matter. That which is proper is only to extinguish them and to conquer them so that those who are still domesticated will not join them and those who are in rebellion will not aspire to greater misdeeds."[25]

These same sentiments were echoed in 1663 in Bahia by the Viceroy, Count of Óbidos, who wanted the great fugitive redoubt of Palmares destroyed as "punishment and example in order to put an end to the hopes of the other slaves." He wanted no quarter given to those who resisted and the settlement burned to the ground so that nothing remained but "the memory of its destruction for the ultimate "disenchantment of the slaves" of Pernambuco and Bahia.[26]

Such extermination was usually carried out by military expeditions conducted by private individuals with local backing or by government troops. Private contracts were sometimes made with backwoodsmen with stipulated rewards for each slave captured. Bush captains, Indian auxiliaries, government-sponsored military columns—all were designed to confront the threat of the fugitive communities to the slave regime.

Mocambo Ethnography: The Case of Buraco de Tatú

The varied and disparate documents that mention the activities of escaped slaves in Brazil reveal little about the social and political organization within the fugitive communities. For this reason the documents pertaining to the destruction of the *quilombo* known as the Buraco de Tatú (Armadillo's Hole) are of singular importance; for although by no means complete they do provide a glimpse into what may have been the history of a typical Bahian *mocambo*.[27]

In 1763 a Portuguese-led military expedition destroyed the

Buraco de Tatú, located just east-northeast of the city of Salvador, near the present-day bathing beaches of Itapoam. Responding to complaints and disturbed by *mocambo* activities, Dom Marcos de Noronha, Count of Arcos and Viceroy of Brazil, began in 1760 a campaign to eliminate fugitive communities. In that year, he appointed Joaquim da Costa Cardoso as captain major of the conquest of savage gentiles (capitão mor da conquista do gentio barbaro) and apparently entrusted him with mounting a punitive expedition.[28] Although Costa Cardoso's commission indicated that hostile Indians were his main objective, he also displayed considerable interest in destroying "various quilombos of Negroes in the outskirts of the city."[29] Neither their numbers nor their location at the time can be determined, but in addition to Itapoam there were also *mocambos* in Cairú and Ipitanga.

The Buraco de Tatú had existed for twenty years. Like most Bahian *mocambos* its economy was basically parasitic, based on theft, extortion, and sporadic raiding. The principal victims, however, were not white sugar planters, but rather the blacks who "came every day to the city [Salvador] to sell the foodstuffs they grow on their plots."[30] The most attractive women were also taken back to the *mocambo*. The chronic lack of women in the Brazilian slave force was reproduced and exacerbated in the *mocambos*. Fugitives preferred to take black or mulatto women, and there are few references to the abduction of European women. No such charge was made against the inhabitants of the Buraco de Tatú.[31]

Despite the actions of the fugitives, there were freedmen and slaves who out of necessity or sympathy cooperated with the Buraco de Tatú. João Baptista, a mulatto farmer, worked with the runaways and supplied them with firewood.[32] He was apparently not alone in his practices. Blacks in the city of Salvador aided the *quilombo* by helping the fugitives to enter the city by night in order to buy powder and shot. Such contact was unsettling to slaveowners and royal officials, who feared increased escapes or a general uprising. As in other instances, whites also cooperated with the *quilombo*—in their case to avoid harm to life or property.

The actions taken against non-*quilombo* blacks and the cooperation between whites and the escaped slaves, although coerced, indicates that the Buraco de Tatú fugitives had no intention of a total war of liberation against all the slaveowning segments of the population. *Quilombos*, in fact, might provide focal points in more general slave rebellions as they did in Bahia in the early nineteenth century, but in general, the goals of the fugitive communities seem to have been the more immediate and practical ones of survival beyond the control of white society. Slave resistance in all its forms may have been a threat to the slave system, but despite the implications of *quilombo* existence for the slave "class," planters and colonial officials perceived enough divisions among the slaves to risk arming *engenho* slaves in order to combat fugitives, as the Conde do Ponte suggested in 1807.[33]

The Buraco de Tatú was destroyed on September 2, 1763, and from the military descriptions of that action and a plan drawn by the attackers to illustrate those reports it is possible to infer much about the internal life of this community. The *quilombo* was a well-organized village laid out in a rectilinear pattern of six rows of houses bisected by a large central street (see figure 4). There were thirty-two rectangular residence units (B) and since there were approximately sixty-five adults in the *quilombo*, we can assume that these units represent houses rather than compounds. The close correlation of two adults per house suggests a monogamous pattern, but the evidence is unclear since the accompanying documents make no mention of children. When children born in a *quilombo* were captured they often became the property of the expedition's leader, and this may explain their absence from the judicial records.[34] Taken as a whole, the monogamous marital pattern, the rectangular house shape, and the even rows of houses suggest a reproduction of a plantation *senzala* (slave quarters) rather than any specific African pattern. Conversely, the large central street equally dividing the rectangular houses and the existence of what may have been a ceremonial, or a "palaver," house in front of a plaza (H) are all elements found among northwest Bantu groups such as the Koko, Teke (Anzico), and Mabea.[35] The surviving documents, in fact, give little indication of the ethnic origins of the inhabitants of the Buraco de Tatú. At least one inhabitant was a *crioulo*. Another was referred to as a *mandingueiro*, a term that in the mid-eighteenth century simply meant "sorcerer," but could also suggest Mandinga origins for at least this fugitive. The most reasonable assumption is that no one African group inhabited this *mocambo*.

Like many fugitive communities in Brazil, the Buraco de Tatú was cleverly fortified. Entry into the *mocambo* was made difficult by an extensive defensive network. The rear was protected by a swampy dike about the height of a man. The three sides of the village were protected by a maze of sharpened stakes (L) driven into the ground and covered to prevent detection by an unsuspecting intruder. This defense was augmented by a series of twenty-one pits

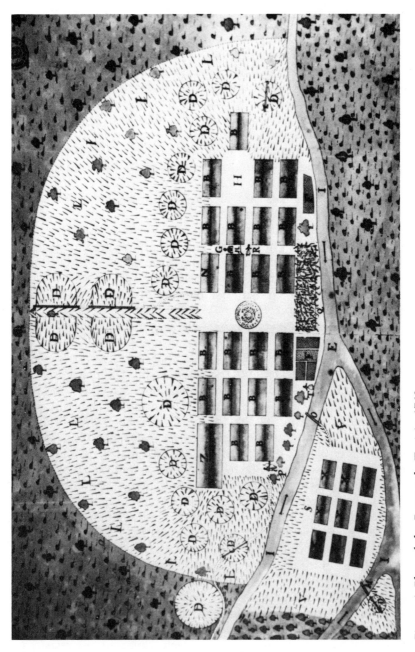

Figure 4. Plan of the Buraco de Tatú in 1763.

(D) filled with sharpened spikes and disguised by brush and grass. Leading into the *mocambo* was a false road especially well protected by spikes and camouflaged traps. Only when the watchman (N) placed planks (C, O, M) over some of the obstacles did entry and exit become possible. The Portuguese noted the effectiveness of this defense and took pains to point out the problems it created to the crown. It was a defense quite unlike that of the palisaded Angolan *quilombo* described by Father Antonio Cavazzi in 1680.[36] Still, covered traps and sharpened stakes were used for village protection in Africa from Nigeria southward to the old Kingdom of Kongo and were also used at Palmares and by other fugitive communities.[37]

In the predatory economy of the Buraco de Tatú agriculture was not a major activity. The plan does show a trellis of *maracuja* (Q) and a number of small gardens perhaps equivalent to the dawn gardens of the Kongo, but these seem to be devoted to herbs rather than staple crops. No *roças* or farmlands are indicated in the area around the *mocambo*. These fugitives probably exacted foodstuffs as tribute from their neighbors and may have supplemented their diet with fish since the village was located near the coast.[38] A few aspects of the *quilombo's* internal life can be gleaned from the report of its destruction. Politically, the Buraco de Tatú had two chieftains or captains. Antonio de Sousa was a war-captain, and a second leader, Theodoro, controlled the *quilombo* itself ("tive administração do quilombo"). Each leader had a consort who was called a queen. Nine houses were separated from the main village. This separation may simply indicate latecomers or the divided political leadership, or may even suggest the possibility that this was the residence of a lineage unable to live in the main village or even an age group of young males required to live apart. This latter possibility is doubtful, however, since the Portuguese would have found this situation notable enough to mention and the records are silent. The religion of the inhabitants is unknown. Two individuals were mentioned as sorcerers, one of them an old woman (R). Women are traditionally the leaders in the Yoruba cults (*candomblé*) still practiced in Bahia, but the dates of this *mocambo* (1743–63) precede the large-scale importation of Yoruba slaves in Brazil.

The Buraco de Tatú was destroyed on September 2, 1763. Under the leadership of Joaquim da Costa Cardoso a force of two hundred men including a troop of grenadiers, but made up mostly of Indian auxiliary militia and Indians from a village in Jaguaripe, carried out the attack. Their battle orders were to remain in the field until, "the quilombo has been destroyed, the blacks captured, the resisters killed, the woods searched, the huts and defenses burned, and the trenches filled in."[39] Indian guides were used to scout the *quilombo's* defenses before the assault was launched. The attack probably came from the unprotected coastal side of the village. Surprise worked to the attackers advantage until an old woman (T) raised the alarm. The defenders, some of whom were armed with bows (P) were greatly outnumbered and overwhelmed. The hero of the defense was José Lopes, who fired two shots at the attackers and, who shouted defiantly that it would take more than two hundred men to capture him. He was mistaken. Four fugitives were killed and sixty-one taken prisoner. No casualties were reported among the expeditionary troops.

Upon their capture the fugitives were incarcerated in Salvador. Thirty-one whose only crime was to escape slavery were, in accordance with a Royal Order of March 3, 1741, branded with the letter F (*fugido*).[40] After their masters paid the costs of capture to the royal treasury, the slaves were returned to captivity. Some were singled out for exemplary punishment. Antonio de Sousa, captain of the *quilombo*, was sentenced to public flogging and life in the galleys. His friend, Miguel Cosme, "reported to be a great thief," received a sentence of flogging and six years at the oars. Theodoro and José Lopes were both whipped in public and sent to the galleys for ten years. José Piahuy, "a great backwoodsman and thief," received two hundred lashes and a four-year term at the oars while the crioulo Leonardo received a like number of stripes. João Baptista, the mulatto farmer and accomplice of the fugitives, was sentenced to five years of penal exile and a stiff fine.[41] The two queens received relatively light sentences.

The Buraco de Tatú provides an example that recapitulates many aspects of the history of fugitive communities in Brazil. Relatively small in size (less than 100 inhabitants) and located close to centers of population, these communities developed syncretic traditions fusing Brazilian and African elements. Their inhabitants seem also to have been of various origins, Brazilian-born and Africans of different ethnic backgrounds. Although they stole from slaves and free people of color as well as whites, some freedmen willingly cooperated with the fugitives. The punitive military expedition and the use of Indians within it represented the usual colonial response to the *mocambos*. Living by their wits and daring, the fugitives of the Buraco de Tatú maintained their independence for twenty years until their actions and the threat of their very existence caused the colonial authorities to exterminate their community. In many ways, the history of the Buraco de Tatú seems to be typical of the history of fugitive communities in Brazil.

Minas Gerais: A Mining Economy

The patterns of *quilombo* formation and the responses of colonial society that we have examined thus far in the case of Bahia were to a large extent reproduced in the mining areas of south central Brazil, although with certain differences as might be expected given the different social and economic formation of the region. The discovery of rich deposits of gold in the mountainous region that came to be known as Minas Gerais and the subsequent development there of a society based on slave labor created conditions that particularly favored slave runaways and the formation of *mocambos*.[42] Slaves made up between one-third and one-half of the total population of the captaincy during most of the eighteenth century and free people of color constituted by 1821 another 40 percent of the total.[43] Together, then, the Afro-Brazilian population—slave and free—eventually made up about three-quarters of the inhabitants. Slaves performed virtually every task, but above all they did most of the mining. They were expensive and highly valued. So long as they were productive and turned over the gold they found to their masters, slaves often had considerable autonomy of movement in the mining district.[44] The large sea of slaves and free coloreds provided a potentially friendly environment for runaways. The discontinuous nature of settlement and the mountainous topography provided large inaccessible tracts for hideouts and even in the many urban concentrations, the large free population of color made the detection of fugitives difficult. Moreover, because fugitive slaves could often provide gold that they had stolen or found, some whites were willing to cooperate with the *mocambos* or to protect fugitives. Finally, in the lawless and restive conditions of early Minas Gerais slaves were often armed by their owners and participated in the various antigovernment movements and in the civil disturbances of the War of the Emboabas.[45]

All of these conditions contributed to an unstable situation of slave control as well as feelings of insecurity and fear among royal officials, municipal councils, and the white population in general. Rumors of planned slave revolts circulated in 1719, 1725, and 1756, but the main problem continued to be *mocambos*. Throughout the eighteenth century governors, miners, royal officials, and town councils complained of thefts, murders, abductions, and other crimes committed by *calhambolas,* the inhabitants of *mocambos.* The response in Minas replicated that of the coastal plantation zones. In Minas, as in Bahia, attempts to use free Indians as slave catchers and the deployment of Indian villages and later of royal troops for this purpose had little impact. Moreover, Minas had distinct problems. Its free population was generally unruly. In the early years of settlement the area experienced a short civil war and a number of antigovernment tax riots. The miners at first also refused to pay a tax for fugitive control.[46] Not until 1744 were royal judges in Minas Gerais authorized to raise money (up to 300 *oitavas* of gold) to pay for anti-*quilombo* operations.[47]

The activist and racist Conde de Assumar (1717–21) made *mocambo* control a central concern of his governorship. Like his predecessor, he suggested the arming of Indians and their use as slave catchers. In 1717, he suggested the creation of *capitães do mato* and by 1722 these posts had been established and a set of standing orders (*regimento*) had been issued with a sliding scale of rewards for the return of fugitives depending on the distance the captain had to travel.[48] The difficulty of recovery from *mocambos* is reflected in the fact that a fugitive caught within a league of the residence of the bush captain fetched 4 *oitavas* of gold while one taken from a *quilombo* (defined as an encampment of more than four Blacks with houses set up) brought 20 *oitavas.*[49] A modern study of local sources was able to identify 117 known *quilombos* in the region before 1800 and appointments of almost 500 slave catchers during the eighteenth century.[50]

Assumar and various municipal councils in Minas Gerais were so preoccupied with the problem of slave control and *mocambos* that they were willing to suggest or try a variety of stringent and extraordinary measures aimed not only at the fugitives, but at the free colored population as well. Assumar was responsible for an attempt to limit the number of manumissions in the region, claiming that the grants of liberty led to slave thefts and prostitution. He also suggested that the large number of free coloreds who controlled property in the area threatened the social hierarchy, and he ordered that free colored residents be prohibited from owning slaves and that no free black could serve as a godparent for a slave. These measures were impossible to enforce but they demonstrated Assumar's fear of a social order in which the lines of race and class had become blurred. For the threat of *mocambos,* he had other remedies. Unlike Bahia, where anti-*quilombo* operations were left to bush captains or to officially sponsored expeditions, under

Assumar anyone wishing to attack a *quilombo* could do so and carry whatever arms were necessary.[51]

Such measures indicate a level of insecurity and fear in the mining zones seemingly exceeding that of the plantation areas. Assumar was perhaps an extreme example of such concern, but he was not alone. Local town councils in Minas also attempted to come to grips with threats to the social order by various ordinances aimed at controlling the free colored population and by actions against fugitives. A number of anti-*mocambo* operations were organized by town councils. In 1735, the *câmara* (town council) of Vila Rica called for the cutting off of a hand as a punishment for fugitive slaves.[52] Perhaps the most infamous action was the barbarous suggestion of the town council of Mariana that fugitives when caught have their Achilles tendon severed, allowing them to hobble to work, but making flight almost impossible. This suggestion met with a rebuff by the Viceroy, The Count of Arcos, as an unchristian measure but, of course, he did not live in Minas Gerais. It should be noted that this suggestion by the *câmara* of Mariana often cited by historians was part of a more general appeal arguing that the free colored of the captaincy aided the escaped slaves in their crimes and that measures should be imposed limiting manumissions, curtailing the movement of the free colored population, and prohibiting them from bearing or even owning arms.[53]

These attitudes and fears sometimes had dire consequences. In 1716, a *quilombo* with 80 to 100 blacks who were raiding the roads near Vila Real and Vila Nova da Rainha was unsuccessfully attacked by a punitive expedition. A second force of 150 men was organized by the two towns; it destroyed the *quilombo*, killing a number of the defenders in a rage after these had surrendered. The royal judge refused to prosecute the guilty for fear that men would not join such expeditions in the future.[54] The Overseas Council in Lisbon lamented theses "excesses," but supported the judge, although in the regimento for bush captains it warned against the excessive use of force.[55] Still, for the most part *quilombos* and fugitive slaves were beyond the norms of civil society. In 1738, a petition from residents of Vila Rica to be exempted from prosecution for the death of *calhambolas* met with a favorable response from the governor.[56]

All of the traditional methods of *mocambo* and fugitive control were tried in Minas Gerais, along with a few that were extraordinary. The large population of free coloreds in the captaincy and the many poor "vagrants" presented in themselves a threat to the social order, but one that might be effectively mobilized against the *qui-lombos*. Efforts to enlist them in anti-*quilombo* activities were made on various occasions.[57] But these efforts did little to stem the problem. The free poor and the fugitive slaves were both manifestations of the inherent conditions of this society.

Quilombos, then, were an endemic problem in Minas Gerais. They were numerous and sometimes attained large size, although here too it is difficult to know much about their internal organization since we must depend on the descriptions of *quilombo* destruction. For example, an account of an expedition that rescued some white children from a *quilombo* noted that the "mulatto entitled king, a concubine, and four slaves remained at large."[58] Governor Gomes Freire de Andrada described an attack against a "small" *quilombo* of over a hundred blacks made in 1746. He noted that three assaults were necessary to overcome their resistance and that twenty or so were killed, over seventy men as well as a large number of women were captured. This "small" *quilombo* must have contained between one and two hundred people.[59] The two largest *quilombos* of Minas—that of Ambrósio, destroyed in 1746 and the Quilombo Grande, attacked and eliminated in 1759—held large numbers of fugitives, the latter perhaps containing over a thousand inhabitants.[60] These, however, were exceptionally large in size.

Minas Gerais, therefore, despite its differing economic basis and social and racial configuration, reproduced and intensified many of the conditions that led to *mocambo* formation in the zones of export agriculture. The early frontier conditions, the considerable freedom of movement allowed to slaves in mining, the urban network, and the racial composition of the region all contributed to the formation of fugitive communities in the region. The response of colonial government to this problem in Minas Gerais and the techniques used to combat it were similar to those applied elsewhere in the colony. It is striking that the term *quilombo* was far more frequently used in Minas Gerais than in Bahia, where *mocambo* was preferred, although by the mid-eighteenth century both terms were in use. The word *quilombo*, in fact, came to mean an encampment of any group of outlaws, so that in 1737 an official in Vila Rica could report preparations to destroy a "quilombo of whites, in flight for various atrocious crimes (brancos omiziados por crimes atroces)."[61] However, the term was used primarily to describe fugitive slave communities; and it has become a symbol of slave resistance in Brazil and, in more modern times, of a movement for equality for blacks in Brazil.

The linguistic difference between Bahia and Minas Gerais is to some extent chronological and it is related to the history of the great fugitive community of Palmares, which for almost a century had resisted all efforts to destroy it. Palmares became a symbol for royal administrators of how any fugitive community might become a real threat to civil society in a society so based on slavery. When the Count of Assumar wrote in 1719 that: "the blacks (of Minas) may be tempted to repeat the acts of the Palmares of Pernambuco, emboldened by their multitude," he was voicing a real fear.[62] While Palmares was atypical in its size and its duration, its history can not be separated from that of the other fugitive communities, if only because of its influence on how slaveowners and royal officials viewed the problem. Moreover, because of its longevity and size and the long contact of colonial society with it, Palmares offers some opportunities to penetrate the internal dynamic of a fugitive community.

Rethinking Palmares

In dealing with the question of fugitive communities in Brazil it is necessary to keep the *quilombo* of Palmares in mind. Palmares, located in the interior of Alagoas, was by far the longest-lived and largest fugitive community. For almost the whole seventeenth century (1605?–1694) it persisted despite determined attempts to eliminate it by the Dutch and Portuguese colonial governments and by local residents of the neighboring captaincies. Because of its reputed size (over twenty thousand inhabitants), longevity, and the continual colonial contact with it, we know more about its internal structure than we do about most of the *mocambos*. Still, the documentation on Palmares is not extensive and it tends to concentrate on the last decade of its existence and its final destruction.[63] Therefore much remains unknown about it. That fact has not deterred authors from attempting to write its history or for romanticizing it into a "Black Troy," or a "republic." More recently, it has taken on a symbolic importance for Afro-Brazilians in their struggle for racial and social equality.[64]

It has long been recognized that Palmares was based on a number of traditional African forms of political and social organization, although like most fugitive communities it combined these with aspects of European culture and specifically local adaptations.[65] Palmares was not a single community but a number of *mocambos* united to form a neo-African kingdom.[66] Various eyewitness accounts reveal much about Palmares' internal organization, although we must recognize that Palmares also had a history and the organization and institutions noted at the end of the seventeenth century were not necessarily those of the earlier period. Moreover, the size of Palmares also changed over time. A mid-seventeenth century account described Palmares as divided into two main settlements with many smaller ones, placing the population of the various settlements in Palmares at about eleven thousand. A later and often repeated estimate raised that figure to twenty thousand. This latter number seems exaggerated. During most of the seventeenth century Pernambuco and its adjacent captaincies had about two hundred *engenhos* with an average of a hundred slaves per mill. In other words, the estimate for Palmares of twenty thousand inhabitants would equal the number of all slaves in the sugar economy of the region.[67] Although this number seems unlikely, Palmares was undoubtedly the largest fugitive community to have existed in Brazil.

During its long history, Palmares was constantly under attack. The Dutch mounted three expeditions against it and after Portugal regained control of the Northeast in 1654 the war continued. Between 1672 and 1680 there was a military expedition almost every year. The fugitives resisted valiantly, but this constant pressure caused them to sue for peace with a recently arrived governor of Pernambuco in 1678. The "king" of Palmares, Ganga Zumba, had in fact tried this policy whenever a new governor arrived. Like the maroons of Jamaica, he had promised loyalty to the Portuguese crown and return of any new fugitives in exchange for recognition of the *quilombo's* freedom. The Portuguese accepted these terms but soon violated them, and in Palmares itself a revolt took place in which the accomodationist Ganga Zumba was overthrown and killed by his nephew Zumbi.[68] The war continued. Expeditions went almost annually against the fugitives in the 1680s but with little success. The defenders of Palmares became masters of guerilla warfare, adept at the use of camouflage and ambush. Frustrated, Portuguese colonial administrators adopted a new tactic. Hardened Indian fighters and slavers from São Paulo who had been used in Bahia to open the interior were now contracted to eliminate Palmares. Their assault began in 1692, and for two years with the aid of local troops and the indispensable Indian allies they slowly reduced the perimeter of the main *mocambo's* defenses. The final battle was fought in February 1694. Two hundred fugitives were killed, five hundred captured, and another two hundred reportedly committed suicide rather than surrender. Zumbi, wounded and in flight, was betrayed, captured, and decapitated. Palmares was no more, but as late as 1746, slaves were still fleeing to the site of Palmares and once again forming into fugitive groups.

European observers did not always understand what they saw, but from their descriptions it is clear that Palmares was an organized state under the control of a king with subordinate chiefs in outlying settlements. While some accounts speak of an election process, the leadership of one village by Ganga Zumba's mother and the succession of Zumbi, Ganga Zumba's nephew to the throne suggests the existence of a royal lineage.[69] The ceremonial postures and demonstrations of obedience required in the king's presence all point to forms of African kingship. The Palmares's fugitives lived by agriculture, although like other *mocambos* they also traded for arms and other commodities with those whites who lived on the borders. Like most of the *mocambos* they also raided for women, cattle, and food. As in many African societies, slavery existed in Palmares. Those who came to Palmares by choice were considered free, but those taken in raids were enslaved. The villages of Palmares were protected by palisades, walls, or by a network of hidden traps much like those described and shown in the description of the Bahian *mocambo* of Buraco de Tatú. Religion in the encampments was a fusion of Christian and African elements, although here too there may have been far more African features than observers realized.

In many ways Palmares seems to have been an adaption of African cultural forms to the Brazilian colonial situation in which slaves of various origins, African and *crioulo* came together in their common opposition to slavery. Within Palmares people called each other *malungo,* or comrade, a term of adoptive kinship also used among slaves who had arrived together on the same slave ship.

In Palmares we can see the attempt to form a community out of peoples of disparate origins. Such an attempt had to be made by all fugitive communities, but in the case of Palmares there are some specific features that help to explain its particular history as well as the history of slave resistance in colonial Brazil as a whole. The search for "African" elements at Palmares and in the cultural "survivals" of slaves or fugitives as a whole has too often focused on specific cultural or ethnic identities. In fact, much of what passed for African "ethnicity" in Brazil were colonial creations. Categories or groupings such as "Congo" or "Angola" had no ethnic content in themselves and often combined peoples drawn from broad areas of Africa who before enslavement had shared little sense of relationship or identity. That these categories were sometimes adopted by the slaves themselves indicates not only the slaves' adaptability, but also the fact African societies had considerable experience with, and a variety of institutions for the integration of disparate peoples and the creation of solidarities across ethnic lines.[70]

There is, I believe, a deeper story in Palmares and one with broad implications for the subsequent history of slave resistance in Brazil. A key to the problem lies in the etymology of the word *quilombo*. This term came to mean in Brazil any community of escaped slaves, and its usual meaning and origin is given as the Mbundu word for war-camp. By the eighteenth century the term was in general use in Brazil, but it always remained secondary to the older term *mocambo*, a Mbundu word meaning hideout. In fact, the word *quilombo* does not appear in any contemporaneous document until the end of the seventeenth century except for its mid-century use by the poet Gregório de Mattos, who employed it with the meaning of any place where blacks congregated. The first document I have seen with the term *quilombo* used for a fugitive community is dated 1691 and it deals specifically with Palmares.[71] The chronology and the connection with Palmares are not accidental. Within the term *quilombo* is encoded an unwritten history that only now because of recent research in African history can be at least partially understood.

While Palmares combined a number of African cultural traditions and included among its inhabitants *crioulos*, mulattoes, Indians, and even some renegade whites, or *mestiços*, as well as Africans, clearly the traditions of Angola predominated. Its residents referred to Palmares as *angola janga* (little Angola) in recognition of that fact, and in a complaint of 1672 the municipal council of Salvador referred to the "oppression we all suffer from the gentiles of Angola who live in Palmares."[72] But, within the context of Angolan history, what is the significance of that connection for the history of Palmares?

The kingdom of Ndongo, which the Portuguese came to call Angola in the late sixteenth century was a land in turmoil, invaded from the coast by the Portuguese and from the interior by bands of marauding warriors from central Africa.[73] The dissolution of the old Kingdom of Kongo and the Lunda state in Kitanga created a period of military struggle and disruption that destroyed villages and uprooted peoples. Powerful groups of uprooted warriors calling themselves "Imbangala" or "Yaka" and called by the Portuguese, "Jaga," swept into present-day Angola, disrupting existing states and eventually creating a series of new polities.[74]

The precise origins and cultural traditions of the Imbangala and even the relationship of the designations Jaga, Imbangala, and Yaka have been a matter of debate among Africanists for some time, but some aspects of Imbangala/Jaga society were noted by contemporary observers that are of direct interest to historians of slave resistance in Brazil, and especially to those interested in Palmares.[75] First, the Imbangala raiders lived on a permanent war-footing. Reportedly, they killed the babies born to their women, but integrated adopted children into their ranks so that over time they came to be a composite force of large numbers of people of various ethnic backgrounds united by an organized military structure. That organization and a reputed military ferocity made them the scourge of the region, highly effective and greatly feared. Imbangala-Portuguese relations were alternately hostile and friendly. Between 1611 and 1619, Imbangala lords served as mercenaries for the Portuguese governors and supplied a flow of captives to the slave traders at Luanda.[76] New states were formed by an Imbangala fusion with the indigenous lineages as the Imbangala conquered or created a number of kingdoms among the Mbundu peoples of the Congo-Angola region. Two of these states were the kingdom of Kasange and the kingdom of Matamba, ruled by Queen Nzinga, with whom the Portuguese first fought until the mid-seventeenth century when an alliance was formed. These states battled each other for control of the Kwango river basin, a struggle that opened up this region to increased slaving.[77]

As the Imbangala moved southward into Angola in the early seventeenth century they encountered among the Mbundu people an institution that they adopted to their purposes.[78] This was the *ki-lombo*, a male initiation society or circumcision camp where young men were prepared for adulthood and warrior status. The Imbangala molded this institution to their own purposes. Torn from ancestral lands and gods, sharing no common lineage, living by conquest and according to European observers rejecting agriculture, the traditional basis of societies in this region, the Imbangala needed an institution that provided cohesion to the disparate ethnic elements comprising their bands. The *ki-lombo*, a military society to which any man by training and initiation could belong, served that purpose. Designed for war, this institution created a powerful warrior cult by incorporating large numbers of strangers who lacked a common ancestry. The Imbangala *ki-lombo* was distinctive because of its ritual laws. Lineage and kinship, so important to the other basically matrilineal peoples of the region, were denied within its confines and although European observers spoke of infanticide, strictly speaking, women could leave the confines of the *ki-lombo* itself to bear their children. What was prohibited was a legal matrilineal link within the *ki-lombo* that might challenge the concept of a society structured by initiation rather than by kinship. Historian Joseph Miller believes that the Imbangala "killing" of their own children was a metaphor for the ceremonial elimination of kinship ties and their replacement with the rules and proscriptions of the *ki-lombo*.

The creation of a social organization based on association created risks. The inhabitants of the *ki-lombo* stood in a special spiritual danger since they lacked the normal lineage ancestors who might intercede with the gods on their behalf. Thus a chief figure in the *ki-lombo* was the *nganga a nzumbi*, a priest whose responsibility was to deal with the spirits of the dead. The Ganga Zumba of Palmares was probably the holder of this office, which was in effect not a personal name but a title. There are other echoes from the descriptions of Angola that seem suggestive. In the Imbangala, *quilombo* leadership depended on some kind of popular acclaim or election just as some of the Brazilian accounts suggest.[79] Most curious is the observation of Andrew Battell, who lived among the Imbangala and who noted that their chief luxury was palm wine and that their routes and camps were influenced by the availability of palm trees. His comment makes the association of the maroon community with a region of Palmares (the word means palm trees) seem more than coincidental.[80]

If the founders of Palmares had used the Imbangala *ki-lombo* as the basis for their society, their version of it was incomplete or at least a variation on the basic model. A number of features associated with the Imbangala *ki-lombos* had no parallel in Brazil. The Imbangala were always referred to as cannibals who practiced cannibalism and human sacrifice to terrorize their enemies. These practices were strictly controlled as was the preparation of *magi a samba*, a paste made from human fat and other substances which supposedly made the *ki-lombo* warriors invincible. A strict set of ritual laws (*kijila*) surrounded the *ki-lombo*. Women were prohibited from the interior compound of the *ki-lombo* and there were strict ritual proscriptions against menstruating women. None of these customs are mentioned in the surviving documentation on Palmares.

The use of the term *quilombo* in reference to Palmares does not necessarily mean that all the ritual aspects of that institution as they were practiced in Angola were present in Brazil or that the founders or the subsequent leaders of Palmares were necessarily Imbangala.[81] Many aspects of the Imbangala *ki-lombo* could be found in other Central African institutions like the *kimpasi*, secret initiation camps of the Kongo, which also created new social bonds by association.[82] Much of what was inherent in the *ki-lombo* would have been understood by non-Imbangala. As noted, Imbangala dynasties and institutions were incorporated in a number of Mbundu states, and the *quilombo* came to symbolize the sovereignty of these states. Our best source in this regard is Antônio de Oliveira de Cadornega, the principal chronicler of seventeenth-century Angola. Cadornega used the term *quilombo* to describe Jaga troops, *quilombos de Jagas*, or *gente e quilombos de Jagas*, but also as a descriptive term for the kingdoms of Matamba and Kasange.[83] The use of the phrase "kingdom and quilombo" of Matamba was a general descriptive use of *quilombo* that referred to these Imbangala influenced polities but did not necessarily suggest the full existence of the original institution nor its ritual practices. *Quilombo* was becoming a synonym for a kingdom of a particular type in Angola.

Given the poor documentary record of Palmares much of the above hypothesis is admittedly tenuous, but I believe there is enough evidence to suggest that the introduction of the term *quilombo* into Brazil in the late seventeenth century was not accidental and that it represented more than simply a linguistic borrowing. If true, then we must deal with the African aspects of Palmares not as "survivals" disembodied from their original cultural milieu, but a far more dynamic and perhaps intentional use of an African institution that had been specifically designed to create a community among peoples of disparate origins and to provide an effective military organization. Surely, the fugitive slaves of Brazil fitted such a description, and the attacks made upon them by colonial governments made the military organization of the *quilombo* essential for survival. The success of *quilombos* varied as greatly as the *quilombos* themselves in size, leadership, longevity, and internal organization. Taken together, Palmares and the smaller fugitive communities constituted a continuous commentary on the Brazilian slave regime.

NOTES

1. This chapter has appeared in Portuguese as "Mocambos, Quilombos, e Palmares: A Resistência escrava no Brasil colonial," *Estudos Econômicos* 17 (1987), 61–88. It includes portions of my earlier article, "The Mocambo: Slave Resistance in Colonial Bahia," *Journal of Social History* 3 (Summer 1970), 313–33.

2. The series of slave revolts in Bahia between 1807 and 1835 has been studied by João José Reis in "Slave resistance in Brazil, Bahia, 1808–1835," *Luso-Brazilian Review* 25:1 (Summer, 1988), 111–44. See also Stuart B. Schwartz, *Sugar Plantations in the Formation of Brazilian Society* (New York, 1985), especially Chapter 17: "Important Occasions: The War to End Bahian Slavery," 468-88. On the Malês see João José Reis, *Rebelião escrava no Brasil* (São Paulo, 1986).

3. For a general overview of the subject see Clovis Moura, *Rebeliões da senzala*, 3d. ed. (São Paulo, 1981), and his *Os quilombos e a rebelião negra*, 2d. ed. (São Paulo, 1981). See also, José Alipio Goulart, *Da fuga ao suicídio. aspectos de rebeldia dos escravos do Brasil* (Rio de Janeiro, 1972). There has been a considerable development of the regional historiography of the *quilombos*. For example, on Pará there is Vicente Salles, *O Negro no Pará* (Rio de Janeiro, 1971); on Rio Grande do Sul, Mário José Maestri Filho, *Quilombos e quilombolas em terras gauchas*, (Porto Alegre, 1979); on Minas Gerais, Waldemar de Almeida Barbosa, *Negros e quilombos em Minas Gerais* (Belo Horizonte, 1972); on Bahia, aside from the above mentioned article by Schwartz, there is much material contained in Pedro Tomás Pedreira, *Os quilombos brasileiros* (Salvador, 1973). Many other works dealing with slavery in general at the local or regional level contain information on *quilombos*. See, for example, Ariosvaldo Figueiredo, *O Negro e a violência do Branco* (Rio de Janeiro, 1977) on Sergipe. The classic works on Palmares remain Edison Carneiro, *O quilombo dos Palmares* (São Paulo, 1947) and M. M. de Freitas, *O reino negro de Palmares*. 2 vols. (Rio de Janeiro, 1954), to which should now be added Décio Freitas, *Palmares: a guerra dos escravos* (Porto Alegre, 1973).

4. The distinction between *mocambo* resistance and *"petite marronage"* was recognized in Brazil. In December 1698 the crown, in response to a petition from the town council of Olinda, ordered that slaves who fled from one plantation to another could not be imprisoned like those who fled to Palmares. (AHU, Conselho Ultramarino, cod. 257, f.1). See the discussion in Gabriel Debien, "Le marronage aux Antilles Françaises au xviiie siécle," *Caribbean Studies* 6:3 (1966), 3–44, a portion of which appears in Richard Price, *Maroon Societies* (New York, 1973), 107–34; and the classic account of Yvan Debbasch, "Le marronage: essai sur la désertion de l'esclave antillais," *L'Année Sociologique* (1961), 1–112; (1962), 117–92. Gerald W. [Michael] Mullin, *Flight and Rebellion: Slave Resistance in Eighteenth Century Virginia* (New York, 1972) is an excellent study of the motivations, backgrounds, and actions of fugitive slaves.

Century Virginia (New York, 1972) is an excellent study of the motivations, backgrounds, and actions of fugitive slaves.

5. This is a major theme addressed on a broad scale in Eugene Genovese, *From Rebellion to Revolution: Afro-American Slave Revolts in the Making of the Modern World* (Baton Rouge, 1979). For Haiti the subject has become a major issue as is evidenced in Leslie F. Manigat, "The Relationship between Marronage and Slave Revolts and Revolution in St. Domingue-Haiti," *CPSNWPS*, 420–39.

6. The term "gentiles" (*gentio*) was applied to Indians beyond Portuguese control and thus still pagan. It was a pejorative term and had the implied meaning of "barbarian" (*barbaro*) to which it was often joined. ARSI, Bras.8 (StL VFL Roll 159).

7. For a particularly sadistic master in eighteenth-century Bahia see Luiz R. B. Mott, "Terror na Casa da Torre: tortura de escravos na Bahia colonial," in *Escravidão e invenção da liberdade*, ed. João José Reis, (São Paulo, 1988), 17–32.

8. See my discussion of Bahian slave demography in *Sugar Plantations in the Formation of Brazilian Society* (Cambridge, 1985), 338–78.

9. Marion D. deB. Kilson, "Towards Freedom: An Analysis of Slave Revolts in the United States," *Phylon* 25 (1964) 175–87; see also Orlando Patterson, *The Sociology of Slavery* (London, 1967), 274–80.

10. D. João de Lencastre to Câmara of Cairú (10 Dec. 1697), APB, Cartas do governo 150. In 1667 Gov. Alexandre de Sousa Freire asked the governor of Pernambuco for forty black militiamen to be used with Bahian blacks and Indians against *quilombos* in Cairú and Camamú. (AHU, Bahia pap. avul. caixa 10, 1st ser. uncatalogued).

11. See the discussion in Stuart B. Schwartz, ed., *A Governor and His Image in Baroque Brazil. The Funeral Eulogy of Afonso Furtado de Castro do Rio de Mendonça by Juan Lopes Sierra*, trans. Ruth Jones (Minneapolis, 1979), 11–14, 43–49. Sebastião da Rocha Pitta, *História da America Portugueza (1724)"* (Lisbon, 1880), 192–97.

12. King to Gov. Vasco Fernandes Cezar de Meneses (12 Feb. 1723), AHU, Conselho Ultramarino codice 247.

13. Consulta, Conselho Ultramarino (9 Nov. 1692), *DHBNR* 89 (1950), 206. The *quilombo* activity in Camamú in this period created fears of a general slave uprising. Governor Antônio Luiz Gonçalves Câmara Coutinho wrote to the Conselho Ultramarino that "em Camamú se levantarem huns mulatos e convocarem asi grande quantidade de Negros querendose fazerse senhores daquella villa." See BA, 51-IX-30 (Bahia, 23 June 1692).

14. José Lopes da Cruz, capitão interino de Sergipe to Gov. of Bahia (26 Sept. 1767), APB, Cartas ao governo 198.

15. BI, Correspondência de Alvaro e Gaspar de Sousa (17 Aug. 1612), f.81.

16. *ACB*, I,4. The terms *capitão do campo* and *do matto* were used interchangeably. By the late seventeenth century letters patent were granted for positions as *capitão mor das entradas dos mocambos*. See for example,

ACS, 124.1 f.126 (10 Nov. 1687) and AHU, Bahia pap. avul. caixa 26, 1st uncat. (1 July 1718). Governor Fernando José de Portugal wrote in 1788 of the necessity of the capitães das entradas and pointed out that the royal treasury spent nothing on their maintenance since it was the slaveowners who paid for their services according to a law of January 28, 1676. ["a fazenda real nada dispende com estes postos pois os senhores dos negros que fogem são os que satisfazem as diligencias em virtude de hum regimento dado aos capitães de assaltos em 28 Jan. 1676"] Portugal to Martinho de Melo e Castro (30 April 1788), *Inventários de documentos relativos ao Brasil*, ed. Eduardo Castro e Almeida, 8 vols. (Rio de Janeiro,1914), III, doc. 12.917.

17. BGUC, cod. 706 (7 March 1703); cod. 709 (5 May 1703), f.140; cod. 711 (5 March 1744), f.123; and ACB, I (13 Feb. 1637), 328–29.

18. *ACB*, I 326 (27 Jan. 1637). There are many instances of capitães do mato exceeding their rights or causing trouble. The captain major of Sergipe de El-Rey complained in 1806 of a certain Daniel Dias who was trying to purchase an office as a "capitão das entradas" simply to increase his power and who went about the captaincy drunk and who was by his habits and actions "unworthy of the uniform he wore." [só para ingrosar mais seos despotismos pois he de numero dos valentes daquele e de custumes pessimos e continuamente anda inbriegado, e se fas pelo seu procidimentos e custumes indigno da farda que tras.] See APB, Cartas ao Governo 208 (Sergipe, 16 Nov. 1806).

19. In the sixteenth century the Duke of Aveiro and the Count of Linhares both absentee landowners in Brazil sought to bring Indians in to their plantations for labor and defensive purposes. See AGS, sec. prov. 1487, (7 Oct. 1603); ANTT, CSJ, maço 8 doc. 9 (28 Aug. 1585); mao 16, *provisão*, 1586.

20. "Información q. hize por mandado de VMg. sobre unos capitulos q. Duarte Gomez de Silveira Vezino de Parahiba embio a la Mesa de Consciência," AGS, sec. prov. lib. 1583, fs.382–89.

21. The *santidade* movement is discussed in some detail in *Sugar Plantations*, 47–49.

22. Serafim Leite, "Enformação dalgumas cousas do Brasil por Belchior Cordeiro," *Anais da Academia Portuguesa da História* 2d. ser. 15 (1965), 175–202.

23. In a provocative essay Thomas Flory has suggested that a desire for the lands cleared and developed by *mocambo* fugitives was also a major impulse for colonial society's attack upon them. His evidence is drawn mainly from the Palmares case. Moreover, the fact that many *mocambos* were in inaccessible areas and usually not in lands devoted to the principle export crops tends to argue against this hypothesis, although a desire to obtain improved lands is certainly plausible in some cases. See Thomas Flory, "Fugitive Slaves and Free Society: The Case of Brazil, *Journal of Negro History* 54:2 (Spring, 1979), 116–30.

24. BA, 51-IX-30 (23 June 1692), f.13v.; Diogo de Campos Moreno,

"Report of the State of Brazil, 1612," edited by Engel Sluiter, *HAHR* 29 (1949), 518–62.

25. *ACB* I (25 Nov. 1640), 477–78.

26. Óbidos to Gov. Francisco de Brito Freyre (9 Sept. 1663), BNRJ, 8,1,3, fs. 3v-4.

27. Lucinda Coutinho de Mello Coelho, "O quilombo Buraco de Tatú," *Mensário do Arquivo Nacional* 10:4 (1979), 4–8. Some further details were added by Pedro Tomás Pedreira, "Sobre o Quilombo Buraco de Tatú," *M.A.N.* 10:7 (1979), 7–10.

28. ANTT, Chancelaria D. José I, livro 70, f.257v. (11 Jan. 1762).

29. AHU, Bahia pap. avul. no. 6451.

30. Ibid. n.6449. There is a copy of the document in IHGB, 1.119 (Correspondência do Governador da Bahia 1751-82). The document was also printed in *Inventário dos documentos relativos ao Brasil*, ed. Eduardo Castro de Almeida, 8 vols. (Rio de Janeiro, 1914), 2 (Bahia 1763-86), 44–45.

31. The rescue of two young white Paulista girls and their brother from a *quilombo* in Minas Gerais is the subject of a report of 1737 in which the author wrote: "it was a painful act to see the tears and lamentations with which the children were received (by their mother) mixing at the same time joy and sadness." See ANTT, Ms. do Brasil 11, 153-154v. (9 Jan. 1737); ms. do Brasil 4 (8 March 1737). Sexual fear of slaves seems to play a relatively minor role in the anti-*quilombo* campaigns, although traces of these sentiments sometimes emerge.

32. "Certidão da sentena condemnatória dos negros do quilombo Buraco de Tatú (12 Jan. 1764)," AHU, Bahia pap. avul. n.6456.

33. Conde do Ponte to Visconde de Anadia (27 April 1807), APB, Cartas do Governo 177.

34. *ACB* 1:119 (24 Jan. 1629).

35. See George P. Murdock, *Africa: Its Peoples and Their Culture History* (New York, 1959), 276. See also Richard W. Hull, *African Cities and Towns before the European Conquest* (New York, 1976), 33–49.

36. Antonio Cavazzi de Montecuccolo, *Istoria descrizione de tre Regni Congo, Matamba, et Angola* (Bologna, 1687), 205–7.

37. Georges Balandier, *La vie quotidienne au Royaume de Kongo du xvi au xviii siècle* (Paris, 1964); J. Van Wing, *Études Bakongo* (Louvain, 1921), 148. Raymond Kent, "Palmares: An African Kingdom in Brazil," *Journal of African History* 6 (1961), 161–75.

38. It is clear that some *mocambos* practiced agriculture. This is indicated in various documents such as that on the *quilombo* of Orobó of 1796 reprinted in Donald Pierson, *Negroes in Brazil* 2d. ed. (Carbondale, Ill., 1967), 49. Such practices, however, were difficult unless the *mocambo* was isolated and relatively permanent.

39. AHU, Bahia pap. avul. n.6649.

40. BGUC, cod. 707, Livro de registro da Relação.

41. AHU, Bahia pap. avul. n.6649.

42. There is now a significant literature on *quilombos* in Minas

Gerais. Aside from Almeida Barbosa, *Negros e quilombos em Minas Gerais,* noted above, see also A. J. R. Russell-Wood, *The Black Man in Slavery and Freedom in Colonial Brazil,* (New York, 1982); Julio Pinto Vallejos, "Slave Control and Resistance in Colonial Minas Gerais," *Journal of Latin American Studies* 17 (1985), 1–34. Carlos Magno Guimãres, *A negação da ordem escravista* (São Paulo, 1988), is particularly valuable for its list of *quilombos* in Minas Gerais and of letters patent for slave catchers. See also his summary article "Os Quilombos do século do ouro," *Estudos Econômicos* 18 (1988), 7–45. Some of his findings and other new materials are presented in Kathleen Joan Higgins, "The Slave Society in Eighteenth-Century Sabara: A Community Study in Colonial Brazil" (Ph.D. diss., Yale University, 1987,) 258–307. Still valuable is C. R. Boxer, *The Golden Age of Brazil: 1695–1750* (Berkeley, 1962).

43. A. J. R. Russell-Wood, "Technology and Society: The Impact of Gold Mining on the Institution of Slavery in Portuguese America," *Journal of Economic History* 34:1 (March, 1974), 59–83. The demographic structure of Minas Gerais has been analyzed in a series of studies by Iraci del Nero da Costa such as *Populações mineiras* (São Paulo, 1981); *Vila Rica: População (1719–1826)* (São Paulo, 1979) and Francisco Vidal Luna, *Minas Gerais: Escravos e senhores* (São Paulo, 1981). See also their jointly authored *Minas colonial: economia e sociedade* (São Paulo, 1982).

44. This point is emphasized by Higgins, "The Slave Society," 258–307. I believe, however, that the high numbers of fugitives and *quilombos* may be a characteristic of frontier regions in general as much as a result of the peculiar structure of Minas Gerais. There is some indication that the frequency of *quilombo* formation began to decline as the slave population became demographically more stable and a shift was made from mining to mixed agriculture.

45. Vallejos, "Slave Control," 6–8; Russell-Wood, *The Black Man,* 42.

46. Consulta, Conselho Ultramarino (22 Dec. 1718), IHGB, Arq. 1.1.25.

47. Provisão (2 Dec. 1744), ANRJ, Cod. 542, f.24–25.

48. On Assumar's campaign against *quilombos* see Francisco Antônio Lopes, "Câmara e cadeia de Villa Rica," *Anuario do Museu da Inconfidência* (1952), 103–251, which reprints important documents. Assumar's comment on the failure of Indians to stop *quilombo* formation under his predecessor is found in AHU, Minas pap. avul. crown to Conde de Assumar (12 Jan. 1719).

49. Regimento dos capitães do mato was issued in 1715 and then reissued in 1722. The version that remained in force was that of 17 December 1724. See ANTT, Mss. do Brasil 28, 307–9v.

50. Guimarães, *A negação da ordem escravista,* 129–71.

51. See the pertinent documentation in Lopes, "Câmara e cadeia," and also Russell-Wood, *The Black Man,* 42.

52. Russell-Wood, *The Black Man,* 42–43.

53. APB, Ordens rgias 55, f.99-99v.

54. "Ouvidor do Rio das velhas da conta . . .," IHGB, Arq. 1.1.24.

55. Regimento dos capites do mato, ANTT, Mss. do Brasil 28, fs.307–309v.

56. Laura de Mello e Souza, *Desclasificados do Ouro*, (Rio de Janeiro, 1982), 113.

57. Mello e Souza, *Desclasificados*, 72.84.

58. ANTT, Mss. do Brasil 11, fs.153–54.

59. Conselho Ultramarino to Gomes Freire (6 May 1747), AHU, Rio de Janeiro pap. avul. caixa 22.

60. Almeida Barbosa, *Negros e quilombos*, 31–53.

61. Assumar to crown (20 April 1719) cited in Vallejos "Slave Control," 15.

62. See the discussion in Higgins, "The Slave Society in Eighteenth-Century Sabara," 258–62.

63. The classic accounts of Palmares are Edison Carneiro, *O quilombo dos Palmares*, 3d. ed. (Rio de Janeiro, 1966), originally published in Spanish as *Guerras de los Palmares* (Mexico City, 1946); Décio Freitas, *Palmares: A guerra dos escravos* (Porto Alegre, 1971), now in a 4th edition of 1982 and originally published in Spanish as *Palmares-la guerra negra* (Montevideo, 1971). There is the older but still useful work of M. M. de Freitas, *O reino negro de Palmares* 2 vols. (Rio de Janeiro, 1954).

64. Indications of the symbolic meaning of Palmares can be seen in works such as Clovis Moura, *Brasil: as raízes do protesto negro* (São Paulo, 1983); Abdias do Nascimento, *O negro revoltado* (Rio de Janeiro, 1968), and his more recent *Quilombismo* (Petrópolis, 1980). Two motion pictures, "Ganga Zumba" (1963) and "Quilombo," (1984), both directed by Carlos Diegues have taken up this theme. In 1984, a conference was held in Alagoas to commemorate the history and significance of Palmares.

65. The African aspects of Palmares have fascinated scholars since Nina Rodrigues wrote his still useful description of that community in 1906. See *Os africanos no Brasil* (São Paulo, 1933). The most consistent attempt to identify the African aspects of Palmares was made by Raymond Kent, "Palmares: An African State in Brazil," *Journal of African History* 6 (1965), 161–75, but while Kent touches many important issues, his translations and ethnographic discussions can not always be trusted.

66. German anthropologist Stephan Palmié has pointed out that the structure of the "kingdom" of Palmares paralleled that of contemporaneous Bantu states such as the kingdom of Kongo. Stephan Palmié, "African States in the New World? Remarks on the Tradition of Transatlantic Resistance" (ms., 1988).

67. Francisco de Brito Freyre, *Nova Lusitania. História da guerra brasilica* (Lisbon, 1675), 280–82. (I have used the facsimile second edition, Recife, 1977).

68. Décio Freitas, *Palmares* presents a fascinating biography of Zumbi as a remarkable man, captured as a child in a raid on Palmares and then raised and educated in Latin and Portuguese by a priest in Porto Calvo. In

1670, at the age of fifteen, the youth fled back to Palmares and later rose to leadership. The precise sources of this account are not made clear by Freitas.

69. There are also accounts of "elections" in Angolan *quilombos*. See António de Oliveira Cadornega, *História das guerras angolanas*, 3 vols. (Lisbon, 1940), II, 221.

70. Palmié, "African States," 10–11. See also his "Ethnogenetic Processes and Cultural Transfer in Afro-American Slave Populations" (ms., 1989). Palmié drew considerable inspiration from Igor Kopytoff, "The Internal African Frontier: The Making of African Political Culture," in *The African Frontier*, ed. Igor Kopytoff (Bloomington, Ind., 1987), 3–84.

71. The absence of the word *quilombo* in reference to early fugitive communities is noted in Kent, "Palmares," 162–63. See also Mario José Maestri Filho, "Em torno ao quilombo," *História em Cadernos*, (Mestrado de História-Universidade Federal do Rio de Janeiro), 2:2 (1984), 9–19.

72. Livro das Atas da Câmara do Salvador (1669-84), 23, cited in Pedro Tomás Pedreira, "Os quilombos dos Palmares e o senado da câmara da cidade do Salvador," *M.A.N.* 11:3 (1980), 14–17.

73. David Birmingham, *Trade and Conflict in Angola* (Oxford, 1966), presents a detailed description of these events. See also his synthesis in "Central Africa from Cameroun to the Zambezi," in *Cambridge History of Africa*, eds. J. D. Fage and Roland Oliver 5 vols. to date (Cambridge, 1975–), 4, (1975), 325–83. See also Jan Vansina, *Kingdoms of the Savanna*, (Madison, 1968), 64-70, 124–38.

74. Joseph C. Miller, *Kings and Kinsmen: Early Mbundu States in Angola*, (Oxford, 1976), contains an excellent description of the Imbangala and their institutions.

75. On the debate, see Joseph C. Miller, "The Imbangala and the Chronology of Early Central African History," *Journal of African History*, 13:4 (1972), 549–74; "Requiem for the Jaga," *Cahiers d'etudes africaines* 13:1 (1973), 121–49; John Thornton, "A Resurrection for the Jaga," *Cahiers d'études africaines* 18 (1978), 223–28.

76. Beatrix Hintze, "Angola nas garras do tráfico de escravos," *Revista Internacional de Estudos Africanos* 1:1 (1984), 11–60.

77. See Roy Glasgow, *Nzinga* (São Paulo, 1982); Joseph C. Miller, "Kings, Lists, and History in Kisanje," *History in Africa* 6 (1979), 51–94.

78. Miller, *Kings and Kinsmen*, 151–75, 224–64, provides an intense analysis. The classic sources on the Jaga *ki-lombo* are Cadornega and Cavazzi de Montecuccolo.

79. Cadornega, *História*, II, 221.

80. E. G. Ravenstein, *The Strange Adventures of Andrew Battel of Leigh in Angola and Adjoining Regions*, (London, 1901).

81. The Jaga origins of Palmares have concerned scholars for many years. Nina Rodrigues was content to point out the Bantu origin of the titles, personal names, and toponymy of Palmares. M. M. de Freitas argued that since the Palmarinos were such inveterate warriors they must have been Jagas. Freitas argued "that the first runaway was of the sacred caste

of the Jagas and the founder of the Palmares' dynasty. (o primeiro quilombola era da casta sagrada dos jagas e o fundador da dinastia palmarina), (I,278). Kent, "Palmares," argued that the Jagas were probably not the originators of Palmares.

82. John K. Thornton, *The Kingdom of Kongo* (Madison, 1983), 61, 107.

83. Cadornega, *História*, 1, 89; 2, 222.

5 Opening the Family Circle: Godparentage in Brazilian Slavery

To penetrate within the slave community has been among the most difficult tasks that historians have set for themselves. The relative lack of documentary materials that expose the most mundane aspects of life, especially among slaves, has historically created a situation in which secondary evidence such as the comments made by travelers or casual observers has served as the basis for an understanding of these aspects of life. It is a situation that has often left slaves mute. Thus, rare glimpses of the inner workings of the slave communities revealed in legal documents or other sources have become all the more valuable; but these materials are usually too fragmentary to provide a sound basis for generalization. In many areas, therefore, historians are forced to examine a series of events such as marriages or running away, and then from the patterns of individual characteristics and behavior viewed in the aggregate attempt to extract the significance and meaning of the events. Where slaves came into contact with the institutions of government—the church, the municipality, the judicial system—records were kept and thus an opportunity to recapture some aspects of the inner workings of the slave communities exists. The problem here, as in all historical writing, remains one of interpretation and point of view because the significance of these encounters to the slave and to the institution were often quite different.

The question of the slave family in Brazil—its existence, structure, stability, longevity, and role within the life of slaves and the history of their descendants—has long been a matter of interest, but only recently one of serious research. The dismissive comments

of some nineteenth-century observers and abolitionists about prom-
iscuity, the lack of family ties, and the family's fragility in the face
of sale and disruption were echoed and embellished by later historians and social scientists who sought either to condemn slavery
or to explain subsequent negative contemporary patterns in the
Afro-Brazilian community.[1] The result was to create an image of a
dysfunctional and fragile slave family.

In the past decade, stimulated to some extent by the debate
over the black family in the United States and especially the work
on the slave family and the slave community by Herbert Gutman,
John Blassingame, and Eugene Genovese, students of Brazil have
begun to reexamine the slave family.[2] The approaches and methods
of Brazilian slave family studies have been greatly influenced by
the historiography of North American slavery and by the serious
development of the family history as a separate branch of inquiry
in Western Europe. These advances have provided new methods of
analysis and a new set of questions for historians, but models developed in other historical contexts must always be adapted and
adjusted to Brazilian realities, and the definition of the slave family
and its functions should reflect them.

In this chapter I examine a form of fictive kinship, *compadrio*
or ritual godparentage, within Brazilian familial and spiritual life.
By examining the manner in which slaves participated in the system
of ritual godparentage, I seek to view the slave family within a
context wider than the generational, consanguineal, and legal dimensions that usually set the limits for this type of study. Moreover,
I demonstrate that within the institution and relations of godparentage, where one might expect to find clear demonstrations of
paternalistic attitudes expressed by masters toward their slaves,
scant evidence of those attitudes exists. Masters and their relatives
rarely served as religious sponsors and spiritual guardians for their
own slaves, and their absence in these roles calls into question the
supposed paternalism of the Brazilian slaveowners.

Godparentage and the Slave Family

The various forms of fictive kinship have long been a subject
of intense interest among anthropologists who have often viewed
the ritualized kinship created through the act of Christian baptism
as a central feature of the extended family in the Iberian world.[3]
In the eyes of Christian society, *compadrio*, as it was called in
Portuguese, established spiritual links between the godparents and

the newly named and initiated Christian and, in the case of a baptized child, between the godparents and the biological parents.

Such links also had a social dimension outside the framework of the church. They could be used to reinforce existing kinship ties or solidify relationships with persons of similar social status, or they could establish vertical ties between socially unequal individuals. Godparentage relationships could be established in a variety of ways: at marriage, confirmation, or even at certain festivals such as St. John's Day, when by joining hands and leaping over a bonfire together, people could become "compadres da fogueira."[4] The church frowned on these popular creations of *compadrio*, but the practice continued. The act of baptism, however, remained the most important moment when godparentage and coparentage ties were created.

Over the centuries, the church sought to regulate the norms of baptismal sponsorship, and although popular practices such as choosing multiple sets of godparents, having the officiating priest serve as sponsor at baptism, or selecting the Virgin or a local female patron saint as godmother were prohibited by the Council of Trent, they were slow to disappear.[5] In Brazil, church practice was codified at a synod in 1707 and published in the *Constituições primeiras do Arcebispado da Bahia* in 1720.[6] According to this code, baptism was to be given to newborn infants by a parish priest within eight days of birth. Each child was to have only one godmother (over the age of twelve) and one godfather (over the age of fourteen). The parents of the child were forbidden to serve as his or her godparents, as were members of religious orders (except those in orders of knighthood). The baptism of newly arrived and unacculturated slaves (*escravos boçais de lingoa não sabida*) called for special religious instruction to ensure that they understood their obligations as members of the church.[7]

In the context of Catholicism, baptism was the primary means by which an individual, slave or free, became a member of Christian society. However, slaves had a variety of ways to establish links of association or forms of kinship both within the structures of the dominant society and outside of them. Ties created by African ethnicity, language, religion, and politics continued to operate in Brazil as the ethnically organized rebellions of the early nineteenth century demonstrate. Even the voyage from Africa, the "middle passage," created conditions for the formation of fictive kinship. As I mentioned earlier, the term *malungo*, or shipmate, was used for one who had crossed on the same vessel and denoted a recognized kinship link. These ethnic and cultural ties forged out of common experience and condition as slaves could sometimes be incorporated into those institutions and associations of Brazilian society. Religious sodalities such as the Brotherhoods of Our Lady of the Rosary were widespread throughout Brazil and represented one of the principal means of association and cultural expression available to people of color. But, of course, like all other associations and institutions sanctioned by the dominant society, membership in a religious sodality was reserved to those who had been accepted into the Christian community by the rite of baptism.

The baptism of slaves was considered a responsibility of all slaveowners since one of the principal justifications of enslavement was the conversion of the heathen and the salvation of their souls. The fundamental law code of Portugal and its empire, the *Ordenações filipinas* (1603), ordered all slaveowners to baptise their African slaves above ten years old within six months and those under that age within one month of acquiring them or forfeit them to the crown.[8] The children born to slave women in the lands of the king of Portugal were to be baptized at the time and in the manner that other children received the sacrament. Failure to have them baptized would result in confiscation by the crown. Attempts were made to baptise slaves on the ships before they departed from Angola, and by 1702 plans were put forward to use free people of color as preachers on the African coast to carry out conversions and prepare slaves for baptism.[9] Slaves arriving from areas on the African coast not under Portuguese control frequently arrived unbaptized. Thus, Brazilian parish registers recorded both the baptisms of recently arrived Africans, usually adults, as well as those of children born as slaves in Brazil.

For various reasons royal officials and slaveowners sometimes circumvented the law.[10] In Minas Gerais, the profoundly racist governor, Dom Pedro de Almeida, Count of Assumar, prohibited slaves from serving as godparents for other slaves. He feared that this relationship would strengthen the power of slaves and weaken the ties of dependence on the masters.[11] His prohibitions seem to have been largely ignored. By the early nineteenth century, the practice of slave baptism had become customary and social pressures were exerted both by masters and other slaves to reinforce the act.

Acceptance into the guild of the church ("gremio da igreja") was presented to slaves as a necessary step in the improvement of their situation. Henry Koster, who resided in Pernambuco wrote in 1816 that newly arrived slaves were not fully accepted by their com-

rades until they had been baptised and received a Christian sur-
name. His comments are revealing:

> The religion of the master teaches him that it would be extremely
> sinful to allow his slave to remain a heathen: and indeed the Portu-
> guese and Brazilians have too much religious feeling to let them ne-
> glect any of the ordinances of their church. The slave himself likewise
> wishes to be made a Christian; for his fellow bonds-men will, oth-
> erwise, in every squabble or trifling disagreement with him close their
> string of opprobrious epithets with the name *pagam* [pagan]. The un-
> baptized negro feels that he is considered as an inferior being; and
> although he may not be aware of the value which whites place upon
> baptism, still he knows that the stigma for which he is upbraided,
> will be removed by it; and therefore he is desirous of being made equal
> to his companions. The Africans who have been long imported, im-
> bibe a Catholic feeling; and appear to forget that they once were in
> the same situation themselves. The slaves are not asked whether they
> will be baptized or not. Their entrance into the Catholic church is
> treated as a thing of course: and indeed they are not considered as
> members of society, but as brute animals, until they can lawfully go
> to mass, confess their sins, and receive the sacrament.[12]

The numerous parish registers in Brazil offer an excellent opportunity to study the historical patterns of godparentage established in the baptism of slaves and by extension, to discuss aspects
of family life among Brazilian slaves. While there has long been
scholarly interest in *compadrio* in Brazil, few studies using historical materials had been done before 1984 when my colleague,
Stephen Gudeman, and I published a series of findings based on our
analysis of godparentage and *compadrio* relationships among slaves
in two rural parishes in Bahia during the period 1780–90.[13] Since that
time, interest in the topic seems to have increased. John Monteiro
has included observations about *compadrio* in his analysis of Indian
slaves in early São Paulo while Eliana Goldschmidt has examined
the godparentage of slaves in eighteenth-century São Paulo.
Kathleen Higgins has devoted a portion of her thesis on Sabará, Minas Gerais, to an analysis of some three hundred slave baptisms in
1727 and 1731–32. Ana Maria Lugão Rios has examined almost three
thousand baptisms among slaves from coffee estates in Paraíba do
Sul (Rio de Janeiro) between 1871 and 1888. While the nature of the
data, the questions posed, and the methods of analysis in these various studies do not permit detailed comparisons, together these
studies suggest some patterns that characterized the baptism of
slaves in Brazil and the formation of ties of fictive kinship.

The Gudeman-Schwartz study of the Bahian Recôncavo sugar plantation region with its dense, mostly African, slave population found that certain patterns in the selection of godparents could be observed. For example, since masters did not serve as godparents for their own slaves and only rarely did relatives of the slaveowner fill those roles, Godparentage was not generally used to reinforce the paternalistic aspects of the master-slave relationship. Almost invariably, slaves did not serve as godparents for free-born children or for those of *libertos* (freed ex-slaves), but, in contrast, slave children had free, freed, and slave godparents. A sort of ranking of sponsorship that replicated the color and status hierarchy of society operated so that whites almost always had white godparents, *pardos* (brown-skinned) children had mostly white but a few black or *pardo* sponsors, and blacks had mostly white but also a significant number of *pardo* and black godparents. For recently arrived adult slaves, other slaves were far more likely to serve as godparents than in the case of children. Slaveholders tended to equalize the status of the godfather and godmother, but not always; and when free persons served as godparents for a slave, they were usually from a status beneath that of the slave's own master. Finally, that study noted that legitimacy and gender also had an impact on the selection of sponsors. Legitimate children were more likely to have higher status godparents and a "normal" arrangement in which both a godfather and a godmother were present, while illegitimate children might have no godmother registered. Male children were more likely than girls to have a free godparent.

These patterns of slave godparentage observed in eighteenth-century Bahia could be logically questioned in terms of their typicality and their specificity to a historical place and time. Bahia was, after all, closely tied to the export economy and the transatlantic slave trade. The parishes examined were sugar-producing zones, and sugar production had expanded in this period. There were large numbers of slaves, many were Africans or the children of Africans, and the region had a significant number of relatively large slaveholdings. For comparative purposes then, it will be useful to examine both the patterns of slave godparentage at a different point in time in Bahia and also to examine them in different regions of Brazil and particularly in an area not tied as closely to the export economy and to the international slave trade. In this chapter I present some findings drawn from Curitiba, Paraná, an area far to the south of Bahia and characterized by a nonplantation economy. Then, using the parish registers and a local census from the rural parish of Iguape, Bahia in the 1830s, a half century after the date of the previous study, I reexamine and expand some of the earlier findings. Finally, using those findings and comparative materials from parallel studies of Minas Gerais, São Paulo, Rio de Janeiro, and the city of Salvador, I suggest the existence of some widespread Brazilian patterns of slave godparentage that have implications for discussions of the relationships between masters and slaves and for relationships and strategies within the slave communities.

A Different Brazil: Slave Baptisms in Curitiba

The parish of Nossa Senhora da Luz dos Pinhais de Curitiba had been established in 1654 as part of the southward expansion of São Paulo, and it remained the central focus of settlement on the upland plains around Curitiba, or what came to be called the "campos curitibanos," well into the nineteenth century.[14] This settlement was from the outset, "a slave-based society based on the use of the labor of Indians and Africans or their descendants and *mestiços*."[15] Founded originally as part of the Paulista thrust in search of mines, the area remained a marginal settlement only loosely connected to the export sector, and in character quite unlike the sugar parishes of Bahia. Gold production remained an important activity, but by 1710 the Jesuit Antonil noted the development of cattle herds on the plains around Curitiba. By 1750, however, the local economy had moved definitely toward the production of cattle and agricultural commodities.

This shift from mining to cattle production around Curitiba was not characterized by any change in the dependence on coerced labor. A small-scale slave society, Curitiba had about 5,500 free persons and 1,334 slaves in 1779 and by the late eighteenth century, 6,400 free persons and 1,400 slaves.[16] Slaves comprised roughly 20 to 25 percent of the population throughout most of this period and into the nineteenth century.

The characteristics of the slave population of Paraná differed from those of the Northeast. By 1850, when Curitiba had become the provincial capital, the demand for domestic labor had increased and the proportion of women in the population was relatively high. In 1830, the sex ratio was 105 men for every 100 women.[17] Curitiba, unlike Bahia, was characterized by a relatively equal number of slave men and women and a high proportion of children in the slave population. A census of 1804, however, revealed that children were rarely found on the almost 500 properties that had from 1 to 3 slaves. They were much more characteristic of the slaveholdings of 15 or more captives. Thus, to a large extent infant baptisms in Curitiba were done in the context of larger slaveholdings.[18] Finally, it should be noted that by 1830, almost 85 percent of the slaves in Paraná were *crioulos* rather than Africans, and, unlike Bahia, there was little dependence on the Atlantic slave trade. The reinforcement of African cultural patterns by newly arrived captives was far more difficult here than it was in Bahia. Moreover, most purchases of slaves were made by owners with less than four slaves so that the impact of the newly arrived slaves was often physically or geographically circumscribed by their dispersion on small properties.[19]

In contrast to Bahia, the first and most distinctive aspect of this labor force was the continued presence of Indians under a variety of arrangements. With the growth of the sugar economy in the late sixteenth and early seventeenth centuries, Bahia had made the transition from Indian to African workers.[20] However, frontier regions like Paraná, lacking capital and involved in economic activities where returns to investment were limited, could afford few relatively expensive African slaves. Thus, the settlers continued to depend on Indian labor, a tradition already well established among the first Portuguese inhabitants of São Paulo, who had long exploited indigenous peoples as a labor force.[21]

Despite laws and prohibitions against Indian slavery in Brazil dating from 1570 forward, Paraná depended primarily on Indian workers from its inception to the 1730s. Parish registers provide evidence of this fact. Between 1685 and 1750, the parish registers contain baptismal entries for 975 Indians and 634 blacks, but an examination of the relative proportions of the two groups reveals that the transition from Indian to Africans really dated from the last thirty years of the period. Until 1709, when 11 children and 17 African adults were baptized, the number of blacks appearing in the registers was negligible. Not until 1740 did the number of Africans and Afro-Brazilians baptized finally exceed the number of Indians.

Between 1751 and 1777 the proportion of Indian and African or Afro-Brazilian baptisms was inverted from the previous era with 694 Blacks and 192 Indians registered. In addition, in the registers of slave baptisms, thirty *libertos* (former slaves) also appear. In the period 1781–85, over 200 slaves were baptized in the parish for the first time and similar levels continued until 1850. From 1780 to 1800, during the period in which Curitiba began to serve as a major transit point for the herds of mules and cattle moving from Rio Grande do Sul in the south to the growing markets of São Paulo and Rio de Janeiro, the proportion of Indians in the registers fell to less than 10 percent of the number of black and mulatto slaves, while the number of *libertos* increased to over 15 percent between 1800 and 1820.[22] Indians, with three exceptions disappeared from the registers. In effect, the baptismal registers simply reflected the transition of the labor force from Indian to African, which accompanied the growth of the region's economy and its links to expanding markets.

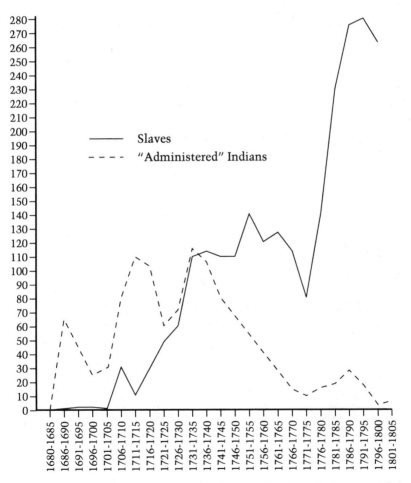

Figure 5. Baptism of Captives. Parish of Nossa Senhora da Luz Curitiba, 1685–1805.

The terminology of Indian servitude in Paraná is in itself an interesting and suggestive problem.[23] Until 1697, the terms *servito* or *servico* were used in the registers for Indians in a state of servitude. Both terms were diminutive forms of *servo* the classical term for a serf—but not a slave.[24] Whether the use of the diminutive indicates the influence of Spanish speakers or whether it connotes a certain proximity and sentiment of attachment, as it sometimes does in both Spanish and Portuguese, is a moot point. What is noticeable, however, is the manner in which the diminutive was replaced between 1702 and 1723 by the term *servo* and then, after the later date, by the phrase *administrado*. This latter term reflected the legal restrictions placed on the enslavement of Indians who were instead placed under the "temporary administration" of a master. The designation "slave" (*escravo*) for Indians only appeared after 1729, and then only rarely.

This changing terminology is suggestive, perhaps indicating a growing separation or distancing between masters and their servants and a changing perception of the relationship and its justification on the part of those masters. This change was accompanied by the shift to a predominantly African slave force and one in which the paternalist fiction was less compelling. It suggests that as the num-

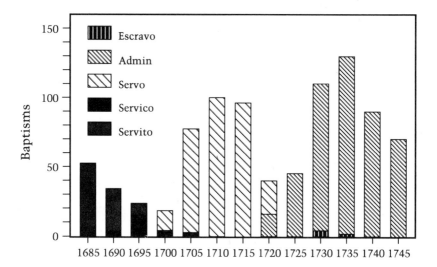

Figure 6. Changes in the Terminology of Indian Labor.

bers of African and Afro-Brazilian slaves began to increase in the region Indians were increasingly thought of as slaves.

Labor conditions and treatment of Indian *administrados* differed little if at all from those of black slaves. A number of authors have argued that *administrados* were in fact slaves and considered as such. But the baptismal records indicate that in ideological and religious terms at least some masters made distinctions between Indians and Africans. In the years 1685–1750 there were only four cases (3 percent) in which a master served as the godparent for his or her black bondsman and in six instances (4 percent) relatives of the master were sponsors. For Indians, however, the master served as godparent in thirty cases (9 percent) and relatives of the master in another 40 (12 percent). These numbers indicate a general attitude toward Indians considerably different from that expressed toward blacks. After all, the justification of "administering" Indians was the civilizing effects of placing them in contact with Christians who would instruct them in proper behavior as members of the church and of civil society. Thus, if masters took their role seriously there would be no incongruity, and, in fact, there would be considerable reason to serve as both master and as baptismal sponsor of Indians under their tutelage. The four blacks treated in the same way seem to be exceptions occurring in the early period when the transition to black slavery was under way. In the period 1750–1820, no black slaves were sponsored by their own masters and in only 5 percent of their baptisms did a relative of their master serve as godmother or godfather. Quite clearly, with the shift to black slavery a different pattern of godparentage had emerged, one similar to that observed in Bahia in which the roles of master and godparent were viewed as contradictory. The pattern of baptism in Curitiba before 1780 also indicates that *administrados* (Indians) and *escravos* (blacks) were perceived differently in terms of their relationship to the master.

From 1820 until the abolition of slavery in 1888, the separation of the statuses of master and godfather remained the predominant rule of godparent selection. Only few exceptions could be found. Of 444 cases sampled in that period, in only three instances did masters sponsor their own slaves and one of these dated from the 1880s when, although born to a slave mother, the child was legally free. It is difficult to ascertain the extraordinary circumstances that led masters to sponsor their own slaves. In an earlier study of the urban parish of Conceiçao da Praia in the city of Salvador, the one case (1/201) found by David Smith between 1649 and 1698, was that of an unbaptized child from the Mina coast. Being neither an African pagan adult nor a Brazilian-born infant, this child was atypical in a number of ways.[25]

The separation of statuses implied by these statistics indicate the failure of a paternalism to overcome the proscriptions inherent in conflicting spiritual and economic roles. Paternalism was also not often provided by having some other member of the slaveowners' family serve as sponsor. In Curitiba, from 1685 to 1850, only 2.3 percent (41/1,764) of the godparents were related to the baptized slaves' owners. Before 1870 relatives of the masters did not serve as godparents in more than 5 percent of the cases. Close personal ties of affection may have existed between a few masters and their families and certain slaves; but the baptismal registers suggest that these were rare exceptions, and that they were as uncommon in Curitiba as they were in Bahia or in Minas Gerais, where Higgins found no cases of masters sponsoring slaves in her sample of 200 baptisms in the 1730s.[26]

Certain other patterns of godparent selection emerge from the study of Curitiba. There existed a strong preference for free godparents, especially for free godfathers. This pattern was modified in the period 1750–99 when the proportion of free sponsors fell below half and that change may be due to the large number of adults who were introduced in these years. Adult slaves in Brazil rarely had free godparents. After 1800, the former pattern reemerged. In general, in Curitiba as in Bahia the proportion of free godparents for slaves remained above two-thirds. Married couples sometimes served as sponsors for slaves as did men and women who were related, but most common were unrelated free sponsors.

In table 4, I present the structure of godparentage in Curitiba from 1800 to 1869. Of the 504 baptisms sampled, over 70 percent

Table 4. Godparents for Baptised Slaves
Nossa Senhora da Luz dos Pinhais, Curitiba
1800–1869

| | | Godmother | |
		Free	Slave
Godfather	Free	357 (70.8%)	38 (7.5%)
	Slave	19 (3.8%)	90 (17.8%)

were sponsored by two free godparents, under 20 percent of the baptized were presented by two slaves, and when the two godparents were of unequal legal status, the baptized were twice as likely to have a slave godmother and a free godfather than the reverse.[27]

After the Law of Free Birth in 1871, the patterns and customs of slavery were subject to new considerations. Since all children born to slaves after that date were legally free but were required to remain in the service of their owners until reaching the age of majority (twenty-five) or being freed by the payment of compensation, there was a change in the perception of status. Moreover the relative proportions of free, freed, and slave was also changing as more and more slaves became free. The previous tendency to have free godparents intensified in the period from 1870 to the end of slavery in 1888, when almost 90 percent of the baptized children in Curitiba had free godparents. Clearly, there were simply fewer slaves to chose among. Moreover, children baptized in this period were recognized as *ingenuos,* legally free although still under the control of their mothers' owners, and it was probably thought unseemly for them to have slave sponsors.

From the middle of the eighteenth century until the 1870s, when slaves were chosen, in most cases they were not slaves of the same owner as the baptized. This situation reflected the relatively small size of slaveholdings in the area and it also suggests the ability of slaves to form links across the boundaries of property in the face of structural attempts to limit such ties. While there were certainly variations from place to place and time to time, and even from estate to estate, I believe that the patterns of selection suggest considerable participation of the slaves themselves in the choice of baptismal sponsors.

The data from Curitiba corroborate many of the findings from eighteenth-century Bahia. The most common pattern of godparentage for children born to slaves was the selection of a free godfather and godmother, neither of whom were the master or related to the master. The next most common pattern was the selection of two slaves to serve as the sponsors. When the status of the sponsors differed, the preference was always for a free godfather and a slave godmother, a pattern also observed in Bahia in the sixteenth century as well. Here, perhaps was recognition of the social importance of a free godfather who might serve as a protector or intercessor in the future, but a parallel practical strategy to deal with the possibility that in case of a mother's death, the slave godmother might have to assume the upbringing and nurturing the child. Rarest of all combinations was a slave godfather and free godmother.

In table 5, I summarize the findings from Curitiba and place them in comparison with available comparable data from other studies. While there are certain differences and variations, a general pattern emerges.

The survey of slave baptisms in Curitiba also revealed that despite ecclesiastical prohibitions, the custom of providing sometimes only one godparent or of invoking one of the saints as a sponsor continued. When only one godparent was present it was usually the male. In about 5 percent of the Curitiba slave baptisms a godmother was absent or the role was filled by the Virgin. On occasion, two males would be listed as godfathers. Such arrangements, while long practiced in Iberia before the Council of Trent, and continued in some places thereafter, persisted in Brazil, especially in the baptism of slaves or lower-class free persons. Evidence of this practice was found in both Bahia and Curitiba well into the nineteenth century.

The data from Curitiba indicate that the Bahian patterns are not exceptional and that despite considerable variations in the size and relative proportions of the slave population, differences in the nature of production and stages of economic development, the patterns of ritual godparentage for slaves were similar. An unwritten set of rules guided Brazilian masters and slaves in sponsorship that implied for masters an acceptance of both slavery and spiritual sponsorship. For slaves, these patterns suggest an adaptation to their circumstances and an attempt to use the institution of godparentage to improve their condition or to strengthen familial ties. While certain patterns seem generalized, variations or changes due to demographic circumstances or historical conditions were always possible.

Santiago de Iguape, Bahia, 1835

Having now compared the patterns of slave godparentage from Gudeman and Schwartz's earlier study of eighteenth-century Bahia with the those in Curitiba, it will be useful to return to Bahia at a different historical moment to see whether the differences observed are simply those of two regions with different economic and demographic structures, or if changes in historical circumstances are also reflected in the patterns of godparentage.

Let us turn to Bahia in 1835, about half a century after the

Table 5. Baptism of Slaves

Locale	Date	# of Cases	Master as Godparent	% Free Godfather/Godmother		% Slave Godfather/Godmother	
Bahia—city	1649–98	201	1	80	75	13	33
Bahia—rural	1780–90	264*	0	72	64	24	36
Bahia—rural	1835	169*	3	49	55	51	45
Bahia—rural	1723–1816	38**		33	26	64	74
Bahia—rural	1835	62**		17	40	83	60
Curitiba							
[Indians]	1685–1750	336	30	83	72	17	28
[Blacks]	1685–1750	154	4	78	64	24	36
	1751–73	180	0	53	49	47	51
	1780–99	150	2	51	58	49	42
	1800–20	164	0	73	66	27	34
	1821–49	234	2	81	77	19	23
	1850–69	113	0	80	78	19	18
	1870–88	97	1	92	90	8	5
Paraíba do Sul	1872–88	2,668	9	38	12	62	88

*Children only
**Adults only

data of the original Gudeman-Schwartz study. The parish of Santiago de Iguape, which lay in the heart of the Bahian Recôncavo, the agricultural zone surrounding the Bay of All Saints, provides a focal point.[28] It contained a number of large sugar plantations, but also some small properties where sugar and tobacco were produced. The existence of a detailed house by house census of the parish in 1835 and a complete set of parish registers from the same date enable us to place the observed patterns of godparentage in a broader social and demographic setting. When the census of the region was carried out, Iguape counted some 7,404 inhabitants of which 3,978 (54 percent) were slaves.[29] In Santiago de Iguape, as in much of the Bahian Recôncavo, the majority of the population was composed of people of color. Over half the population was slave and another 40 percent were free people of color. A total of only 590 whites comprised about 8 percent of Iguape's inhabitants, less than 20 percent of the free population.

In the year of the census, 169 children of slaves and 62 adult Africans were baptized. In comparison with the 1780–90 Bahian data analyzed in the Gudeman-Schwartz study, the most notable difference in the pattern of godparentage among the 169 slave children baptized in Iguape was the lower proportion of free godparents. For both godfathers and godmothers, that figure fell below 50 percent, and even if freed persons are added to the total, the figure remains below the earlier findings for Bahia and is more in line with those from the late eighteenth century in Curitiba. Although more research is needed here, this pattern indicates a growing sense of community among the slave population and a decreasing sense of dependency on the part of slaves or of paternalism on the part of the free.

Why should this be the case? Between 1807 and 1835 Bahia was rocked by a series of slave revolts that severely threatened the very basis of slave society. Tensions, suspicions, and repression characterized these years, a period in which the struggle for national independence and the political definition of the new nation was also taking place after 1822. It is therefore not surprising to find a lessening of the social bonds between free and slave or across color lines as reflected in the choice of godparents.[30]

Iguape, in fact, had been the center of much of this tension. In January 1827 slaves on the Engenho São José do Açu had fled en masse and the municipal judge in the nearby town of Cachoeira had mobilized the militia to stop the "contagion" from spreading to the sixteen other sugar mills in the district. His report emphasized the vulnerability of the town surrounded as it was by an "infinite number of slaves."[31] Two months later slaves on one of the four plantations of Pedro Rodrigues Bandeira had killed the overseer and his brother. Fearing a general rising, the district defense forces were again mobilized.[32] In the following year, the fears became reality when in September 1828 slaves on a number of estates rose and killed those who opposed them, murdering the family of one planter and burning the buildings. The band then attacked nearby estates, killing free and slave who opposed them. Over twenty people were killed and forty wounded in these attacks and slaves from other estates fled to join the rebels. When the rebels were finally dispersed or captured it was very difficult to bring charges in these "horrendous crimes" because "the rebels were only new slaves whose names were still not known and from different engenhos."[33] Whatever the origins of the rebels and despite the fact that many slaves did not join them, there were good reasons in Iguape for a growing distrust and distancing between slave and free.

This tension did not, however, completely change the previous patterns of godparent selection. The census from Iguape permits an examination of the pool of possible godparents. If only women over the age of twelve and men above the age of fourteen are counted then the total population "at risk" of serving as godparents was 5,446. While whites and *pardos* were about 39 percent of the possible godmothers they served in about 55 percent of the baptisms, if we assume that all those whose color was unreported in the documents were, in fact, whites or *pardos.* Men of these high status color designations were chosen about equally with blacks. But while white and *pardo* men of suitable age made up 29 percent of the pool, they served in 49 percent of the slave baptisms. Free persons were slightly favored in godparentage selection. Free or freedmen served in 49 percent of the baptisms as godfathers but since they constituted only 35 percent of the pool of eligible godfathers their participation was disproportionate. Free and freed women served in over half of the baptisms of infant slaves, which was their proportion in the pool of possible sponsors. Still, the marked preferences for persons of higher color and free status noted in the previous Bahian study and in most periods in Curitiba are not as apparent in Iguape (see table 5). Slaves sought other slaves as their coparents. With few whites available or willing to serve, there appears to have been less advantage to have a free person of color as a godparent.

In the matter of adult baptisms, the Iguape data from 1835

parallels the earlier findings from Bahia. The Bahian baptisms from the 1780s indicated a distinct pattern in the baptism of adult slaves in which, unlike those involving children, other slaves or more rarely *libertos* were more likely to serve as sponsors. This same pattern was observed in Minas Gerais in Higgins study of Sabará during the gold mining boom and in Smith's earlier analysis of slave baptisms in Salvador in the seventeenth century in which of 39 baptisms of "pagan" adults, 64 percent of the godfathers and 81 percent of the godmothers were slaves. Clearly, in terms of integration into the church and into the secular world of this slave society, other slaves assumed or were given a major role in the integration of newly arrived Africans.

That conclusion is also supported by an analysis of the adult baptisms in Iguape during 1835. In that year, 62 Africans were baptized, over half of them Yoruba-speakers, or Nagô. Of the 124 possible godparents, only 16 (12 percent) were free persons, and of these only three were whites. The majority of slaves were sponsored by other slaves. Over 80 percent of the godfathers and 60 percent of the godmothers were other slaves. Moreover, there appears to have been a strong "ethnic" preference among the Yoruba to have godparents from the same group or, to a lesser extent, from slaves born in Brazil, but rarely from other African peoples.

Masters as Godparents

Finally, the Iguape data support the central finding of the Gudeman-Schwartz study that masters did not serve as the spiritual sponsors for their slaves. This pattern seems to hold true for the most part in the data presented here from Bahia in 1835, in the records from Curitiba before 1870, and in the few other studies done elsewhere in Brazil. Occasional exceptions did occur. How frequent and important they were remains a question. In his study of Campinas, Robert Slenes has suggested that the godparentage bond between master and his slaves' children was not uncommon, although he has yet to publish the quantitative evidence for this assertion. Nevertheless, data from Curitiba reveal a few cases, especially after 1871 in which such relationships, or more frequently between relatives of the owner and slaves, were also created. In Curitiba, the percentage of godparents who were related to the master never rose above 6 percent until the period after 1870, when it reached 8 percent of the total. Studies from São Paulo and Paraíba do Sul also note some exceptions. But it should be emphasized that in all these studies the ratio of masters who served as sponsors for their own slaves was under 1 percent of the total. The records of godparentage provide very little evidence of a paternalistic attitude of Brazilian slaveowners toward their slaves.

How can the few cases be reconciled with our original thesis about the incompatibility of ownership and spiritual parenthood? Perhaps the increasing frequency of such ties can be explained by changes in the nature and perception of slavery and possibly by a decreasing role of religion in the definition of everyday life. We can speak of a colonial model in which with only the rarest exceptions, the status of slaveowner and godparent were kept separated because of the perceived incompatibility in the two roles. Within this colonial model, however, distinctions must be drawn between the relationship with Indians who were legally free, although "temporarily" under the protection of Portuguese masters, and Africans and Afro-Brazilians who were legally enslaved. This model would have extended throughout the colonial period and into the first decades of the nineteenth century during the creation of the independent nation of Brazil after 1822.

By the mid-nineteenth century, exceptions to the perception or rule of incompatibility began to increase because religion and the theological meaning of *compadrio* had less impact in the lives of the slaveowning class. In 1871, the Law of Free Birth would have changed the rules governing this relationship. After that date, all children born to slave mothers were considered free and in a state of tutelage until reaching the age of majority. The master-slave relationship, which had formerly been perceived as contradictory to spiritual sponsorship was now replaced by a new status of "temporary bondage" or apprenticeship. This status, despite its sometimes obvious fictional nature, presented justification for masters to now be viewed as mentors or protectors, and therefore in positions not incompatible with the role of godparent. In some ways, after 1871 slave children as *ingenuos*—the term used for these legally free but still bonded people—was not unlike that of Indians in the eighteenth century under the "administration" of settlers. In both cases, the responsibilities of paternalism and tutelage, real or feigned, muted the economic relationship and this connection was reflected in the act and meanings of religious sponsorship.

What is striking then is not the increasing frequency of such ties but in the majority of cases, their continued absence. For both the "administered" Indians in the eighteenth century and that of *ingenuo* children in the last years of slavery, the proportion of spiritually paternal or maternal owners or their relatives remained under 10 percent. In Lugão Rios's study of slaves on coffee estates in Paraíba do Sul from 1872 to 1888, she found only nine instances (9/2,668) when masters sponsored their own slaves. The vast majority of children born to captive mothers, and even more so of slaves baptized as adults, did not have the spiritual guidance or sponsorship of their owners or of their owners' relatives.

The process by which godparents were chosen by slaves or selected by owners remains unknown. Surely, there were variations that placed the initiative sometimes in the hands of slave and sometimes in those of the masters. While certain patterns of selection appeared somewhat constant, such as the choice of other slaves as sponsors for recently arrived Africans and a preference among certain African peoples for ritual sponsors from their own "nation," variations in the patterns of selection over time suggest changes in the dynamics of master-slave relations, attitudes toward the slave community, and in the value placed on reinforcement or enlargement of the slave family in its ritual as well as its legal and consanguineal dimensions.

If these variations were, in fact, the result of changes in demographic, economic, and historical circumstances, then this discussion of godparentage suggests that a separation of the study of the inner workings of the slave community, (*escravidão*) and of slavery as an economic and social system (*escravismo*) is misguided. The formation of *compadrio* relations at the heart of family and spiritual life, like all else within slavery, reflected the essential relations of power within society and economy as a whole. The life lived, the choices made, and the strategies adopted by those who endured slavery were continually shaped and constrained by the pervasiveness and power of the dominant social and economic system and can not be understood without reference to it.

NOTES

1. I have reviewed some of this literature in "The Slave family and the Limitations of Slavery," in *Sugar Plantations and the Formation of Brazilian Society* (Cambridge, 1985), 379–412. A fuller discussion of the major features and findings in the history of the slave family in Brazil is José Flavio Motta, "Família escrava: Uma incursão pela historiografia" (Pa-

per presented to Conference on Slavery and Abolition, São Paulo, 1988). See also Robert Slenes, "Lares negros, olhares brancos: Histórias da família escrava no século xix," *Revista Brasileira da História* 8:16 (1988) 189–203; and his "Escravidão e família: Padrões de Casamento e estabilidade familiar numa communidade escrava (Campinas, século xix), *Estudos Econômicos* 17:2 (1987), 217–28. On travelers' observations, see Iraci del Nero da Costa, "Os viajantes estrangeiros e a família escrava no Brasil," (Paper presented to Conference on Slavery and Abolition, São Paulo, 1988).

2. Herbert Gutman, *The Black Family in Slavery and Freedom, 1750–1925* (New York, 1976); John Blassingame, *The Slave Community* (New York, 1972); Eugene Genovese, *Roll Jordan Roll: The World the Slaves Made* (New York, 1974).

3. The classic articles by Sidney Mintz and Eric Wolf, "An Analysis of Ritual Co-Parenthood," *Southwestern Journal of Anthropology*, 6 (1950), 341–68, and George M. Foster, "Confraria e Compadrazgo in Spain and Spanish America," *Southwestern Journal of Anthropology*, 9 (1953), 1–28, were important statements about the origins and historical changes of ritual godparenthood. Much of the large body of anthropological writing on the topic, however, concentrates on structural or ideological aspects and does not deal with change over time. Probably the most extensive recent study is Hugo Nutini and Betty Bell, *Ritual Kinship: The Structure and Historical Development of the Compadrazgo System in Rural Tlaxcala* 2 vols. (Princeton, 1980–84). The second volume was published by Nutini alone. A recent study on Brazil is Itamar de Souza, *O compadrio: da política ao sexo* (Petrópolis, 1981).

4. Attempts to limit the practice of establishing *compadrio* at the St John's Day bonfires were codified in the *Ordenações filipinas* of 1603. See Liv. 5, tit. 90. For modern observations see Charley Wagley, *Introduction to Brazil* (New York, 1963), 190–92.

5. Stephen Gudeman, "The Compadrazgo as a Reflection of the Natural and Spiritual Person," *Proceedings of the Royal Anthropological Institute* (1972), 45–71; Francisco Chacón Jiménez, "Identidad y parentescos ficticios en la organización social castellana de los siglos xvi y xvii. El ejemplo de Murcia," in *Les parentés fictives en Espagne (xvi–xvii siècles)*, ed. Augustin Redondo (Paris, 1988), 38–50. Interesting historical work has been done on the institution in Italy, see for example, J. Bossy, "Padrini e madrine: Un'istituzione sociale del cristianesimo populare in occidente," *Quaderni storici* 41 (1979); Margherita Pelaja, "Segmenti orizzontali: Madri e madrine a Roma nell'800," in Lucia Ferrante, et. al., *Ragnatele di rapporti. Patronage e reti di relazione nella storia delle donne*. Turin: Centro documentazione donne di bologna, 1988), 417–34.

6. Sebastião Monteiro da Vide, *Constituiçõens Primeyras do Arcebispado da Bahia . .*, (Coimbra, 1720). I have used the edition of Lisbon, 1765.

7. *Constituições primeiras*, tit. x; tit. xiv, n. 50; tit. xviii.

8. *Ordenações do Reino de Portugal,* V, tit. xcix. If a slave refused baptism, the owner was required to inform the parish priest and the slave was required to state his desire to remain unbaptized before witnesses in order for the slaveowner to avoid confiscation of the slave.

9. APB, Ordens régias, 4, doc. 100 (5 March 1697); 13, doc. 72 (7 March 1702).

10. In sixteenth-century Spain, newly baptized Muslim converts were required to have "Old Christian" godparents thus limiting the ability of converted relatives from serving in those roles. See Bartolomé Bennasar, "Les parentés de l'invention: enfants abandonnés et esclaves," in Redondo, *Les parentés fictives en Espagne,* 95–100.

11. Kathleen Higgins," Slave Society in Eighteenth Century Sabará: A Community Study in Colonial Brazil" (Ph.D. diss., Yale University, 1987), 148–50. Dom Pedro de Almeida was an able administrator with broad colonial experience but he was a profound racist who harbored the most negative views about blacks and feared their potential to destroy the colonial regime. He became a strong advocate of restrictions on manumission, inheritance, and free association for people of color, free and slave, as a way of subordinating them.

12. Henry Koster, *Travels in Brazil,* 2 vols. (Philadelphia, 1817), 2: 198–99.

13. "Cleansing Original Sin: Godparentage and Slave Baptism in Eighteenth Century Bahia," in *Kinship Ideology and Practice in Latin America,* ed. Raymond T. Smith (Chapel Hill: University of North Carolina Press, 1984). It has also been published in Portuguese. See Stephen Gudeman and Stuart Schwartz, "Purgando o pecado original: compadrio e batismo de escravos na Bahia no século xviii," in *Escravidão e invencão da liberdade,* ed. João José Reis (São Paulo, 1988), 33–59. The earlier studies are Stuart B. Schwartz, "Indian Labor and New World Plantations: European Demands and Indian Responses in Northeastern Brazil," *American Historical Review* 83:1 (1978), 43–79; Donald Ramos, "A Social History of Ouro Preto" (Ph.D. diss., University of Florida, 1972); David G. Smith, "Cor, ilegitimidade e compadrio na Bahia seiscentista: Os livros de batizado da Conceição da Praia" (Paper presented to third Congress of Bahian History, 1973); Robert Slenes, "Coping with Oppression: Slave Accomodation and Resistance in the Coffee Regions of Brazil, 1850–1888" (Paper delivered to Southern Historical Association, 1978); Robert Slenes and Pedro Carvalho de Mello, "Paternalism and Social Control in a Slave Society: The Coffee Regions of Brazil, 1850–1888" (Paper to 9th World Congress of Sociology, 1978). Subsequent to 1984 are Higgins, "Slave Society in Eighteenth Century Sabará," (1987) which devotes a section of a chapter to godparentage; Eliana Maria Rea Goldschmidt, "Compadrio de Escravos em São Paulo colonial," *Anais de Sociedade Brasileira de Pesquisa Histórica* 7 (1989), 81–83; Ana Maria Lugão Rios, "Famílias escravas e transição: Paraíba do Sul, 1872–1920," Master's thesis, Universidade Federal Fluminense, 1990.

14. The research supporting these statements was organized under

my direction in the Seminar on Social History at the Universidade Federal dô Paraná in 1983. Participating members of the seminar were: António Carlos Ruiz Albergaria, Nelci Lopes da Silva, Cezar Augusto Carneiro Benavides, Estela Maris Araldi, Ana Lucia Cruz, Jorge Luiz da Cunha, Mariza Ribeiro de Oliveira, and Ana Carolina de Paula Muller. The seminar members selected approximately fifty-year periods from 1685 to 1888 and examined the registers of the parish of Nossa Senhora da Luz of Curitiba. Each member presented his or her results in the seminar where the general trends, problems of data, and implications were discussed.

15. "Uma sociedade escravocrata fundada na utilização do trabalho dos indios e africanos ou seus descendentes e mestiços." Octavio Ianni, *As metamorfosis do escravo* (São Paulo, 1962).

16. These figures are taken from the *Mapas de população* cited in Ianni, *As metamorfosis,* 87–88. For alternate and lower figures based on parish registers see, Ana Maria Burmeister, "A população de Curitiba no século xviii" (Ph.D. diss., Universidade Federal do Paraná, 1974). See also Iraci del Nero da Costa and Horácio Gutiérrez, *Paraná. Mapas de habitantes, 1798–1830"* (São Paulo, 1985).

17. Horácio Gutiérrez, "Casamentos nas senzalas. Paraná, 1800–1830," (paper to 1st Seminar, Centenário da Abolição do Escravismo, São Paulo, 1986).

18. Horácio Gutiérrez, "Demografia escrava numa economia não-exportadora: Paraná, 1800–1830," *Estudos Econômicos* 17:2 (1987), 297–314.

19. Horácio Gutiérrez, "Crioulos e africanos no Paraná, 1798–1830," *Revista Brasileira de História* 8:16 (1988), 161–88.

20. Stuart B. Schwartz, "Indian Labor and New World Plantations," 68–71.

21. See John Monteiro, "São Paulo in the Seventeenth Century: Economy and Society," (Ph.d. diss., University of Chicago 1985), 393–96 argues that the transition to African labor in São Paulo took place in the early eighteenth century, but that it was slow and incomplete. See also his "From Indian to Slave: Forced Native Labour and Colonial Society in São Paulo in the Seventeenth Century," *Slavery and Abolition* 9:2 (1988), 105–27; "Celeiro do Brasil: escravidão indígena e a agricultura paulista no século xvii," *História* 7 (1988), 1–12. For comparative purposes see Dauril Alden, "Indian versus Black Slavery in the State of Maranhão during the Seventeenth and Eighteenth Centuries," *Bibliotheca Americana* 1:3 (1983), 91–142.

22. On the market for mules see Herbert S. Klein, "A oferta de muares no Brasil central: O mercado de Sorocaba," *Estudos Econômicos* 19:2 (1989), 347–72.

23. I have discussed the use of the term *negro da terra* or "black of the land" for Indian slaves in Bahia in Schwartz, "Indian labor," 66–68. A parallel discussion appears in Monteiro, "From Indian to Slave," 114. He also notes the use in São Paulo of such terms as *gentio de cabello corredio* (straight-haired heathen) by the end of the seventeenth century.

24. Jesuit writers in Brazil consistently used the Latin term *mancipium* for slave rather than the cognate *servus*.

25. The child, Gonçalo, was described as "nigrinho mina que viera sem se baptizar." His master and godfather was Bernardo Vieira Ravasco, a dominant figure in the city's life and the brother of the famous Jesuit Padre Antônio Vieira, See Smith, "Cor, ilegitimidade, e compadrio," 7.

26. Higgins, "The Slave Society," 173.

27. Because of inconsistencies in the data, I have excluded cases involving libertos and "fictitious," godparents such as saints. Together these cases amounted to less than 1 percent of those sampled. Data in this table was collected by Nelci Lopes da Silva, Jorge Luiz da Cunha, Estela Maris Araldi, and Antonio Carlos Ruiz Albergaria.

28. See Kátia M. de Queirós Mattoso, *Bahia: A cidade do Salvador e seu mercado no século xix* (São Paulo, 1978), 39–60 for a discussion of Santiago de Iguape.

29. "Relação do numero de fogos e moradores do districto de Santiago Maior do Iguape," APB, Policia 6175. The census of 1835 was brought to my attention by Bert Barickman who is presently completing a doctoral thesis at the University of Illinois. The census has been integrated with parish register data and is presently being analyzed by students at the Social History Research Laboratory, University of Minnesota. A first result of this project is Arlene Díaz and Jeffrey Stewart, "Occupational Status and Female-Headed Households in Santiago Maior do Iguape, Bahia, 1835" (Paper presented to Social Science History Association, 1989).

30. See João José Reis, *Rebelião escrava no Brasil* (São Paulo, 1986), 13–87, for a discussion of the period and the conditions in Bahia. Also see his historiographical discussion in "Um balanço dos estudos sobre as revoltas escravas da Bahia," in *Escravidão e invenção da liberdade* ed. João José Reis (São Paulo, 1988), 86–140.

31. Juiz de Fora, Antônio Vaz de Carvalho to President of the Province (Cachoeira, 17 January 1827), APB, Pres. da prov. Juizes Cachoeira, maço 2270.

32. Nuno Eugenio de Subtil to Presidente da Provincia (Cachoeira, 25 March 1827), APB, Pres. da Prov. Juizes Cachoeira 2270.

33. Juiz de Fora Antônio Vaz do Carvalho to Col. Manuel Ignacio de Cunha e Meneses (1828), APB, Pres. da Prov. Juizes Cachoeira 2270; Juiz de Fora José Pais Cardoso da Silva to Pres. da Prov. (24 September 1828), Ibid.

6 Reconsiderations

Two themes serve as central threads joining the disparate essays presented in this volume. These two themes intertwine in complex ways and while sometimes seeming to conflict they actually represent a tension that runs through much of the modern historiography of slavery, not only in Brazil but elsewhere as well. The first theme is the pervasive and pernicious nature of slavery as a social and economic system, and as a structure that, so long as it remained vigorous, determined the contours of all else in Brazilian life. In effect, to consider the history of slavery in Brazil is to deal with the history of Brazil itself.

For almost four centuries slavery played such a central role in the historical development of the country that it was virtually impossible to separate any aspect of human experience from it. The institution of slavery provided a structure to social and economic relations, a setting for political decisions and actions, and a context for cultural phenomena. No one who lived in Brazil was ever far from the shadow it cast or free from its influence. Women or men, laity and ecclesiastics, free workers or slave, local markets as well as international trade, no aspect of Brazilian life remained untouched by the phenomenon. John Mawe, an English traveler to Brazil, wrote in 1812 that whenever he had a question about how something was done, a slave was sent for to provide the answer. Mawe saw in this dependence the damaging influence of slavery on "progress" in Brazilian life. He reflected: "This aversion to improvement I have often observed among the inhabitants of Brazil; when, for instance, I have questioned a brick-maker, a sugar-maker, a soup-boiler, or even a miner, his reasons for conducting his concern in such an imperfect manner, I have been almost invariably referred to a Negro for answers to my interrogatories."[1]

Slavery was omnipresent. If the power and pervasiveness of

slavery emerges from these essays, so too does the ability of slaves, often under the most difficult of circumstances, to influence the conditions of their lives and to exercise some control over their day to day existence. Whether in seeking manumission, striving for some degree of productive autonomy, creating familial ties and group associations, choosing or accepting godparents, or resisting slavery, the story of slaves as actors and not simply as a category of labor or the object of oppression provides the second theme to these essays as it does to much of the recent historiography of Brazilian slavery. Here we may ask whether recognizing the complexity of human relations within slavery and the varying strategies of slaves and masters to pursue their interests detracts from an understanding of slavery's power as an institution, as an economic system, and as the fundamental structure of social organization.

This tension and contrast between slavery as a pervasive system and the actions of slaves, masters, and others in shaping its contours is really an aspect of a long and unresolved debate among historians and sociologists over the roles of human action or "agency" and social, political, and economic structures in explaining society. Did Napoleon make his age or was he the product of his times? Did the collective action of slaves seeking freedom through manumission create the structures that made manumission possible, or was it the other way around? In a sense, the division between slavery as a system and the internal aspects of slave life and society, between *escravismo* and *escravidão*, is another form of the agency versus structure debate. In the essays presented here, I have sought to demonstrate that this division creates a false dichotomy, prejudicial to an understanding of how slavery worked.

First, clearly the actions of slaves were constrained in many ways by the structure of Brazilian slavery, but that structure was itself partially the product of what was possible to demand or extract from the slaves. In chapter 2, I sought to demonstrate not only how the plantation work regime set the contours of slave life but also how slave goals and aspirations could be used to make that regime function smoothly. I do not wish to deny the agency of slaves nor to denigrate their struggle to improve their lives, but rather to show how masters could use that struggle, at least in the short term, to achieve their own goals. Whether the use of such techniques by the slave owners eventually created a series of contradictions that contributed to the fall of slavery itself is another question. In chapter 2, I also suggested that certain aspirations of the slaves, such as their desire for autonomy in food production, were not constants, but were themselves influenced by market conditions that existed in late eighteenth-century Brazil. Slavery as an institution was also part of the historical process, and slaves did not live in an unchanging "ethnographic present."

These historical events—changing market opportunities, created by international demand for Brazilian products, a growing urban population, and an expansion of the slave trade—provided the context for the following chapter on "Peasants and Slavery." Here I shifted the focus to small-scale food producers who had always been marginal to the export-oriented economy and slavery, but who were drawn into slaveowning when conditions were favorable. The power and pervasiveness of slavery in structuring human action even among these people who had previously been for the most part outside the institution was one conclusion that could be drawn from this evidence.

In the final two chapters of this volume I concentrated on the actions of slaves, but once again within the context of the structures that ordered their lives. In my discussion of slave resistance, it is clear that those structures were not limited to the institution of slavery under which the fugitives had labored, but also included cultural ones brought from Africa and modified or redefined in Brazil. *Quilombos* starkly represented the struggle of human agency against the dominating structure of slavery, but once in flight and rejoined in groups, other structures emerged or were recreated to guide and direct human action.

In the discussion of the spiritual kinship of slaves, the interplay of cultural constraints and the self-interests of masters and slaves are examined in the context of the slave family. Here, within what has come to be seen as an area of life in which slave initiative and action is easily perceived, I argued that patterns observed in the selection of godparents reflected choices made by masters and slaves. Moreover, these patterns changed over time, reflecting the legal status of the captives, the justification of slavery as an institution, and changing relations between free persons and slaves brought about by the violence of slave rebellions and slaveowner repression.

There are some who are made uncomfortable by a recognition of the slaves' ability to be historical actors and to have exercised some influence on their lives; as though such recognition subverts an understanding of slavery as a system, or excuses its basically exploitative and destructive nature.[2] These essays are in no way exculpatory. Rather, I have sought to deal with slavery as essentially a constantly shifting relationship between masters and slaves within the framework of juridical, cultural, and economic realities that formed its structure. This relationship reflected the unequal distribution of power within society to be sure, but in many ways those enslaved constantly sought to shape their lives and reshape the limitations on their hopes. To lose sight of this struggle is to surrender too much to a system that had already extracted more than enough from those who endured it, and continued to do so from those who came after.

NOTES

1. John Mawe, *Travels in the Interior of Brazil* (London, 1812), 135.

2. Jacob Gorender, *A escravidão reabilitada* (São Paulo, 1990). Gorender's volume is essentially an attack on the mounting evidence of slave initiatives and on the evidence of considerable variability over time and within slave regimes. Gorender believes that undue emphasis on these variations has rehabilitated a benign view of slavery and has detracted from an understanding of its brutality and exploitative nature.

INDEX

Abolition, 16, 18, 20

Acontundá, 17

Administrados, 146, 147

Africa: defenses used in, 116; number of slaves from, 69, 70

African martial arts clubs (capoeira), 15

Africans, baptisms of, 144, 145; and contacts with Christian conversion, 17; ratio of, to crioulos, 41; freed, 18

Afro-Ásia, 17

Afro-Brazilians: baptisms of, 144, 145; percentage of, in Minas Gerais, 118

Afro-Indian cooperation, 111

Agregados, 71

Agriculture: commercialization of, 76, 77, 78, 80; expansion of, 79; export, 74, 75, 76, 80, 85, 89; functions of, 66; peasant, 66; plantation, 76; slash and burn, 76; slave-based, 68, 92; small-scale, 75, 79, 80, 81, 90, 163; subsistence, 71, 76, 85

Aimoré Indians, 107

Alagoas, 104, 122

Alden, Dauril, 9, 13, 22, 30

Alencastro, Luiz-Felipe de, 12, 22–23

Almeida, Pedro de, Count of Assumar, 119, 120, 122, 140, 158n11

Almeida Barbosa, Waldemar de, 14, 23

Alqueires, 61; definition of, 62n3

Alves Filho, Ivan, 23

Amaral Lapa, José Roberto do, 7, 23

Ambrósio, quilombo of, 121

American Revolution, 68

Andrade, Carlos Otávio de, 34

Andrews, George Reid, 19, 23

Angola, 80, 125, 126, 127, 128

Antonil, André João, 40, 143

Aragão, Garcia Davila Pereira de, 56n11

Arcos, Count of. See Noronha, Marcos de, Count of Arcos

Areias, 76

Arquivo Nacional, 20; Departamento da Imprensa Nacional, 23

Assumar, Count of. See Almeida, Pedro de, Count of Assumar

Atibaia, 76

"Atlantic Revolution," 15

Aufderheide, Patricia Ann, 15, 23

Aveiro, Duke of, 131n19

Azevedo, Paulo Cesar de, 20, 23

Backwoodsmen (bandeirantes), 108

Bahia, 14, 41, 75, 84, 154; and anti-quilombo operations, 119; compadrio relationships in, 141, 148; food and provisions, 79, 82, 89; fugitive communities in, 104; linguistic differences with Minas Gerais, 121–22; and manioc production, 85, 91; mocambos in, 106–7; number of slaves in 72, 105; and pardos, 71; and slave imports, 68; slave revolts in, 152; and slave sex ratios, 73–74; and slaves for small-scale farming, 90, 92; and sugar 9, 80; and use of word mocambo, 121; Yoruba cult in, 16, 17

Bahian Recôncavo. See Recôncavo

Bandeira, Pedro Rodrigues, 153

Bantus (people), 114
Baptismal registers, 145
Baptisms 140, 141, 144–45, 151, 158n10;
    adult, 153–54; code for, 139; refusal
    of, 158n8
Barbados, 40
Barbosa, Francisco de Assis, 20, 29
Barickman, Bert, 160n29
Barros de Castro, Antônio, 7, 8, 23
Barros dos Santos, Ana Maria, 14, 23
Baskets (*tipitís*), 61, 62n3
Bastide, Roger, 23; *African Religions in
    Brazil,* 16
Battell, Andrew, 127
Bay of All Saints, 152
Beans, 78, 86, 88
Beiguelman, Paula, 4, 23
Benedictine Order, 56n6
Benedictines, and Santana, 58–59n42
Berrance de Castro, Jeanne, 24
Bethell, Leslie, 12, 24
Binder, Wolfgang, 31
"Black Troy," 122
Blackburn, Robin, 20, 24
Blacks (*escravos*), 147
Blassingame, John, 138
Boiling houses (*fábricas*), 42, 43, 47
Boipeba, food sources for, 84–85
Borges Martins, Roberto, 10, 24
Boschi, Caio César, 17, 24
Boxer, Charles R., 4, 24
Brazil: and contraband trade with Eng-
    land, 68; exports from, 68; popula-
    tion groups in, 71; population map
    of, 70; slave imports to, 74; studies
    on, 40; sugar production in, 40; syn-
    od of 1707, 139
"Brazil system," 83
"Brazilian Brazilianists," 6
"Brazilianists," 5
Brotherhoods of Our Lady of the Rosa-
    ry, 140
Brunel, A., 26
Buraco de Tatú (Armadillo's Hole), de-
    struction of, 112–13, 114, 116–17, 124
Bush captain (*capitão de campo*): and
    anit-*quilombo* operations, 119; as
    fugitive slave hunters, 109; types of,
    110

Cacao, 68

Cachoeira, 17, 152
Cadornega, Antônio de Oliveira de, 128
Cairú: and Aimoré Indians, 107; black
    militiamen against, 130n10; food
    sources for, 84–85; and fugitive
    slaves, 108; and manioc production,
    90, 91; and *mocambos,* 105, 113
Calendar, religious, 43
Camamú: and Aimoré Indians, 107;
    black militiamen against, 130n10;
    food sources for, 84–85; and fugitive
    slaves, 108; and *mocambo* forma-
    tion, 105
Câmara Coutinho, Antônio Luiz Gon-
    çalves, 130n13
Caminho de Viamao, 78
Campinas, 18, 154
Campos (Rio de Janeiro), 15, 47
"Campos curitibanos," 143
Campos Graf, Márcia Elisa de, 21, 24
Camps, initiation, 128
Cano, Wilson, 10, 24
"Capitão das entradas," 131n18
Capitães do campo, 130n16
Capitães do mato, 109, 119, 130n16,
    131n18
*Capitães mor das entradas dos mo-
    cambos,* 130n16
Capitalism, development of, 7
Carcanhas (*calcanhas*), 63n7
Cardoso, Ciro Flamarion S., 7, 8, 9, 24
Cardoso, Fernando Henrique, 4, 24
Caribbean, plantation colonies of, 65
Carneiro, Edison, 14, 16, 24
Carneiro da Cunha, Manuela, 7, 18, 20,
    24–25
Carreira, Antônio, 12, 13, 25, 29
Carvalho de Mello, Pedro, 9, 13, 25
Carvalho Franco, Maria Sylvia de, 18,
    25
Casting nets (*tarrafa*), 61, 62n1
Cattle, 77, 78, 81, 85; *fazendas,* 78;
    shift of production to, in Curitiba,
    143
Cattle ranches, slaves on, 39
Cavazzi, Antonio, 116
Celeiro Público. See Public granary
Centro de Estudos de Demografia His-
    tórica da America Latina, Univerity
    of, São Paulo, 8
Charque. See Meat, dried salted

Cheese, 81
Chiavento, Juilo José, 14, 25
Children, number of, 58n35
Christiano, Jr., 20
Circumcision, 126–27
"Clayed" sugar, 40
Clocks, 43
Coastal shipping (*cabotagem*) 75
Coffee, 68, 76; plantations, 73, 75, 80, 156; planters in Vassouras, 83
Color, hierarchy of, 44
"Compadres da fogueira," 139
Compadrio. See Godparentage
Conceião da Praia, parish of, 147
Congo, Manuel, revolt of, 15
Conrad, Robert Edgar, 12, 18, 19, 20, 25
Conselho Ultramarino, 130n13
Constituicões primeiras do Arcebispado da Bahia in 1720, 139
Constraints, cultural and moral, 42
Cordeiro, Belchior, 111
Corn. *See* Maize
Cortes de Oliveira, Maria Inês, 17, 25
Cosme, Miguel, 117
Costa Cardoso, Joaquim da, 113, 116
Cotton, 68, 72, 80, 81, 89
Council of Trent, 150; and baptismal sponsorship, 139
Couples, Azorean, as small-scale farmers, 78, 79
Crioulos, 47, 48, 114; and ration of to Africans, 41; definition of, 41; and earnings used for escape, 47; in Paraná, 144
Culture, Afro-Brazilian, 16
Curitiba (Paraná), 8, 21, 77, 78, 142, 153, 154; and masters as godparents, 148; population of, 143, slave sex ratio in, 143–44
"Curitibanos, campos gerais," 77
Curtin, Philip D., 12, 25

Daily quotas (*tarefas*), 42, 43, 45, 47, 48, 61, 62n2
Davis, David B., 3, 4, 25
Dean, Warren, 14, 25
Degler, Carl, 3, 18, 25
Demographic conditions, negative, 11
Demography, historical, 8
Dependency theory, 65–66
Diamonds, 80

Dias, Daniel, 131n18
Dias, Henrique, 112
Dias Tavares, Luís Henrique, 12, 25
Diegues, Carlos, 134n64
Diet, and ratio of manioc to maize, 67
Dos Santos, D. M., 16
Drescher, Seymour, 20, 26
Dutch Brazil, 12

East Africa (Mozambique), slaves from, 73
Eisenberg, Peter L., 14, 18, 19, 26
Elbein dos Santos, Juana, 16, 26
Elkins, Stanley, 3, 26
Ellis, Myriam, 14, 26
Eltis, David, 13, 26, 73
Engenhos, 40; living conditions on, 41; social hierarchy of, 48
Enlightenment, 7
Ennes, Ernesto, 14, 26
Escravidão. See Slavery, internal nature of
Escravismo. See Slave system, impact of
Espírito Santo, 19
Estudos Econômicos, 11, 16
Eveleth, Phyllis B., 26
Export products, 81
Exports, slave-produced, 68

Fábrica, workers in, 44
Falcon, Francisco C., 7, 26
Fernandes, Florestan, 4, 10, 23, 26
Fernando, José de Portugal, Governor, 131n16
Ferreira da Câmara, Manoel, 85
Ferreira de Almeida, Vilma Paraíso, 19, 26
Figueiredo, Ariosvaldo, 14, 27
Figueiredo, Manoel da, 52
Filho, Alves, 14
Firewood, 61, 62n6
First-birth, age of, 56n35
Florentino, Manolo G., 11, 27
Food production, 69, 85
Food supply, shortage of, 84, 86, 88, 89
Fragoso, João Luis, 11, 27
Free people of color, 18, 94n13; as godparents, 142, 153; mortality rates of, 71; numbers of, 71, 118; as preachers, 140; and slave ownership, 119;

Free people of color, *continued*
  terms for, 71
Freitas, Décio, 14, 27
Freitas Brandão, Júlio de, 7, 27
French Antilles, 40
Freyre, Gilberto, 3, 6, 10, 16, 20, 27;
  Casa grande e senzla (*The Masters
  and the Slaves*), 2; criticism of, 4
Fuba, 67
Fugitive communities (*mocambos, lad-
  eiras, magotes, quilombos*), 103; de-
  scription of, 117; goals of, 113–114.
  See also Mocambos; Quilombos
Fugitive slaves, 103, 104, 108, 112; ac-
  tivites of, 109; aid to, 113; branding
  of, 117; description of, 105; detec-
  tion of, 118; expeditions against,
  107; punishment of, 117, 120; and
  "Treaty of Peace" of Santana, 53

Galloway, J. H., 19
Gama Lima, Lana Lage, 15, 27
Ganga Zumba, "king" of Palmares,
  123, 127
Ganga Zumba, mother of, 124
"Ganga Zumba" (motion picture),
  134n64
Garden plots, 45, 46, 47, 49
Gebara, Ademir, 19, 27
Genovese, Eugene, 3, 15, 27, 43, 138
"Gentiles," 130n6
Gentio de cabello corredio (straight-
  haired heathen), 159n23
Giacomini, Sonia Maria, 18
Godparentage (*compadrio*), 11, 138, 139,
  155, 156; pattern of, 149–150, 152,
  153
Godparents: free, 148, 149, 152; selec-
  tion of, 147–48, 156, 163; and rank-
  ing of sponsorship, 142; for slaves,
  148
Goiás, 14, 71
Gold, 39, 80, 118
"Golden Law" (May 13, 1888), 1
Goldhammer, Arthur, 31
Goldschmidt, Eliana, 11, 27, 141
Gomes de Silveira, Duarte, 110
Gomes, Freire de Andrada, Governor,
  121
Gonçalves Salvador, José, 12, 27

Gorender, Jacob, 8, 27; *O escravismo
  colonial*, 7
Goulart, José Alípio, 27; *Da fuga ao
  suicídio*, 14
Goulart, Mauricio, 12, 27
Graham, Richard, 10, 13, 19, 27–28
Gregório Luís (slave), 53, 59, 60
"Guarapuava, campos de," 78
Guaratinguetá, 77
Gudeman, Stephen, 11, 28, 141, 142,
  150, 152, 154
Guindadeiras, 63n7
Gutiérrez, Horácio, 9, 10, 28, 33
Gutman, Herbert, 138; *The Black Fam-
  ily in Slavery and Freedom*, 10

Hahn, Steven, 20, 28
Haiti, and fugitive slaves, 104
Harris, Marvin, 3, 4, 28
Harvest (*safra*), 41, 43
Hell, Jurgen, 7, 28
Hides, 68, 80
Higgins, Kathleen, 141, 148, 154
Historians, cliometric, 13
Historiography, Brazilian, 5; North
  American, 10
History, postemancipation, 3; profes-
  sionalization of, 5
Hogs, 81
Holidays, 81
Holidays, religious, 42
Holloway, Thomas H., 15, 28

Ianni, Octávio, 4, 28
Iguape. *See* Santiago de Iguape
Ilhéus, 50, 51, 88; food sources for, 85;
  and fugitive document, 59; and *mocambo* formation, 105; *ouvidor* of,
  90; rebellious slaves in, 84
Imbangala (people), 126, 127
Incentives, system of, 48
Indians, 2, 109, 123; baptisms of, 144,
  145; as part of labor force, 111, 144,
  146; as slave catchers, 108, 110, 119;
  as slaves, 13, 144, 147; treatment of,
  147
Indigo, 68
Infrastructure, development of, 75, 76,
  77
Ingenuos, 155; definition of, 149

Inquisition, 56n11; records of, 17
Institute of African Studies, University of Bahia, 16–17
Instituto de Pesquisas Econômicas, University of São Paulo, 9
Ipitanga, *mocambos* in, 113
Itapoam, *mocambos* in, 113

Jagas (people), 126, 128; and Palmares, 135–36n81
Jaguaripe, 85–86, 90
Jamaica, 49, 123; and fugitive slaves, 104, 112
Jesuits, 52, 56n6; and the Indians, 110; and Santana, 51, 58–59n42
João Baptista (farmer), 113, 117
Joaquim (slave), 56n9
Judicial records, use of, 15

Karasch, Mary C., 9, 14, 18, 28
Kasange, kingdom of, 126, 128
Ki-lombos, 126, 127; ritual laws of, 127–28
Kiernan, James, 18, 28
Kimpasi, 128
Kiple, Kenneth, 9, 28–29
Kitanga, Lunda state in, 125
Klein, Herbert S., 3, 18, 19, 29; *Middle Passage*, 12
Kokos (people), 114
Kolchin, Peter, 20, 29
Kongo, kingdom of, 125; initiation camps of, 128
Koster, Henry, 46, 47, 48, 140; on baptism, 141; on slave provisions, 49–50
Kuznesof, Elizabeth Anne, 9, 29
Kwango river basin, 126

Labat, Jean Baptiste, 40
Labor force, urban, 14
Lacombe, Américo Jacobina, 20, 29
Lara, Silvia Hunold, 15, 29
Latour da Veiga Pinto, Françoise, 13, 29
Lauderdale Graham, Sandra, 18, 29
Law of Free Birth (1871), 149, 155
Leff, Nathaniel H., 19, 29
Leonardo (crioulo), 117
Levy, Bárbara, 18, 29
Libby, Douglas Cole, 13, 30

Libertos (former slaves), 18
Ligon, Richard, 40
Linhares, Count of, 51, 131n19
Linhares, Maria Yedda, 18, 30
Lisbon, Overseas Council in, 120
Lissovsky, Maurício, 20, 23
Lopes, José, 117
Lugão Rios, Ana Maria, 141, 156

Mabeas (people), 114
Machado Monteiro, Helena, 15, 30
MacLachlan, Colin M., 7, 13, 30
Maestri Filho, Mário José, 14, 21, 30
Maeyama, Takashi, 8, 30
Magi a samba, 127
Maize, 67, 78, 86; production of, 93n7; purchases of, 88
Majuro, Frédéric, 31
Malê rebellion of 1835, 15, 47, 103
Manchester, Alan, 12
Mancipium, 160n24
Mandingas (people), 114
Mandingueiros, 114
Manioc, 67, 82, 83, 84, 88, 90, 99n61, 105; cultivation of, 52, 84, 89; daily quota of, 61; flour, 49, 69, 82, 85, 86, 88, 89; harvest and production of, 89, 90, 91, 93n7, 98n51
Mantiqueira range, 80
Manumission, 17, 18, 71, 94n14, 162; as an incentive, 48; limitation in number of, 119; refusal of, 47; self-purchase of, 46, 47, 56n13
Maragogipe: manioc production in, 90, 91; as source of foodstuffs, 85–86
Maranhão, 12, 54, 59, 60, 68
Marchiori Bakos, Margaret, 19, 30
Marcílio, Marcia Beatriz, 10
Marcílio, Maria Luiza, 13, 30–31; *La ville de São Paulo*, 8
Marcos dos Santos, Ronaldo, 19, 31
Mariana, *câmara* of, 120
Marinho de Azevdeo, Celia Maria, 20, 31
Martins, Roberto B., 31
Martins Filho, Amilcar, 10, 31
Marxism, 7
Mascarenhas, Jorge de, Marquis of Montalvão, 112

Masters: as godparents, 142, 147, 148, 154; relatives of, as godparents, 142, 147, 148; and slaves, 2, 15, 163–64
Matamba, kingdom of, 126, 128
Matheus, Morgado de, 76
Mattos, Gregório de, 125
Mattos de Castro, Hebe Maria, 19, 31
Mattoso, Katia M. de Queirós, 11, 14, 17, 18, 31
Maurits, Johan, of Nassau, 84
Mauro, Frédéric, 7
Mawe, John, 161
Mbundu states, 128
Mbundus (people), 126
Meat, dried salted (*charque*), 14, 49, 79, 80, 81
Medeiros dos Santos, Corcino, 12, 31
Mello e Souza, Laura de, 17, 18, 31
Menard, Russell, 13, 31
Medonça, Afonso Furtado do Castro do Rio, 108
Mentalities, 17
Mesquita Samar, Eni de, 10, 31–32
Mestiços, 71
Metcalf, Alida C., 11, 32
Mezan Algranti, Leila, 15, 32
Miller, Joseph, 12, 31, 127
Mills: operation of, 41; work rhythm in, 43
Minas Gerais, 14, 59, 73, 75, 76, 143; adult baptisms in, 154; and *acontundá*, 17; and circumvention of the law, 140; and free people of color, 120; free population of, 81; and fugitives, 104, 109, 120; growth of, 10, 71; insecurity and fear in, 118; linguistic differences with Bahia, 121–22; and maize, 67; and masters as godparents, 148; and markets, 80; mining in, 118; and *pardos*, 71; peasantry in, 71, 81; population of, 118; and *quilombos*, 121; and small-scale agriculture, 81, 90, 92; and slave sex ratios, 73; slaves and slavery in, 9, 80, 81, 82
Mines and mining, 14, 39, 76, 80, 120, 143
Miscegenation, 2
Mocambos, 104; and abduction of women, 113; in Bahia, 106–7; de-struction of, 110, 111, 112, 120, 131n23; formation of, 121; location and size of, 108; as social protest, 109; white cooperation with, 118
Moedeiras, 63n7
Monteiro, John, 32, 141
Moradores, 71
Mott, Luis R. B., 14, 17, 20, 32–33
Moura, Alexandre de, 109
Moura, Clóvis, 5, 14, 33
Mulattoes, 47, 48
Mule trains (*tropas*), 77, 81
O mundo que o português criou, 2
Muslims: baptism of converts, 158n10

Nagos (people), 154
Napoleon, 162
National Council of Scientific and Technological Development, The (CNPq), 1
National Guard, 17
Ndongo, kingdom of, 125
Negro da terra, 159n23
Nero da Costa, Iraci del, 9, 10, 33, 38
"New Road" (Caminho novo), from Rio to Minas Gerais, 76
Nganga a nzumbi, 127
Nina Rodrigues, Raymundo, 16, 33
Nizza da Silva, Maria Beatriz, 10, 33
Noronha, Maros de, Count of Arcos, 113, 120
Nossa Senhora da Luz dos Pinhais de Curitiba, parish of, 143, 145, 148, 159n14
Novais, Fernando A., 6, 7, 13, 26, 33
Novinsky, Anita, 33
Nzinga, Queen, 126

Obidos, Count of, 112
Olinda, town council of, 129n4
Oliveira Portocarrero de Castro, Helio, 13, 33
Ordenações filipinas (1603), 140
Oscar, João, 14, 33

Palacin, Luís, 14, 34
Palmares, *quilombo* of, 14, 103, 104, 108, 116, 122–25, 135–36n81
"Palmas, campos de," 78
Pará, 12, 14

Paraguayan War, 19
Paraíba, river valley of, 14
Paraíba do Sul (Rio de Janeiro), 19, 141, 154, 156
Paraná, 4, 75, 77, 78; data from, 9; and dependence on slavery, 68; and Indian labor, 144, 146; population of, 97n38; and shift to African slave force, 146; slave sex ratio in, 143; as supplier to internal markets, 78
Paranaguá, 12, 78
Paraty, 18
Pardos, 71, 153
Parish registers, 141, 144
Paternalism, 148, 152
Patriarchalism, 5
Paty do Alferes, Barao do, 36
Peace treaty, 60, 61–62
"Peasant breach," 8, 49–50, 83
Peasantry: growth of, 68, 86; and manioc, 67, 89, 92; in Minas Gerais, 81; origin of, 66; and provisioning, 67, 74, 75; as a "telluric" population, 66; terms for, 66, 71, 93n4; variation in situation of, 71–72
Pedreira, Pedro Tomás, 14, 34
Pedro II, King of Portugal, 19
Peixoto de Lacerda, Francisco, 36
Pereira da Costa, Claudio José, 61
Pereira dos Santos, Mariano, 21
Pereira Toledo Machado, Maria Helena, 15, 34
Pernambuco, 12, 14, 19, 82, 84, 85, 109; as consumer of *charque,* 79; and *pardos,* 71; population of, 123; and slave sex ratios, 74; sugar planters of, 80
Pessoa de Castro, Yeda, 16, 34
Petite marronage, 104, 129n4
Piahuy, José, 117
Piauí, 14
Pilatti Balhana, Altiva, 8
Pinaud, João Luiz, 15, 34
Pinheiro, Paulo Sérgio, 34
Pinto Venâncio, Renato, 8, 34
Plantations, work regime on, 162
Planters: and export crops, 83; and purchase of foodstuffs, 82, 85; and social control, 83–84
Plate, River, 78

Police records, use of, 15
Pombal, Marquis of, 67
Ponte, Conde do, 114
Pontes, Felisberto Brant, Marquês de Barbacena, 58n32
Popular culture, 17
Population: growth of, 69; and slave ratio, 79
Porto Calvo, 134–35n68
Porto Seguro, 88
Portugal, Fernando José de, 88
Portugal, and Brazilian exports, 80
Postma, Johannes Menne, 12, 34
Povolide, Count of, 86
Prado, Jr., Caio, 7, 34
Prefeitura Municipal do Salvador, 20
Priests, as sponsors, 139
Prisoners, auction of, 110
Prohibitions, religious, 42
Prostitution, 119
Public granary (*Celeiro Público*), 87, 88, creation of, 86
Putnam, Samuel, 27

Queirós Mattoso, Katia de, 17
Querino, Manuel, 16, 34
"Quilombo" (motion picture), 134n64
Quilombo Grande, 121
Quilombos, 14, 112, 163; Angolan, 116; definition of, 119, 121, 125, 128; formation of, 133n44; illustration of, 115; numbers of, 119; rutitual aspects of, 128
"Quinta comarca," 77
Quota system. *See* Daily quotas (*tarefas*)

Race relations, differences in, 3
Ramos, Artur, 16, 34
Ramos, Donald, 10, 34
Recife, 68, 72
Recôncavo, 84, 85–86, 142, 152
Reis, Jaime, 19, 34
Reis, João José, 8, 15, 17, 21, 34–35
Reis de Queiroz, Suely R., 14, 16, 19, 35
Religion, role of, 155
Religious brotherhoods (*irmandades*), 17, 140

Republic, centenary of establishment
of, 2
Revisionism, 4
Rewards, for return of fugitives, 119
Ribeiro Júnior, José, 12, 35
Ribeira da Vasabarris, and manioc production, 91
Rice, 54, 78, 86, 88, 98n52
Rio de Janeiro, 12, 17, 18, 78, 143; and
Angola, 73; and autonomy of Africans, 54; captaincy of, 75; consumer
of *charque*, 79; and domestic labor,
18; food prices in, 83; and grain exports, 70; growth of, 72, 75, 77; and
manumission, 18; markets of, 80,
145; Province of, 14; slave crime in,
15; slave demography in, 9; and
slave imports, 68, 73; and slave sex
ratios, 73
Rio Grande do São Pedro. *See* Rio
Grande do Sul
Rio Grande do Sul, 4, 14, 19, 75, 77;
cattle from, 79, 145; and dependence on slavery, 68; growth of, 79;
markets of, 78, 80; slave population
of, 73; and slave sex ratios, 73
Rothwell, Arthur, 26
Routes, transport, 80–81
Rum, 82
Russell-Wood, A. J. R., 7, 17, 35
São Cristóvão, and manioc production,
91
São Gonçalo (Rio de Janeiro), 82
São João, Indians from, 110
São José do Açu, 152
São Luis de Maranhão, 72–73
São Paulo, 14, 15, 19, 78, 143; and dependence on slavery, 68; godparentage of slaves in, 141, 154; growth
of, 72, 77; and Indians 123, 141,
144; markets of, 145; peasantry (*caipira paulista*) of, 71, 75–76; popula-
tion structure of, 9; and slaves for
small-scale farming, 90, 92; and subsistence agriculture, 76; and sugar
and coffee exports, 76; women in,
18
"São Paulo School" of scholars, 4
Sabará, 141, 154
Saes, Décio, 19, 35

Saints, as sponsors, 150
Salaries, 44
Salles, Ricardo, 19
Salles, Vicente, 14, 35
Salt, royal monopoly on, 79
Salvador, 54, 75, 84, 143, 147; and autonomy of Africans, 54; baptisms
in, 154; *câmara* (town coucil) of, 86,
99n60, 99n61, 109, 112, 125; *Celeiro
Público* of, 86, 87, 88; food prices
in, 83; food sources for, 84–85;
growth of, 72; Malê rebellion in, 15,
47
Salvador, Vicente do, 92
Santa Catarina, 75
Santana de Paranaíba, 51, 77; and the
Benedictines, 58–59n42; Brazilian-
born slaves at, 52, 53; document
concerning, 50, 59–61; family life of
slaves, 52, 53; and the Jesuits, 51,
58–59n42; level of productivity, 51;
and expanded manioc production,
92; revolt of slaves at, 51, 53; sex
ratio of slaves, 52, 53; size of slave
force, 51; treaty of, 50–51, 61–62
Santiago de Iguape (Bahia), parish of,
143, 152, 153, 154, 160n29
Santidade religion, 111
Santo Amaro, *câmara* of, 89
Santos, 76
Sawyer, occupation of, 62n5
Scarano, Julita, 17, 35
Scholars, Brazilian and Brazilianists, 5
Schwarcz, L. Moritz, 20
Schwartz, Stuart B., 9, 11, 13, 14, 18,
20, 28, 31, 36, 141, 142, 150, 152,
154
Scott, Rebecca, 20, 26, 36
Seminar on Social History, Universi-
dade Federal do Paraná, 159n14
Sergipe de El-Rey, 14, 85, 131n18; and
fugitive slaves, 108; and manioc
production, 90, 91
Serinhaem, 74, 82
Ship owners, and purchase of food-
stuffs, 85
Silva, Eduardo, 8, 20, 29, 35, 36
Silva, Marlene Rosa Nogueira, 14, 36
Silva Dias, Maria Odila Leite da, 18, 36
Silva Ferreira, Manoel da, 51, 59, 61

Silva Lisboa, José da, 82, 85
Silva Machado, João da, (later Baron of Antonina), 78
Silva Maia, José da, 59
Silva Prado, Antônio da (later Baron of Iguape), 78
Silva Santos, João da, 60
Skiles, Jacqueline D., 26
Skills and training, hierarchy of, 48
"Slave Protest," 16
Slave trade, 11, 12, 41, 72, 74, 85, 144
Slavery, as a social and economic system, 161
Slavery, 1, 4, 5, 6, 7, 9; dependence on, 72; documents on, 20; economic history of, 13; expansion of, 68, 75; Freyre's patriarchal model of, 6; influence of, 161; internal nature of (*escravidão*), 6, 156, 162; opposition to, 103, 124; power of, 161–62; profitability of, 9, 13; regional studies of, 14; and social and economic conditions, 15; as a system (*escravismo*), 6, 4, 156, 162, 163
Slaves, 5, 8, 53, 71, 73, 162, 163; African, 11, 44, 139, 159n21; and agriculture, 48, 75, 79, 82, 83, 90, 92, 105, 107; and autonomy, 48, 49, 53, 54; baptism of, 140, 141, 151, 154; cost of, 13; and crime, 15; *crioulo*, 44; and culture, 16; and dried meat production, 79–80; earnings of, 47, 84; and family life, 2, 10, 11, 41, 46; and family names, 52; fertility of, 9, 41, 52, 72; flight of, 103; and forms of kinship, 139; free, 149; and free time, 45, 46, 50, 84; and godparentage, 138, 140, 142, 149, 153; incentives for, 44, 45, 47, 48; numbers of, 72–73, 80, 107, 118; Indian, 159n23; intercaptaincy movement of, 72; and lack of documentary materials, 137; living conditions of, 41, 45, 105; marriage of, 10, 11; mortality of, 9, 41, 72; mulatto, 44; Muslim, rebellion of, 15, 47; *petite marronage* of, 104, 129n4; and property ownership, 46, 48, 49; and provisions, 48, 49, 84; and quotas, 53; rate of illegitimacy, 11; revolts of,

15, 60, 68, 103, 152, 153; and sense of community, 152; sex ratio of, 41, 73–74, 105; sexual fear of, 132n31; and skilled labor, 43, 44, 47; spiritual kinship of, 163. *See also* Fugitive slaves.
Slenes, Robert W., 9, 10, 13, 20, 36, 154
Smith, David G., 148, 154
Smith, Raymond T., 28
Soares de Galliza, Diana, 19, 36
Social banditry (*cangaço*), 109
Sodalities, religious, 140
Sorocaba, 77, 78
Sousa, Antonio de, 116, 117
Sousa, Francisco de, 56n9
Sousa Andrade, Maria José, 14, 36
Sousa Coutinho, Rodrigo de, 89
Sousa Freire, Alexandre de, 130n10
Sousa Martins, José de, 19, 37
Souza e Silva, Joaquim Norberto de, 37
St. Domingue: slave rebellion of 1792, 68
Stein, Stanley J., 37; *Vassouras*, 14
Stolcke, Verena, 19, 37
Studies, postemancipation, 19, 20
Subsistence, 53–54, 55
Sugar, 68, 72, 77, 82, 84, 88, 90 105, 107, 152; areas of cultivation, 86; *engenhos*, 73; export of, 76; plantations, 40–41, 80; planters, 85; production, and slave cooperation, 42; purchases of, 88; shift to, 89
Sugar cane: daily quota of, 61, 62; harvest and processing of, 41, 42–43; and slaves, 39
Supply and price, manipulation of, 86
Sweet potatoes, production of, 93n7

Tannenbaum, Frank, 4, 6, 20, 37; *Slave and Citizen*, 3
Taubaté, 76
Taxes, for anti-*quilombo* operations, 119
Teixeira, Pedro, 52
Teixeira da Silva, Francisco Carlos, 18, 30
Tekes (Anzicos) (people), 114
Theodoro, 116, 117
Thornton, John, 17, 37
Timber, cutting of, 54

Time, concepts of, 43
Titton, Gentil Avelino, OFM, 7, 37
Tobacco, 68, 72, 78, 81, 84, 85, 88, 89,
    100, 152
Toplin, Robert, 3, 18, 20, 37
"Treaty of Peace," demands of, 53–54

United States, slave narratives in, 20
Universidade Federal do Paraná, 8,
    159n14
University of Bahia, 16–17
University of São Paulo, 9
Urban centers, growth of, 72, 75

Vainfas, Ronaldo, 7, 17, 37
Vasconcelos Ferreira de Salles, Gilka,
    14, 37
Vassouras, coffee planters of, 83
Verger, Pierre, 16, 37
Vidal Luna, Francisco, 9, 10, 18, 24, 38
Vieira, Antônio, 160n25
Vieira Ravasco, Bernardo, 160n25
Vila Nova da Rainha, 120
Vila of Belmonte, 60
Vila Real, 120

Vila Rica, 121; câmara (town council)
    of, 120
Vilela Santos, Maria Januária, 38
Viotti da Costa, Emilia, 4, 18, 19, 38

Wallerstein, Immanuel, 7, 38
War of the Emboabas, 118
Wehling, Arno, 12, 38
West Indies, amelioration of slavery in,
    49
Westphalen, Cecilia Maria, 12, 38
Whale meat, 49
Whaling, 14
Wheat, 67, 78, 79, 80
Whites, as godparents, 153
Women, menstruating, 128
Work, rhythms of, 43
Workers, hierarchy of, 43–44

"Yaka" (people), 126
Yams, production of, 93n7
Yoruba cults (candomblé), 16, 17, 116
Yorubas (people), 154

Zumbi (nephew of Ganga Zumba), 123,
    124, 134–35n68

BOOKS IN THE SERIES BLACKS IN THE NEW WORLD

Before the Ghetto: Black Detroit in the Nineteenth Century
David M. Katzman

Black Business in the New South: A Social History of the North
Carolina Mutual Life Insurance Company
Walter B. Weare

The Search for a Black Nationality: Black Colonization and Emigration,
1787–1863
Floyd J. Miller

Black Americans and the White Man's Burden, 1898–1903
Willard B. Gatewood, Jr.

Slavery and the Numbers Game: A Critique of *Time on the Cross*
Herbert G. Gutman

A Ghetto Takes Shape: Black Cleveland, 1870-1930
Kenneth L. Kusmer

Freedmen, Philanthropy, and Fraud: A History of the Freedman's Savings
Bank
Carl R. Osthaus

The Democratic Party and the Negro: Northern and National Politics,
1868–92
Lawrence Grossman

Black Ohio and the Color Line, 1860–1915
David A. Gerber

Along the Color Line: Explorations in the Black Experience
August Meier and Elliott Rudwick

Black over White: Negro Political Leadership in South Carolina during
Reconstruction
Thomas Holt

Keeping the Faith: A. Philip Randolph, Milton P. Webster, and the
Brotherhood of Sleeping Car Porters, 1925–37
William H. Harris

Abolitionism: The Brazilian Antislavery Struggle
Joaquim Nabuco, translated and edited by Robert Conrad

Black Georgia in the Progressive Era, 1900–1920
John Dittmer

Medicine and Slavery: Health Care of Blacks in Antebellum Virginia
Todd L. Savitt

Alley Life in Washington: Family, Community, Religion, and Folklife in the City, 1850–1970
James Borchert

Human Cargoes: The British Slave Trade to Spanish America, 1700–1739
Colin A. Palmer

Southern Black Leaders of the Reconstruction Era
Edited by Howard N. Rabinowitz

Black Leaders of the Twentieth Century
Edited by John Hope Franklin and August Meier

Slaves and Missionaries: The Disintegration of Jamaican Slave Society, 1787–1834
Mary Turner

Father Divine and the Struggle for Racial Equality
Robert Weisbrot

Communists in Harlem during the Depression
Mark Naison

Down from Equality: Black Chicagoans and the Public Schools, 1920–41
Michael W. Homel

Race and Kinship in a Midwestern Town: The Black Experience in Monroe, Michigan, 1900–1915
James E. DeVries

Down by the Riverside: A South Carolina Slave Community
Charles Joyner

Black Milwaukee: The Making of an Industrial Proletariat, 1915–45
Joe William Trotter, Jr.

Religious Philanthropy and Colonial Slavery: The American Correspondence of the Associates of Dr. Bray, 1717–1777
Edited by John C. Van Horne

Black History and the Historical Profession, 1915–80
August Meier and Elliott Rudwick

Paul Cuffe: Black Entrepreneur and Pan-Africanist
(*formerly* Rise to Be a People: A Biography of Paul Cuffe)
Lamont D. Thomas

Making Their Own Way: Southern Blacks' Migration to Pittsburgh, 1916--30
Peter Gottlieb

My Bondage and My Freedom
Frederick Douglass, edited by William L. Andrews

Black Leaders of the Nineteenth Century
Edited by Leon Litwack and August Meier

Charles Richard Drew: The Man and the Myth
Charles E. Wynes

John Mercer Langston and the Fight for Black Freedom, 1829–65
William Cheek and Aimee Lee Cheek

The Old Village and the Great House: An Archaeological and Historical Examination of Drax Hall Plantation, St. Ann's Bay, Jamaica
Douglas V. Armstrong

Black Property Owners in the South, 1790–1915
Loren Schweninger

The Sociogenesis of a Race Riot: Springfield, Illinois, in 1908
Roberta Senechal

Coal, Class, and Color: Blacks in Southern West Virginia, 1915–32
Joe William Trotter, Jr.

No Crooked Death: Coatesville, Pennsylvania, and the Lynching of Zachariah Walker
Dennis B. Downey and Raymond M. Hyser

Black Towns and Profit: Promotion and Development in the Trans-Appalachian West, 1877–1915
Kenneth Marvin Hamilton

Slaves, Peasants, and Rebels: Reconsidering Brazilian Slavery
Stuart B. Schwartz

Reprint Editions

King: A Biography, Second Edition
David Levering Lewis

The Death and Life of Malcolm X, Second Edition
Peter Goldman

Race Relations in the Urban South, 1865–1890
Howard N. Rabinowitz, with a Foreword by C. Vann Woodward

Race Riot at East St. Louis, July 2, 1917
Elliott Rudwick

W. E. B. Du Bois: Voice of the Black Protest Movement
Elliott Rudwick

The Negro's Civil War: How American Negroes Felt and Acted during the War for the Union
James M. McPherson

Lincoln and Black Freedom: A Study in Presidential Leadership
LaWanda Cox

Slavery and Freedom in the Age of the American Revolution
Edited by Ira Berlin and Ronald Hoffman

Diary of a Sit-In, Second Edition
Merrill Proudfoot, with an introduction by Michael S. Mayer

They Who Would Be Free: Blacks' Search for Freedom, 1830–61
Jane H. Pease and William H. Pease

The Reshaping of Plantation Society: The Natchez District, 1860–1880
Michael Wayne

Rice and Slaves: Ethnicity and the Slave Trade in Colonial South Carolina
Daniel C. Littlefield